. . . to live up to its *raison d'être*, criticism should
be partisan, passionate, political, that is to say,
written from an exclusive point of view, but a point
of view that opens up the widest horizons.

—BAUDELAIRE

JAMES MERRILL

JAMES MERRILL

Essays in Criticism

Edited by DAVID LEHMAN
and CHARLES BERGER

CORNELL UNIVERSITY PRESS
Ithaca and London

Copyright © 1983 by Cornell University Press

All rights reserved. Except for brief quotations in a review, this book,
or parts thereof, must not be reproduced in any form without permission
in writing from the publisher. For information address Cornell University Press,
124 Roberts Place, Ithaca, New York 14850.

First published 1983 by Cornell University Press.
Published in the United Kingdom by Cornell University Press Ltd.,
Ely House, 37 Dover Street, London W1X 4HQ.

Excerpt from "Self-Portrait in a Convex Mirror" from *Self-Portrait in a Convex
Mirror* by John Ashbery, copyright © 1972, 1973, 1974, 1975 by John Ashbery,
is reprinted by permission of Viking Penguin Inc. and Carcanet Press.
Excerpts from "The System" and "The Recital" from *Three Poems* by John
Ashbery, copyright © 1970, 1971, 1972 by John Ashbery, are reprinted by per-
mission of Viking Penguin Inc. and John Ashbery.
Excerpts from *Gravity's Rainbow* by Thomas Pynchon, copyright © 1973 by
Thomas Pynchon, are reprinted by permission of Viking Penguin Inc.
"Mind" from *Things of This World* by Richard Wilbur, copyright © 1956 by
Richard Wilbur, is reprinted by permission of Harcourt Brace Jovanovich, Inc.

International Standard Book Number 0-8014-1404-0
Library of Congress Catalog Card Number 82-71603
Printed in the United States of America

Librarians: Library of Congress cataloging information appears
on the last page of the book.

The paper in this book is acid-free and meets the guidelines
for permanence and durability of the Committee on Production
Guidelines for Book Longevity of the Council on Library Resources.

Contents

7

Acknowledgments

Many people befriended this book on its progress from conception to completion. We learned to count on our contributors not only for essays of exceptional merit but also for advice when needed and for unfailing support throughout. We knew we could rely as well on the staff at Cornell University Press, and we would like specially to thank Bernhard Kendler, John Ackerman, and Glen Hartley for their sound judgment and practical assistance. Helen Vendler's suggestions proved valuable. Marcia Brubeck copy-edited the manuscript scrupulously. Stefanie Lehman collaborated on more than a few details. We are indebted to the Society for the Humanities at Cornell University, where David Lehman held a fellowship during the 1980–81 academic year. Finally, in addition to providing the pretexts for this project, James Merrill made our job easier in countless greatly appreciated ways.

Grateful acknowledgment is made to the following for permission to reprint copyrighted material:

Atheneum Publishers for material from *The Country of a Thousand Years of Peace and Other Poems*, New and Enlarged Edition, copyright © 1958, 1970 by James Merrill; for material from *Water Street*, copyright © 1962 by James Merrill; for material from *The (Diblos) Notebook*, copyright © 1965 by James Merrill; for material from *Nights and Days*, copyright © 1966 by James Merrill; for material from *The Fire Screen*, copyright © 1969 by James Merrill; for material from *Braving the Elements*, copyright © 1972 by James Merrill; for material from *Divine Com-*

edies, copyright © 1976 by James Merrill; for material from *Mirabell: Books of Number*, copyright © 1978 by James Merrill; for material from *Scripts for the Pageant*, copyright © 1980 by James Merrill; for material from *From the First Nine: Poems 1946–1976*, copyright © 1982 by James Merrill; and for material from *The Changing Light at Sandover*, copyright © 1982 by James Merrill; all reprinted with the permission of Atheneum Publishers.

Alfred A. Knopf, Inc. for material from *The Collected Poems of Wallace Stevens*, copyright © 1954 by Wallace Stevens.

Faber and Faber Ltd for material from *Poems 1943–1956* by Richard Wilbur; and for material from *The Collected Poems of Wallace Stevens* by Wallace Stevens; reprinted by permission of Faber and Faber Ltd.

Alvin Feinman for permission to reprint lines from his poem "Preambles" in *Preambles and Other Poems* by Alvin Feinman.

Oxford University Press for material from *Five Temperaments* by David Kalstone, copyright © 1977 by David Kalstone.

Abbreviations

Extended quotations from James Merrill's major collections will be followed by parenthetical mention of volume and page number. The following abbreviations are used:

BE   *Braving the Elements*
CLS   *The Changing Light at Sandover*
CT   *The Country of a Thousand Years of Peace and Other Poems* (rev. ed.)
DC   *Divine Comedies*
FP   *First Poems*
FS   *The Fire Screen*
M   *Mirabell: Books of Number*
ND   *Nights and Days*
S   *Scripts for the Pageant*
WS   *Water Street*

Note: *The Changing Light at Sandover* is an omnibus volume containing Merrill's Ouija trilogy in its entirety: "The Book of Ephraim" from *Divine Comedies*, all of *Mirabell*, all of *Scripts for the Pageant*, and an epilogue. In these essays we have elected to make our page references to the original publications (except for quotations from the epilogue), since each part of the trilogy has its own integrity and since it is worth keeping in mind the order in which the parts were written.

In *The Changing Light at Sandover*, pages 3–92 correspond to pages 47–136 of *Divine Comedies*; pages 97–276 correspond to pages 3–182 of *Mirabell: Books of Number*; pages 283–515 correspond to pages 3–235 of *Scripts for the Pageant*. The title of the trilogy's second volume has been changed to *Mirabell's Books of Number*; the epilogue is entitled "Coda: The Higher Keys."

JAMES MERRILL

Introduction

David Lehman

From the beginning, James Merrill's poetic gifts have marked him among his contemporaries. About his technical dexterity and quick wit, there was never much room for disagreement; he handled intricate forms with startling assurance and gave every indication of having inherited the staff of Prospero from Auden. The elaborate conceit came naturally to Merrill. For sheer cleverness it would be difficult to top the apparently effortless gesture that crowns an early sonnet on the myth of Europa and the bull. The latter has proliferated into "tattered bulls on shut church doors," and we are left with a double pun:

> The god at last indifferent
> And she no longer chaste but continent.
>
> [CT, p. 49]

With *Water Street* in 1962 and yet more strikingly with *Nights and Days* four years later, Merrill's poetry became more frankly auto-biographical. With these volumes, too, came a stylistic loosening; the poet's delivery, here and subsequently, relies on colloquial rhythms and conversational ease. These are surprisingly important to his "metaphysical" purposes. In David Kalstone's words, "When Merrill uses an idiom, he turns it over curiously, as if prospecting for ore."[1] Sometimes a simple transposition of letters produces the intended effect: from a worn phrase comes a Japanese brush drawing ("SWIRLS BEFORE PINE") or a moralized landscape ("the lean tree burst into grief").

15

A supple and gently understated style that puts its gift for verbal complication in the employ of a verse autobiography in progress—this is scarcely a mean achievement, but Merrill reached his poetic maturity at a time when some professional readers could acknowledge his gifts only grudgingly. His puns were perhaps *too* perfect, too good to be true. It was thought that the brilliant surface of his poems reflected an aesthete who was either too safely airy or too subversively sensual, depending on the critic's point of view. Perhaps it was inevitable that so stylish a manner would, like Yeats's circus animals, be seen to take all its author's love, and not the things it was expressive of. At any rate a climate of opinion that prized the "barbaric yawp" before all else would have little use for Merrill's bemusedly civilized tone. The reviewer who likened the poet to "Charles Atlas trying to lift a pea" put the case for the prosecution, who—starved for significance and "relevance"—saw all manner and no matter in Merrill's music.[2] Such a response speaks to the poet's subtlety, among other things. To grasp his meaning, to find the figure in his Jamesian carpet, takes a certain amount of hard work—it is definitely not for those who would expect to learn the whole Talmud while standing on one foot.

If it is easy to see why Merrill might have struck some critics as out of step with his time, that by no means condones the extent and seriousness of the misunderstanding. The unkindest cut of all was delivered by the *New York Times* in an editorial protesting the decision to award the Bollingen Prize of 1973 to the author of *Braving the Elements*. Merrill was charged with being a private poet when the times called for public commitment and social consciousness. Let Richard Saez reply: "It is true Merrill has avoided confessional poetry and topical or fashionable subjects. But for readers who understand Merrill's highly-informed language, the poems of *Braving the Elements* deal more memorably and more incisively with liberation, radical violence, kidnapping, space travel, the assassination of political leaders, and the effect of mass-media on the English language than any poetry written in America today."[3] It is an amusing historical irony that it should be Merrill, of all American poets, who might succeed in identifying history with himself. Having felt like a candidate for abduction in the wake of the Lindbergh case, he could publish a depression kidnapping fantasy that was a prophetic step ahead of events: "Days of 1935," whose protagonist feels grateful to his kidnappers, seems eerily aware of the future history of Patricia Hearst. And having grown up in "18 West 11th Street," the house blown up by Weathermen in 1970, gave Merrill a special impetus, and perhaps a special authority, to examine that incident and its implications—and to see his own life pass before him during the slow-motion replay of the blast.

"The time eventually comes, in a good poet's career, when readers actively long for his books: to know that someone out there is writing down your century, your generation, your language, your life—under whatever terms of difference—makes you wish for news of yourself, for those authentic tidings of invisible things, as Wordsworth called them, that only come in the interpretation of life voiced by poetry."[4] For Helen Vendler that time had already come some years earlier; it took, however, a major literary event— the impact of *Divine Comedies* in 1976—to gain for Merrill the wider attention he deserved. With its ninety-page magnum opus "The Book of Ephraim," *Divine Comedies* surprised even those of Merrill's readers who had confidently anticipated his greatness. "Ephraim" seemed as strange, ambitious, and daring a long poem as any American poet had produced in this century. It was, moreover, just the first leg of a three-part journey, a trilogy of the afterworld, apocalypse tomorrow. Without sacrificing grace and nuance, "Ephraim" and the two volumes that followed—*Mirabell: Books of Number* in 1978 and *Scripts for the Pageant* and 1980—took on an unmistakably public character, a willingness to engage the world at its most problematic and least tractable. "Can humanity save itself from destruction?" This, Stephen Yenser reminds us, is the central question articulated by the poem. The trilogy issued ominous warnings of nuclear disaster while it spun out a creation myth and speculated on the possibility of paradise; it claimed the dominion of the atom for poetry even as it appropriated all manner of "pop" phenomena, from science fiction to fictive fact, from the Bermuda Triangle to the bicameral brain. The trilogy's good cheer was everywhere in evidence, no matter how dark or dire its worries. To the poet's customary urbanity had been added the finishing touch—a

Keatsian intensity, capable of making all disagreeables evaporate.

The trilogy's explosive typography (telegraph uppercase denotes otherworldly speakers), its inventive organization (epic and dramatic), its use of the Ouija board as a generative conceit, and its very length (that he should have been able to sustain it so far!)—all testify to Merrill's ingenuity; he has "made it new" with a vengeance. At the same time that it extends the frontiers of literary experimentation, the work also demonstrates the poet's technical mastery. Into the tapestry of the poem are woven a canzone, a villanelle, passages in terza rima, the remnants of a *nouveau roman*, sonnets, sonnet sequences, prose quotations, intricately rhymed pentameter and slithering fourteeners, with an extended masque into the bargain. The nature of the enterprise, its artistry and its cosmic reach, force the reader to receive it on terms we usually associate with Dante or Milton. About the work of few recent poets can such an extravagant claim be made with a sober face. Indeed, of contemporary poets, it is Merrill who most explicitly takes up Wordsworth's challenge: "Paradise, and groves / Elysian, Fortunate Fields—like those of old / Sought in the Atlantic Main—why should they be / A history only of departed things, / Or a mere fiction of what never was?"

More than half the essays assembled here are concerned to identify and to elucidate some of the ways in which Merrill's trilogy presents itself, some of the tasks it sets out to perform. Peter Sacks examines the work as a "triumphantly consoling" elegy that transfigures fear into revelation and loss into the promise of joy regained; Richard Sáez regards it as an apocalyptic epic that invokes a genre but denies its premises in favor of "an eternity of transient moments." In "Merrill and Dante," Rachel Jacoff explores the trilogy in the shadow of its chief precedent; in "Merrill and Pynchon," Charles Berger considers it in the company of *Gravity's Rainbow*, with which it has a "central anxiety" in common. Willard Spiegelman focuses on interruption as both a modus operandi and a major theme. The principle of unity in multiplicity—arguably the trilogy's most fundamental tenet—takes center stage in Stephen

Yenser's meticulous reading of *Scripts,* last and longest of the three volumes.

Against the mistaken notion that the trilogy broke utterly with Merrill's poetic past, a number of the essays take pains to delineate the development of an image, a metaphor, a theme, a device, as it occurs and recurs, with changes and modifications, in the course of Merrill's career. In what sense can it be said that the poet's previous books lead inevitably to the trilogy as to an apex achieved? And to the contrary, how—with what effects, and at what cost—does the trilogy's epic river race far from the lyric tributaries that fed it? These and similar questions are taken up by more than one writer in the pages that follow.

The first few essays in the volume concentrate their attention on early texts that have a particular bearing on Merrill's "sacred books." J. D. McClatchy attends to *Water Street,* that "turning point" in Merrill's career; with McClatchy, Samuel E. Schulman—in his essay on *The Fire Screen* (1969) and *Braving the Elements*—shares an interest in themes of self-possession and dispossession, houses and habitations, makeshift or permanent. Schulman is among those following up on David Kalstone's essay on Merrill in *Five Temperaments,* and so is David Kalstone, who demonstrates how essentially lyric resources came to serve larger autobiographical ends; Kalstone compares poems from each of Merrill's first three volumes with passages in *Mirabell,* the point being that Merrill "performs his most telling acts of self-representation" in the process of "refiguring" certain resonant "objects of desire." That tropes persist, that the unity of Merrill's career is apparent even at those moments when self-revision seems most disruptive, are premises of my own essay also. I propose readings of such poems as "Charles on Fire," with its myth of cracked vessels, and "The Will," which acts as a sort of prologue to the trilogy, akin to the "timely utterance" Wordsworth heard from the mouth of a leech-gatherer, preparing him to receive intimations of immortality.

One of the most pernicious developments in recent critical theory is the rise of the doctrine that authors do not exist: not only are their intentions deemed irrelevant, but their authority in every

sense has been questioned—has in effect been reduced to that of
the stenographer or typist in the creation of a business letter. No
poetry has had more fun with this line of reasoning than Merrill's
in the trilogy. Does he not refer to himself throughout as "scribe"?
Taking dictation from "ghostwriters" is frustrating in fact—or in
jest: the element of humor in Merrill's "divine comedies" is pro-
nounced and complex. He is upbraided for saying so but "JM," as
the poet refers to himself (thus establishing a critically ambiguous
distance between the self as artist and the self as actor), protests
his lot:

> Very pretty, but I'd set
> My whole heart, after *Ephraim*, on returning
> To private life, to my own words. Instead,
> Here I go again, a vehicle
> In this cosmic carpool. Mirabell once said
> He taps my word banks. I'd be happier
> If *I* were tapping them. Or thought I were.
>
> [*M*, pp. 167–168]

Merrill's voices may be seen as parts of a self that has enlarged its
boundaries in order precisely to accommodate them. Whether this
necessarily involves subjugation of the poet's will, and whether
this is cause for jubilation or for concern, provoke differing re-
sponses from contributors to this volume. Surely, however, all can
agree that such questions as these direct our attention to decisions
and revisions made by the author; his method of composition war-
rants special consideration, then, not only because it is so unusual
but because it was itself one of the most important of these deci-
sions. From his privileged position as partner and participant, as
"hand" to JM's "scribe," David Jackson (the poem's "DJ") describes
the Ouija sessions that resulted in the trilogy. Among other par-
ticulars, he discusses the relation between transcripts of those ses-
sions and the finished poem.

Anyone setting out, as we did, to edit a volume of "original"
essays can expect surprises to occur with some regularity. These
prove educative. Whatever their initial aims, contributors find their

essays changing in progress, and the nature of the volume—
however carefully planned—is modified a dozen different times as
each new essay somehow takes its place to support the others.
(This state of affairs is as it should be, given the radical instability
that Merrill seems to make almost a formal principle—and given,
too, his openness to mid-course corrections.) One essayist unknow-
ingly echoes another; points of acute disagreement, or of parallel
effort, stand out. Some conclusions are rather easily reached: there
is a consensus that "The Broken Home" and "Lost in Translation"
are pivotal texts, for example, as is the opening of Book 6 of *Mira-
bell;* the writers again and again insist upon the influence of Proust.
Various pairings are possible, each suggestive of an exchange of
voices not entirely unlike those that JM plays deejay to. One notes
that Sacks discusses the flute and its elegiac quality, that Sáez
treats the soprano voice and its lyric intensity, and that both dis-
cussions (to a greater or lesser extent) touch on the problem of evil,
or theodicy. One compares Kalstone's reading of "Childlessness"
to McClatchy's. One remarks the importance that both Lehman
and Spiegelman assign to Bloom's *Kabbalah and Criticism* for its
help toward an understanding of some of Merrill's narrative pro-
cedures. Rachel Jacoff's analysis of the "Dantesque" is as if written
in the face of Kalstone's statement that "Ultimately Merrill's trilogy
is more Ovidian than Dantesque." Charles Berger observes that
speakers in the trilogy can cut each other off without undercutting
the whole; Stephen Yenser argues that fusion and fission—mir-
rored in Merrill's coupled and split rhymes—are twin aspects of a
single energy source and that, in keeping with the balance it every-
where strikes between unity and duality, the profoundest ques-
tions raised in *Scripts* can only be answered "yes & no." And they
make these arguments—it will seem to the reader—in rejoinder to
Sáez's conviction that the trilogy can't have it both ways, that it
cannot be monist and dualist simultaneously.

The image of the house is dear to Merrill. If one borrows an
architectural idea to describe Merrill's poetic achievement one might
speak of his visible columns and capitals and of the concealed

shrine within. It is a structure one admires first from the nearest angles at hand. To do it justice requires study, however; circumambulation precedes entry, and then one must adjust to the changing light within. Inquiry and wonder and interpretation follow. But one ends where one began, in praise.

CHAPTER 1

Elemental Bravery: The Unity of James Merrill's Poetry

David Lehman

. . . break, blow, burn, and make me new.
—DONNE, "Holy Sonnets"

For nothing can be sole or whole
That has not been rent.
—YEATS, "Crazy Jane Talks With the Bishop"

With the visionary gleam that informs his cosmic commedia, James Merrill appears to have taken a great many readers by surprise. The critic who might once have damned Merrill with faint praise—by extolling him as "merely" a master craftsman—no longer has that luxury, if luxury it is to deny oneself the pleasures of texts in which, as in the novels of Jane Austen and Henry James, an education of the feelings takes place under the tutorship of language. "The Book of Ephraim," *Mirabell,* and *Scripts for the Pageant* are as elegant of surface, as fastidiously well-wrought, as any of Merrill's previous writings, but there should now be less room for misunderstanding. The "poems of science" Merrill has fashioned achieve a remarkable synthesis of levity and gravity; their gay, buoyant atmosphere contrapuntally sets off the seriousness of their hieratic intent. If Merrill's tone remains that of the dandy, his attitude that of the aesthete abroad (who feels "American in Europe and exotic at home"),[1] one can scarcely ignore the news he now brings us

from heavenly circles of limitless circumference, whose centers are
everywhere.

"Mind you, it works best as metaphor," Merrill's vision does, as
he himself remarks of his model of "the psychic atom." Still, the
wedding of science fiction and poetic truths for the sake of dealing
with ultimate questions as well as with the pressures of an im-
mediate reality—this is a larger ambition than we are accustomed
to, and an ambition largely brought off. And surely one must ad-
mire the performance, the skill with which Merrill has approached
a problem memorably defined by one of his voices from beyond:

> DANTE'S LUCK LAY IN HIS GULLIBLE
> & HEAVENLY WORLD   WE MY BOY DRAW FROM 2
> SORTS OF READER: ONE ON HIS KNEES TO ART
> THE OTHER FACEDOWN OVER A COMIC BOOK.
> OUR STYLISH HIJINKS WONT AMUSE THE LATTER
> & THE FORMER WILL DISCOUNT OUR URGENT MATTER
>
> [M, p. 53]

Uncomprehending or dismissive responses are indeed inevitable.
With his Ouija board apparatus, lost continents, and black holes,
this most urbane of poets had made himself vulnerable on several
counts. But I would argue that it is precisely thanks to the taking of
this risk, to the fusion of "stylish hijinks" and "urgent matter," of
comic book and art, that Merrill's great breakthrough has occurred.
It seems to me, moreover, that the breakthrough has come not as
an about-face but as the culmination of a lifetime of trials and
tremors; there is, I will undertake to show, an essential unity to
Merrill's career. Toward the "lessons" of *Mirabell* and *Scripts*, Mer-
rill began doing his homework long ago. He has schooled his
sensibility to aim at high romantic ideals, or at a network of them:
the apprehension of angels on earth, the recovery of paradises
misplaced or extinct, the redemption of time, the outwitting of
mortality.

In securing Merrill's place as an American original, the trilogy
compels us to take a retrospective look at his career and, in doing
so, to question our biases, to wonder how so many could fail for so
long to recognize as virtues this poet's metaphysical wit and his
prodigious formal resources; a melancholy conclusion points to the

devaluation, in our time, of the verbal gestures that give Merrill's poetry its distinctive finish. Like Emerson's Rhodora, these gestures are their own excuse for being, but their existence is far from gratuitous. To the contrary, Merrill's formal choices and his visionary insights present a classic chicken-and-egg problem in causality. His "means" and his "meanings" coincide (*DC*, p. 40); the pun, so characteristic of its author, is as much an instrument of truth as an element of style or a quirk of mind. From the start Merrill's reflexive attentiveness to a word's multiplicity of meanings signaled a concomitant interest in the overtones of an action or event: what life proposed, language disclosed. Pleasurable in itself, Merrill's wordplay is thus inseparable from the tasks his sense of poetic vocation demands of him. The trilogy represents an apotheosis of the effort to extend the scrutiny of self to the point that the examined consciousness—no less than "the life lived" and "the love spent" (*WS*, p. 6)—acquires the shape and clarity of a work of art. By the same token, the earlier books may now be seen to chart the progress of the poet toward a vision as difficult to endure as to earn, the living record of one who transformed himself from "maker" to "creator" with no consequent loss of craft, whose outbreaks from the jail of form result in new forms every bit as exacting as those they supplant, designed to enhance poetic freedoms rather than diminish them.

To call the trilogy a comedy is to fix its mode, not to circumscribe its flight. It might be argued that the comic impulse derives much of its energy from the perceived push-and-pull between gravity (or gravitation) and levity (or levitation), and Merrill's poetry is indeed poised between the thrill of escape from the earth's magnetic force and the relentless insistence of our corporeal natures, dragging us back to earth. The pattern is defined in the comic archetype of the stargazer who falls into a ditch, although in the versions of this motif found in Chaucer, Sidney, and Swift the accent falls on the assertion of our "clayey lodgings" that make a mockery of all spiritual aspiration.[2] Not so in Merrill's poetry. There the "erected wit" stands a good chance of rescuing the "infected will": never has Merrill excluded the possibility of a true transcendence, beyond even the project of uniting sense and soul, Cupid and Psyche, the Sultan and Scheherazade. Even before "Ephraim," his work is rife with intimations of an immortal world in which, at a stroke, two clichés renew themselves—"whatever will be, will be right." (Not for nothing is JM said to be the "faithful representative" of an obscure nineteenth-century editor of the works of Alexander Pope.) "Form's what affirms," Merrill affirms in "The Thousand and Second Night" (*ND*, p. 15), and so, finally, does the comic impulse, with its hope of order restored, its happy ending implicit from the start. It holds out the promise that buoyant chatter can redeem weighty matter, that wit is everlasting and dust but for a time, that the stuff of tragedy, endured and absorbed, can be transmuted—by a conceit Rilke would have enjoyed—into the musical "scale of love and dread" played on a "thinking reed" by "the great god Pain" (*BE*, p. 72).[3]

In his poetry, Merrill characteristically cuts the figure of the suave host whose conversational brilliance and fondness for camp humor disarm the invited guest, so that the pouring of spirits at dinner's end finds him half-drugged already "in laughter, pain, and love" (*ND*, p. 56) or "wit, affection, and despair" (*DC*, p. 108), as the case may be. In "A Tenancy," the poem that closes *Water Street*, Merrill makes this tight-lipped pronouncement:

> If I am host at last
> It is of little more than my own past.
> May others be at home in it.
>
> [*WS*, p. 53]

As "The Book of Ephraim" gathers momentum, the "others" who make their home in Merrill's salon include Zulu chieftains and "pallid Burne-Jones acroliths": like a friendly organism, the poem harbors and offers nourishment to all who call. But I do not mean to dwell overlong on this biological sense of "host"; it is pertinent that *hospes*, the Latin root of the word, signifies "host," "guest," and "stranger," for each fairly describes an aspect of the poet. He has ever been his own "perfect stranger"; he now plays host to a host of spirits, "familiar" and strange at once, while he himself is the guest in a heaven Ephraim defines as "THE SURROUND OF THE

LIVING" (*DC*, p. 103). To be host is not to deny other duties: from his privileged position at "the angelic secretariat," he takes dictation from Auden and other "ghostwriters": but then, Merrill's sense of hospitality is hardly conventional.[4]

An additional sense of host can help correct a common misconception of readers who, upon opening *Mirabell*, will instinctively suspect the poet of pulling their legs. Such a reader will wonder whether Merrill gave strict credence to the messages spelled out by the willowware cup on his Ouija board; perhaps he or she will associate the work's otherworldly population with the mock-heroic machinery of *The Rape of the Lock*, will question the "scientific" basis of the poem, or will simply think the whole thing rather silly. Next, reassured by the way the poet has anticipated these reactions, impressed by the skepticism that marks the poet's persona, the reader will decide that Merrill consulted the board in much the same way that Yeats took note of his wife's sleeptalking, as a kind of Jungian trick, a way of coaxing the imagination. No doubt several of these responses have something to commend them, but committed readers will go further. They will begin to see that for Merrill the Ouija board is no more a trick than the Eucharist would be for devout Catholics. I draw my simile not only from the ecclesiastical sense of "host" but from the value Merrill everywhere places on the forms of ritual, the processes that prepare one to receive a vision of, and communion with, divinity. To be sure, Merrill's religiosity is quite explicitly that of the aesthete. Asked how "real" his "new mythology" seemed to him, Merrill has given this reply: "Literally, not very—except in recurrent euphoric hours when it's altogether too beautiful not to be true."[5] If the relation between beauty and truth proposed here should strike familiar Keatsian chords, that is no accident; the romantic element in Merrill's work—its Platonic confidence, its sensuality of language—will prompt many to see Keats's capable hand pushing Merrill's pen in pursuit of his theme, "an old, exalted one: / The incarnation and withdrawal of / A god" (*DC*, p. 47).

Reviewing Merrill's career, one is struck by the consistency with which the poet has turned to this theme, by the frequency with which his poems function as rituals designed to welcome and witness the divine visitation and to mourn over its aftermath. Not since Rilke has a poet trained his vision with such determination to explore the realms of the angels, confident that superior eyesight can discern their presence here on earth. "Life was fiction in disguise" (*BE*, p. 14), and as a corollary proposition, "the stranger is a god in masquerade" (*ND*, p. 8): subscribing to the defense of masks and fictions mounted by Oscar Wilde in *The Critic as Artist*, Merrill never forgets that the purpose of the disguise is to foster ultimate recognition, that the unmasking scene crowns the masquerade ball. Consider these lines from "A Dedication," the poem that serves as the valedictory close to *The Country of a Thousand Years of Peace*; the poet is communing with the newly-dead Hans Lodeizen, a figure of importance in the trilogy as well:

> These are the moments, if ever, an angel steps
> Into the mind, as kings into the dress
> Of a poor goatherd, for their acts of charity.
> There are moments when speech is but a mouth pressed
> Lightly and humbly against the angel's hand.
>
> [*CT*, p. 83]

Significantly, the angel is rendered as a Shakespearean monarch, bearing a likeness to Henry V in disguise among his troops. "His state is kingly," we are meant to see, and his charity a form of *caritas*; standing and waiting, the poet is struck speechless in his praise.

The "evidently angelic visitor" returns twice in *Water Street*, both times in the context of a work of art half-perceived and half-created by the poet. In "Angel," the figure appears "in finely woven robes, school of Van Eyck," in the painting hanging "above my desk"; in the angel's gestures and "round, hairless face," the poet reads a text "demanding praise, demanding surrender," forbidding profane speech (*WS*, p. 42). In "A Vision of the Garden," the poet recollects the childhood incident when, using his breath for ghostly writing on a chill windowpane, he drew the features of an angel doomed to "fade in mist"—features that will someday, he adds, be embodied in a flesh-and-blood "you" (*WS*, p. 8). Nor is the figure absent from succeeding volumes; if anything there is a proliferation of guises by which he may be apprehended. An unlikely reincarnation occurs in *Braving the Elements,* in "Days of 1935": the poet's remembered fantasy of being kidnapped at age nine by "Floyd and Jean," gangster and moll. To them he becomes, in one of the poem's poignant reversals, deeply attached; and in an eery echo of the "mouth pressed / Lightly and humbly against the angel's hand," the boy struggling with his captor leaves "my toothprints on his hand, / Indenture of a kiss" (*BE,* p. 12).

David Kalstone reports on a hidden agenda to Merrill's career, to which the titles of his volumes attest:

> It would be interesting to know at what point Merrill saw a larger pattern emerging in his work—the point at which conscious shaping caught up with what unplanned or unconscious experience had thrown his way. In retrospect a reader can see that *Braving the Elements* (1972) gathers behind it the titles—with full metaphorical force—of Merrill's previous books. In *The Country of a Thousand Years of Peace, Water Street, Nights and Days,* and *The Fire Screen,* he had referred to the four elements braved in the book which followed them. (*Divine Comedies* extends it one realm further.)[6]

The elements thus braved resurface in *Scripts for the Pageant,* only now they have been elevated into a quartet of angelic essences. "Samos," the magnificent canzone at the heart of that volume, weaves a pattern of the "Promised Land" out of the elements and our ability to engage them; the poem's five recurrent end words are "water," "light," "fire," "land," and "sense" (*S,* pp. 87–88).[7] If there is a teleology at work here—if "sense" somehow leads to "ascents"—one way to measure it is by reference to the poet's progressively more successful attempts at prolonging his brief encounters with those divinely appointed messengers who came at first unbidden and eventually by way of response to his conscious summons. Perhaps the most extraordinary change in Merrill's poetry since *Divine Comedies* is its scale, its epic extension of a lyric impulse; by dint of an arduous soul-making, vessel-breaking progress, Merrill has managed to sustain the epiphanies that had previously proved as delicate and evanescent as Walter Pater's privileged moments or those of Stephen Dedalus.

It had always seemed an implicit truth in Merrill's poetry that the god's incarnation must be followed by his withdrawal. Hence, in works preparatory to "The Book of Ephraim"—in the past that serves as prologue—the ecstatic occasion is tinged with regret at its imminent loss. Beauty, as Stevens put it, is momentary in the mind; the word "moments" occurs no fewer than three times in the nine lines of "A Dedication." Alas, the poet seems to lament, the vision cannot endure—to paraphrase Auden, it does not seriously intend to stay; more exactly, we can endure it only briefly. Yet even in defeat the poet takes away such knowledge as heralds future victory.

"Charles on Fire" (*ND*, p. 25) comes close to making a parable from the (necessarily) interrupted vision, the blaze of brightness that blinds the viewer back into the cave but, once seen, ignites the determination to gain a return match, to stage a second showing. The poem records precisely the sort of epiphany Pater had in mind when he wrote, in *The Renaissance*: "A sudden light transfigures a trivial thing, a weathervane, a windmill, a winnowing flail, the dust in the barn door; a moment—and the thing has vanished, because it was pure effect; but it leaves a relish behind it, a longing that the accident may happen again."[8] Like "A Narrow Escape" (*CT*, p. 28), "Charles on Fire" has a *Symposium* setting—somewhat ironically, given the wise man's reticence at dinner's end. By the time of *Scripts*, the party will have grown into a full-fledged banquet, an ongoing and movable feast that numbers Plato himself among the gregarious "guest-hosts"; but here we are granted only an isolated moment of illumination bracketed by darkness. In a second respect as well, "Charles on Fire" resembles "A Narrow Escape" and the seven other poems Merrill published in 1954 under the title *Short Stories*:[9] it tells a tale in little, claiming the stuff of short fiction for the province of verse, just as "The Book of Ephraim" would later perform the functions of a novel. I quote the poem in full:

> Another evening we sprawled about discussing
> Appearances. And it was the consensus
> That while uncommon physical good looks
> Continued to launch one, as before, in life
> (Among its vaporous eddies and false calms),

Still, as one of us said into his beard,
"Without your intellectual and spiritual
Values, man, you are sunk." No one but squared
The shoulders of his own unloveliness.
Long-suffering Charles, having cooked and served the meal,
Now brought out little tumblers finely etched
He filled with amber liquor and then passed.
"Say," said the same young man, "in Paris, France,
They do it this way"—bounding to his feet
And touching a lit match to our host's full glass.
A blue flame, gentle, beautiful, came, went
Above the surface. In a hush that fell
We heard the vessel crack. The contents drained
As who should step down from a crystal coach.
Steward of spirits, Charles's glistening hand
All at once gloved itself in eeriness.
The moment passed. He made two quick sweeps and
Was flesh again. "It couldn't matter less,"
He said, but with a shocked, unconscious glance
Into the mirror. Finding nothing changed,
He filled a fresh glass and sank down among us.

[*ND*, p. 25]

In "little tumblers finely etched" and "filled with amber liquor," the poet's alter ego serves up a trope for poetry, for that kind of poetic making whose desired end is the burnished artifact, frozen in its elegance, into which go a few rare and expensive drops of "spirits."[10] It is a poetry that keeps up appearances; and, in the sense of "physical good looks," "appearances" are what the after-dinner conversation turns to. At one time, we learn, these may have sufficed, as the delicate objet d'art might once have satisfied its maker. Indeed, the group agrees, uncommonly handsome physiognomy might still be said "to launch one." At this point in the poem, Merrill instinctively renews the somnolent metaphor in "launch": having been christened, having had the queen break a bottle on his hull, the initiate is now sailing somewhat against the current, through the "vaporous eddies and false calms"—the misleading appearances of calm—that are all that stand between him and turbulent waters. The figure is extended in the beat diction of the bearded young man, who issues a crucial proviso: "With-

out your intellectual and spiritual / Values, man, you are sunk."
Both *sunk* and *man*, the two slang words in the statement, work
overtime. Looks might launch the man, but staying afloat is a
"spiritual" matter.

No sooner has our host poured the liquor than the same young
man—ironically, since he has been the one to insist upon the "spir-
itual" side of things—takes a sudden interest in appearances and
fashion, flaming the brandy as is done "in Paris, France." (A lovely
touch, naming the country conveys a sense of the speaker's in-
nocence and enthusiasm; he has the arrogance of youth—of one
who has only recently been "launched.") His action results in an
appearance of a wholly unexpected kind, an emblem of the angelic
realm; in lieu of a toast, there is a divine hush:

> A blue flame, gentle, beautiful, came, went
> Above the surface. In a hush that fell
> We heard the vessel crack. The contents drained
> As who should step down from a crystal coach.

These lines do more than conduct us to the story's denouement. If,
in the poem's terms, the sea represents that element of flux upon
which our material lives toss and turn, fire is the agency of the
spirit, of all that "couldn't matter less." Dancing "Above the sur-
face," the "blue flame" comes as a revelation; it has all the attrib-
utes of an epiphany, that is, a flashing forth of divinity, of dark-
ness made visible. Extending the poem's sailing metaphor, the
"blue flame" also suggests the bluish aura or glow visible around
the masts of a ship during an electrical disturbance: the phenom-
enon known as St. Elmo's Fire, after the patron saint of sailors. The
ship in question is no longer seaworthy, however; it has metamor-
phosed into an altogether different sort of vessel, one that cannot
weather the storm. The glass, though it collaborated with the flames
and the brandy to make the epiphany possible, can neither survive
the moment nor contain it. The glass cracks; the fire that purifies
destroys. But in its flickering instant a social occasion has turned
into a religious mystery, as physical appearances have given way
to a spiritual apparition. From circumstances that must, at least at
first, seem unlikely, Merrill has extracted "the makings of a mira-

cle," in Elizabeth Bishop's phrase; from the milieu of manners, he has derived the forms of ritual and ceremony so dear to him because they connect the realms of art and of spirit. And if, as a result, the host's serving of "spirits" may be taken as a trope for the poetic process, it is the vessel-shattering flame that has turned an inconsequential anecdote into a parable.

Harold Bloom has demonstrated that, as found in the doctrine of the Lurianic Kabbalah, the theme of the cracking of vessels furnishes an antecedent myth for the literary artist's "breaking of forms," an account of creation that the secondary or "belated" artist must reenact. According to the Kabbalah, God first created "kelim, 'vessels,' of which the culminating vessel was *Adam Kadmon* or primal Man." But the creative light was too strong, or the vessels too fragile, for the majority of them shattered instantly to pieces. It is axiomatic—the very products of holy energy cannot contain it, cannot stay whole. Fortunately, by stages one can grow to absorb such heavenly light as, in its original force, cannot but burst the beholder, splintering his vision as if it were no sturdier than a child's eyeglasses lying smashed and forlorn on a worn gymnasium cinderpath. Creation can be restored, the dispersed light gathered, only by a process of restitution that, in Bloom's words, calls for "acts of meditation, acts that lift up and so liberate the fallen sparks of God from their imprisonment in the shards of the *kelippot* [broken vessels of evil]." That these acts of meditation are "at once psychic and linguistic," that "defense mechanisms and rhetorical tropes" accomplish the work of restitution, hammers home (for Bloom) the pertinence of the analogy for an understanding of poetic creation.[11] It would be impossible, in so brief a summary, to do justice to Bloom's reasoning. But even as I have sketchily described it, the myth of blinding light, broken receptacles, and redemptive meditation cannot fail to illuminate a vital aspect of "Charles on Fire" and the tendency it exemplifies in Merrill's poetry.

Indeed, whether or not the allusion lay beyond the poet's conscious intention, "Charles on Fire" seems invested with a knowledge of kabbalistic doctrine. Just as "God's name was too strong for his words" and therefore smashed the *kelim*, so here the "blue flame" shatters one of the "little tumblers finely etched"; just as the divine sparks of light disperse, so here the "contents" drain from the glass. The destruction is holy nevertheless, for it yields the glimpse of an angelic presence, "As who should step down from a crystal coach." The very syntax of this royal simile recalls the moment of Merrill's first angelic encounter:

> an angel steps
> Into the mind, as kings into the dress
> Of a poor goatherd, for their acts of charity.

The visitation has taken place, however unseemly the circumstances, and it has swiftly made itself felt. Precisely where the vessel has cracked, a lane to the spiritual realm has opened—we remember that these lines from Auden's "As I Walked Out One Evening" occur in the "Quotations" section of "The Book of Ephraim":

> *The glacier knocks in the cupboard,*
> *The desert sighs in the bed,*
> *And the crack in the tea-cup opens*
> *A lane to the land of the dead.*
>
> [DC, p. 102]

Now Charles, "Steward of spirits" in both senses, experiences a momentary transfiguration, even as he resumes his duties as host; preparatory to sweeping up the spilled "contents," his "glistening hand" has "gloved itself in eeriness," has added an invisible layer to his skin. Only for a moment, to be sure: and it passes, as the flame itself "came, went," pausing only for the length of a comma. The change in Charles does not survive "a shocked, unconscious glance / Into the mirror," which confirms our host's return to flesh and to the world of looks and appearances; the other "host," the sacred guest, has departed, if he was ever there—he existed by intimation alone, by the proxy work of a simile. And now, with the conclusion of the poem, the metaphor of shipwreck is brought to port: "He filled a fresh glass and sank down among us."

I have analyzed "Charles on Fire" in such detail not only because Merrill's intricate conceits demand and reward the closest possible attention but because this paradigmatic epiphany mirrors so many of the concerns and habits we encounter in the trilogy. There, as here, the consuming wish to entertain the angels (in the additional sense of entertaining an idea) is as fundamental as Merrill's penchant for elevating social gestures, parlor games, apparent accidents, even a guest's gaucheries, into acts and activities of mystical significance, performed, pondered, repeated as rituals, as invitations extended to the divine unknown. Thus from figures on wallpaper, demoniac beings spring to imaginative life; thus a photocopying machine can supply the requisite mirror and flash of light that, in an ironic update of Proust's memory triggers, bring spirits rushing to the scene. Nor does the question of appearances go away after "Charles on Fire."[12] Merrill is still asking it in the celestial context of *Mirabell*: "Will it ever, ever solve itself, / This riddle of appearances in Heaven?" (*M*, p. 11). "This riddle," which can be solved by paradox alone, refigures the diners' dilemma in "Charles on Fire"; it revises that poem's gloomy conclusion on the uneasy relations between spirit and corporeal form. How, JM wonders during one of the early lessons, can his bodiless tutors be said to resemble the bats on his wallpaper? His skepticism merits an "A PLUS" from the spirit of Maria Mitsotáki, who exposes "THE FICTION THAT THEY HAVE APPEARANCES   THEY DO NOT" (*M*, p. 58). Nevertheless, though he exists "in the realm of no appearances," JM's favorite bat promptly turns into a peacock and manifests himself as such (*M*, p. 63). From "Charles on Fire," whose mirror signaled a failed metamorphosis, we have arrived at a place where mirrors—and where the mind's mirrorlike systems of reflection and speculation—enable spirits to "appear," allow contact to be made with them, and can even revamp bat into peacock, "741" into foppish "Mirabell," a number into a name.

In the journey of his making, the Merrill of *Nights and Days* seems in retrospect to have been governed by Hölderlin's wistful observation (in "Brod und Wein"):

> Denn nicht immer vermag ein schwaches Gefäs sie zu fassen,
> Nur zu Zeiten erträgt göttliche Fülle der Mensch.
>
> [For not always can a frail vessel contain them,
> Only from time to time can man bear the plenty of the gods.]

But he has also learned that he must endure—and more, he must work to bring about—the shattering of vessels, the *shevirah hakelim*, before he can embark upon those redemptive acts of meditation that will restore his blissful seat at "the angelic secretariat." He will have to subject to a visionary blaze the vessels of his craft; he will have to stretch to the breaking point the sculptured verse forms that resemble "little tumblers finely etched." In the books that lead up to *Mirabell* and *Scripts for the Pageant,* Merrill has taken just this course. His poetry seems to have burst out of contours lovingly etched; the forms he has mastered he shatters, and out of a gathering of splinters a new heavenly order has emerged. It is surely appropriate that the epigraph of *Scripts* contains a reference to the delicate glass the groom must shatter with his foot during the Jewish wedding ceremony: for the climax of that book occurs when JM and DJ, scribe and hand, break a mirror in order to release the imprisoned spirits of Auden and Maria. It is also to the point that the word "break," in conjugated or participial form, recurs throughout *Mirabell* and more than once signals an actual break in the flow of words, a rupture between verb and object. Two examples:

> Broken—for good?—of its imperious
> Slashing at capitals, our cup points out
> A gentler dictum . . .
>
> [*M*, p. 19]

And, two pages earlier, in an italicized letter addressed to DJ:

> *How about breaking (remember*
> *that old dream?) the trip with a glimpse of Stonehenge*
> *& Avebury?*
>
> [*M*, p. 17]

It is a rupture, we learn, that necessitates the surgery DJ must undergo. He had suffered it when—no accident!—he carried up some flights of stairs the immense Victorian mirror that proved indispensable to the Ouija ceremony; the pain of the breakage constitutes the cost, for him, of admission to the celestial seminars (*M*, p. 69). JM, for his part, has been told he will have an "ARTISTIC BREAKTHRU." But inevitably the message containing this prophecy or promise itself "Breaks off. Is broken off," mid-sentence, before the speaker could complete the thought (*M*, p. 14). Some sort of fragmentation must, it seems, precede or accompany a vision of unity. After all, the author of "The Broken Home" was also, and first, the product of one. No accident: there is a special providence in the fall of a sparrow—or in the breaking of a trance, a limb, a code, a home. "Nothing can be sole or whole," said Crazy Jane to the Bishop, "that has not been rent."

Of this pattern Merrill's story "Peru: The Landscape Game" takes charming notice. An account of a trip to Peru, the story was conceived and composed *before* the trip took place, in the writer's effort to provide proof against disappointment, anticipatory imaginings to compensate for the inadequacies of actuality. The story's generative conceit is "that psychological game in which each person describes a house he then leaves in order to take an imaginary walk. One by one he discovers a key, a bowl, a body of water, a wild creature, and finally a wall. Free association is invited at any stage, and nothing explained until the last player has spoken." What kind of bowl springs to Merrill's mind as, the night before flying to Lima, he plays the game? Not golden but a "mixing bowl, cracked—fearing botulism, I kick it out of my path." A humorous translation of the line occurs a page later, in this exchange:

> "What was it your bowl meant?" K yawned, up in the room.
> "I'm a good mixer. But liable to go to pieces."

In the Jungian code the story proposes as an interpretive key, the bowl stands for Art.[13]

2

Merrill brings to "The Book of Ephraim" a novelist's ambition and sense of scale; elsewhere as well his imagination gravitates toward narrative form. But in Merrill's most ambitious narrative experiments the characters break ranks, the sequence of events snaps; the friction between double-meaninged words causes flames to flare, threatening to disrupt the proceedings. Such disruptions are intentional and inevitable. What makes them so? The ironically self-deprecatory tone Merrill uses when referring to his "Unrelenting fluency" (*DC*, p. 114) hints at an answer. Here is a poet who, mistrustful of his gifts, harbors the suspicion that, as he puts it in "The Thousand and Second Night" (*ND*, p. 14), "fluent passages of metaphor" undermine the text, falsify the experience. Since his events of insight occur as disjunctions, violations, even fractures, the interrupted narrative has emerged as a favored strategy.

For Merrill, breakdown leads eventually to breakthrough. Laboring to find a form that will stretch to assimilate interruptions and intrusions, he has made the most of these threats to his poetic coherence; they present, after all, a fit challenge to his shaping powers, a stimulus toward the construction of new and larger wholes, houses that can stand though divided against themselves. Between the whole and its parts, between the expansive impulse and the contractions of form, between lyric endings and narrative ends, there is at best an uneasy truce. We would do well to keep this complicated dialectic in mind. A poem pauses to make room for a subversive patch of prose; quatrains drift toward and away from sonnets; sonnets, in a poem composed of a series of them, reassert their individual integrity even as the boundaries between them begin to blur. Thus the poems formally enact their underlying tensions. The marvel is that their "Unrelenting fluency" prevails despite the wandering rocks and other obstacles blocking the way.

It is possible to read certain of Merrill's poems as chapters of a life in progress, a *Künstlerroman* in the making; "The Book of Ephraim" is, in Kalstone's words, "only the most explicit and extended of these efforts" toward "a kind of autobiography in verse."[14] In supervising the relations between autobiography and "fiction in disguise," Merrill turns frequently to Proust for guidance.[15] Already in *Water Street*, where a poem "For Proust" has "Scenes of Childhood" for a neighbor, Merrill's devotion to this master is brought to the surface; "The World and the Child," the volume's moving villanelle, features that most primal of Proustian scenes, "the child awake and wearied of," stoical in his dark bedroom while parents and others in the room below talk about him. The influence has deepened in the course of Merrill's career; the poet has even, in the willowware cup he and his partner use as a Ouija pointer, found a worthy substitute for the teacup from which, thanks to Marcel's madeleine, "towns and gardens alike" sprang into being. It is to Proust that, in "Days of 1971," Merrill attributes the "twofold" law said to govern human desire. From Proust, too, Merrill derives one of his distinctive procedures: "To overlook a subject for its image, / To labor images till they yield a subject" (*DC*, p. 120).[16] He rebels against this tendency momentarily in "The Book of Ephraim," but the struggle only confirms the extent of the influence, Proust being the kind of necessary angel with whom the poet must sometimes wrestle, in overnight combat, to emerge the next morning limping into a new name—Jacob's fate in the Bible.

With the instincts of a novelist, whose detached omniscience asserts itself even in a first-person narrative, Merrill enjoys playing shrink to his own analysand, refusing to stay put on the couch. Curiosity and not complaint is this poet's driving force. Accordingly, after the example of Proust, Merrill endeavors to read his days, as though they constituted an unwritten text; he would determine what valences the elements of his life might be said to have; he would leap to poetry from exercises of the involuntary memory. Time is the joker in the deck, the great variable in the formula chalked on the blackboard. Consciousness of a fourth dimension leads the writer to depart freely from accepted chronology, juggling past and present events (and future forebodings) instead of imposing a linear sequence on them:

> Too violent,
> I once thought, that foreshortening in Proust—
> A world abruptly old, whitehaired, a reader
> Looking up in puzzlement to fathom
> Whether ten years or forty have gone by.
> Young, I mistook it for an unconvincing
> Trick of the teller. It was truth instead
> Babbling through his own astonishment.
>
> [*DC*, pp. 114–115]

As Proust did, Merrill relies on his fictions to guide him past astonishment to the truth. He avails himself of the error, the joke, the slip of the pen or pun, the dream: all the subterfuges of the psyche, the witticisms of the soul, as Freud described them in *The*

Psychopathology of Everyday Life, Jokes and Their Relation to the Unconscious, and *The Interpretation of Dreams.*

Jung is given a more prominent place in "The Book of Ephraim," but the trilogy's debt to Freud is arguably the profounder one. So Mirabell acknowledges, honoring Freud for having married myth to science:

> FREUD'S V WORK WAS TO ILLUMINE FOR
> SCIENCE THE DELICATE ENVELOPE OF SOUL: THE PSYCHE:
> MANIFESTATION OF SOUL ENERGIES   IF BREATH IS THE
> SOUL OF THE BODY THEN PSYCHE IS THE BREATH OF THE SOUL
>
> [*M,* p. 143]

What else is Mirabell's "no accident" clause but an uppercase version of Freudian determinism, with myth and metaphysics layered on? At one point in "Ephraim," however, Freud seems to have a special nay-saying part to play: it is JM's shrink, cast in the role of doubting Thomas, who furnishes the skeptical counterturn to the Jungian or Stevensian equation of God and the imagination. Tom would have JM and DJ regard their Ouija sessions as a "harmless" folie à deux; he even prompts the former to come up with a textbook explanation for "these odd / Inseminations by psycho-roulette" (*DC,* p. 74). The trilogy overcomes such denials—Freud puts in a personal appearance to override Tom—but by including them, attributing some of them to himself, Merrill manages to anticipate possible objections to his work and thereby to deflate them. This foresight is more than a shrewd rhetorical strategy. As much as his insouciance under pressure, his reluctance to believe what his celestial informants have to say contributes to the tension between matter and manner (or antimatter) that is one of the trilogy's abiding sources of energy. The result is a species of the comic sublime, the assertion of wit and cultivated sensibility in the very throes of an ecstatic seizure. Such clashes of impulse are fundamental to the enterprise. "The two pioneering forces of modern sensibility are Jewish moral seriousness and homosexual aestheticism and irony," Susan Sontag observes in her "Notes on 'Camp,'"[17] and judging by his treatment of these "forces" in *Mirabell,* one imagines Merrill would concur. The one impulse constantly tests and tempers the other, as the poetry performs the work of reconciliation, housing them under one head just as Ephraim, taking after Joyce's Bloom, embodies a synthesis of Hellenism and Judaism.

Between one Scylla and another Charybdis—between novel and poem, or fiction and life, or artifice and nature—the poet seems often to be navigating. While it causes him some anxious moments, the real or merely apparent antagonism implicit in these dualities can turn into a fruitful exchange, especially when Merrill makes the evolution of a work one of that work's subjects. This he does with wry self-consciousness (as in "The Thousand and Second Night") or by intimation (as when, in "The Friend of the Fourth Decade," the ritual washing of a postcard collection, in the manner of a philatelist eager to dislodge stamps, suggests the process by which a novel "dissolves" into a poetic solution.) By the time of "The Will," in *Divine Comedies*, writing and living have become so bound together as metaphors for one another that Valéry's *il faut tenter de vivre* seems to have evolved into *il faut tenter d'écrire*. In several of these poems Merrill very nearly adopts the posture of novelist manqué that marks his experimental novel, *The (Diblos) Notebook*. It is almost as though he conceived of such works as surrogates for the shipwrecked "big book" that Mallarmé regarded both as the desired destination of all existence and as its vehicle. Merrill's strength of versification, his ability to load every rift with ore, is such that what might appear a liability—the need to predicate a work on an absent but prior text—is converted into an asset: language takes the place of incident, and the writing of a longer prose narrative seems an uneconomical superfluity. Yet such works do seem to lurk somewhere in the background; "The Thousand and Second Night" and "From the Cupola," for example, both include excerpts from *Psyche's Sisters*, a spurious novel by the pseudonymous A. H. Clarendon, whose similarly unwritten *Time Was*, quoted in "The Book of Ephraim," reinforces our impression of him as a stylist in the manner and mode of E. F. Benson.[18]

Among the poems that seem to have presented themselves to Merrill, at least initially, as the stuff of prose, "The Book of Ephraim" is unquestionably the most notable. Its opening section delineates the trilogy's prose origins and poetic alchemy, beginning with an admission of error or weakness:

> Admittedly I err by undertaking
> This in its present form. The baldest prose
> Reportage was called for, that would reach
> The widest public in the shortest time.
>
> [DC, p. 47]

Defeated by deadlines, the poet then considers the novel to be the proper form for his "novel" material, and when here too the attempt is aborted, again he blames himself:

> My downfall was "word-painting." Exquisite
> Peek-a-boo plumage, limbs aflush from sheer
> Bombast unfurling through the troposphere . . .
>
> [DC, p. 48]

Along the way Merrill complains of the inadequacy of "Our age's fancy narrative concoctions"; supernal punmanship engenders psychoanalytical insight as he explains why he dismissed from consideration "the in its fashion brilliant / Nouveau roman," which

> Struck me as an orphaned form, whose followers,
> Suckled by Woolf not Mann, had stories told them
> In childhood, if at all, by adults whom
> They could not love or honor.
>
> [DC, p. 47–48]

The form of "Ephraim" would appear, then, to have been contrived at last resort, all else having failed. And we are right to assume that something other than modesty, something beyond rational planning, accounts for this version of the work's origins. The point is that, in its final state, the poem gathers together various discarded or unrealizable selves: it functions as reportage, fairy tale, novel, even nouveau roman. The flotsam and jetsam of at least one abandoned novel bob up to the surface of "Ephraim"; from details given here and there, an enterprising reader can extrapolate the entire plot of this shipwrecked work. But (to switch metaphors) in doing so he will have visited but one story in a multitiered structure. For the poem also asks to be read as history, as a recollection of the twenty years preceding it—and as a chronicle of 1974, the year of composition, which supplies its share of metaphors:

> Impeachment ripens round the furrowed stone
> Face of a story-teller who has given
> Fiction a bad name (I at least thank heaven
> For my executive privilege vis-à-vis
> Transcripts of certain private hours with E.)
>
> [DC, p. 85]

But in order for "The Book of Ephraim" to make a present of its several pasts, to recover and to redeem its broken pieces, there had to have been something to wreck—something to break, to burn, and to be made new. As a necessary prelude to the final composition, a novel had to be drafted, if not inscribed, then not simply shelved but thrown away, "accidentally on purpose," as children like to say. In *Divine Comedies*, "The Will" documents this crucial transitional phase—the loss or rejection, the loss that is a rejection, of the abandoned novel that became "Ephraim."

Among Merrill's poems "The Will" is scarcely unique in being concerned with the salutary effects of loss. As befits the author of "Midas among Goldenrod," an early poem, Merrill participates in the mythic pattern that Richard Howard sees as central to his generation of poets: he would dissolve his golden touch in water, longing to lose what he had labored to acquire.[19] In fact, it might be equally helpful to use Prospero as his foil, for he vows to drown his book and break his magic staff after having first unleashed and then resolved his tempest in a teacup. For Merrill, the impulse to bring order out of wreckage seems ever accompanied by the desire to reverse the process, to crack the well-wrought urn; within his completed design, there persists a lingering distrust of artifice and design. Consider the punning relation of numbers to words in *Mirabell: Books of Number*. Stephen Yenser explains:

> Thus section 0 begins "Oh very well then," and section 1 echoes its number in both French and English: "UNHEEDFUL ONE." 3's "Trials and tremors" make use of Greek and the reader's choice of several other languages, 4's "Fear" of German, 5's "Go" of Japanese,

6's "She stood" of Russian, 7's "CHILDREN" of Chinese, 9's "NO VEIL" of Italian and Portuguese. 2 and 8 ring changes on the device, the one beginning with the second letter of the Hebrew alphabet (sometimes used in place of the number) in "Bethinking," the other with "8."[20]

What could speak more eloquently of the value this poet attaches to design—and of his steadfastness and ingenuity in keeping to one? Nor are the results merely ornamental; the conceit signifies. It dramatizes the notion that an alphabet of numbers gave birth to the writing; it suggests that language has a mind of its own, an autonomy of genius. Yet, though the correspondences are blessed, though they are produced by imagination and not by mere fancy, the poet reports that he is "Sickened by these blunt stabs at 'design'" when, in *Scripts for the Pageant* (p. 29), he looks back at the numbered portals he had erected for *Mirabell* and sees that book itself as a "Tower of Babel."

The trilogy has its share of deliberate breakdowns, characters stopping in mid-speech, interruptions, abandonments, misgivings, turnings against the self. The fragments do coalesce and cohere; the set pieces fit together, puzzle perfect; yet something about them militates against that sense of completion, of "design." The hybrid form and blend of styles exhibited by the work argue for a poetry of movement, process, and flow, as if for the sake of vitality the poet had to be a quick-change artist. "The Book of Ephraim" presents Merrill at his most protean, constantly changing shape, modulating from the narrator's pentameter to Ephraim's telegraphic style, hopping from sonnet sequence to terza rima. One ingenious section takes the guise of an annotated dramatis personae; another, taking a cue from its initial letter, consists entirely of quotations, mostly in prose, from real or imagined sources. Expediency would seem to be Merrill's rule of thumb:

> Since it had never truly fit, why wear
> The shoe of prose? In verse the feet went bare.
> Measures, furthermore, had been defined
> As what emergency required.

> [DC, p. 48]

As Marianne Moore put it, "ecstasy affords the occasion and expediency determines the form"; form, in effect, follows function. The garments available to the cunning seamstress are various enough to assure that for each speaker, for every situation, the appropriate dress will be found. But clothes are doomed to stay shapeless until worn—it takes a living body to make them come to life, and an "emergency" (in the sense of "an emergent occasion") to bring the wardrobe out of the closet.

"The Thousand and Second Night" prefigures "The Book of Ephraim" with respect to its expedient form. Like the latter, if on a smaller scale, it combines narrative and reflection upon narrative, interrupting its flow to accommodate a sonnet here, a prose paragraph there; there is visible evidence of split seams, but these have been skillfully mended. The poem's controlling image is its final one: an ethereal Scheherazade who merges with her fictions, a lusty Sultan liberated from her spell, left in the dark as to what his own tale might mean. The pair can stand for the soul and the senses, night and day, moon and sun, fiction and action, mother and father, even Psyche and Cupid. Can the poet negotiate a peace these estranged or quarreling couples can live with? Or, as Merrill puts it in *Mirabell*, will "Sultan Biology" come to love nature as Scheherazade, and if so, to what effect? The questions linger in the air long after the crisis that prompted them has found resolution and acedia has given way to resolve. "Form's what affirms," then, without actually settling anything; there is at best a half-rhyme between *form* and what it means to *affirm*. The remark appears in the poem's penultimate section, garbed in one of life's nonfiction disguises, the instructor's trot through a poem:

> Now if the class will turn back to this, er,
> Poem's first section—Istanbul—I shall take
> What little time is left today to make
> Some brief points. So. The rough pentameter
>
> Quatrains give way, you will observe, to three
> Interpolations, prose as well as verse.
> Does it come through how each in turn refers
> To mind, body, and soul (or memory)?

> [*ND*, p. 14]

The tension between narrative "forward motion" and poetic closure establishes itself immediately in "The Thousand and Second Night." The three "rough pentameter / Quatrains" that open the poem lead us to expect a fourth to follow, and it does; but it breaks off abruptly after two clipped lines, forcing us to revise our reading, to regard the opening fourteen lines as a sonnet. The breaking of the form is thus itself formally contained even as it enables the poet to reach out of bounds. (By contrast, "An Urban Convalescence"—the lead poem in *Water Street*—opens with stanzas that approach but fall short of sonnet form, an octave followed by a five-line stanza.) Here is that quatrain and a half which, at second glance, is the sestet of a sonnet; notice how the exclamation at the end simultaneously concludes one movement and announces the start of the next:

> Twenty-five hundred years this city has stood between
> The passive Orient and our frantic West.
> I see no reason to be depressed;
> There are too many other things I haven't seen,
>
> Like Hagia Sophia. Tea drunk, shaved and dressed . . .
> *Dahin! Dahin!*
>
> [*ND*, p. 4]

Of the "three / Interpolations" that follow, the last—a paragraph of prose—illustrates well Merrill's characteristically "vertical" expansion of a spot of time along the "horizontal" vector of the poem's narrative graph. No sooner has the verse announced the surfacing of an "infantile / Memory" than the prose, as if in obedience to a summons, steps dutifully forth. The Proustian click has happened on the poet's walk "across the bridge," a movement the poem enacts; we travel across from the troubled "now" of Istanbul to the healing "then" of memory, from "I" to fictive "he," verse to prose, the "mosque of Suleiman the Magnificent" to the wen on a grandmother's wrist, the "hard mauve bubble" that the mosque recalls:

> And now what? Back, I guess, to the modern town.
> Midway across the bridge, an infantile
> Memory promises to uncramp my style.
> I stop in deepening light to jot it down:

On the crest of her wrist, by the black watered silk of the watch-band, his grandmother had a wen, a hard mauve bubble up from which bristled three or four white hairs. How often he had lain in her lap and been lulled to a rhythm easily the whole world's then—the yellowish sparkle of a ring marking its outer limit, while in the foreground, silhouetted like the mosque of Suleiman the Magnificent, mass and minarets felt by someone fallen asleep on the deck of his moored caïque, that principal landmark's rise and fall distinguished, from any other, her beloved hand.

[*ND*, p. 6]

As in Proust, the apprehended object has retreated from central stage, has evolved into a simile for an object it imperfectly resembles; as in Proust, the simile's value rests in the quickening of memory, the conjuring up of early sensations. By thus disrupting the narrative to accommodate a glimpse of an anterior one, while insisting that the disruptive element itself be formally circumscribed, Merrill argues for the affirmative powers of form. *What* it affirms seems secondary to the blessed realization *that* it does; it speaks to the imagination's provisional success in either sensing or willing an order to things while maintaining fidelity to the appearance of disorder, disunity, dispersal.

The same strategy is at work in "From the Cupola," which together with "The Thousand and Second Night" provides a frame for *Nights and Days*. Again the poet conducts his train of verse to a prose detour; again the prose is in counterpoint to the verse around it, and here it is overtly a surviving fragment from an abandoned manuscript. The verse portions of "From the Cupola" record the breathless exchanges between Psyche and Cupid; the prose functions as a digression, a "breather" during which the poet drops anchor off the coast of a more prosaic island of activity, where campy kitchen conversations take place. Psyche, it seems, lives with her sisters Alice and Gertrude in the Connecticut equivalent of 27, rue de Fleurus; or rather, they live in the imagination of the imaginary Mr. Clarendon:

"Oh, Psyche!" her sister burst out at length. "Here you are, surrounded by loving kin, in a house crammed with lovely old things, and what do you crave but the unfamiliar, the 'transcendental'? I declare, you're turning into the classic New England old maid!"

[ND, p. 47]

Once it has furnished a contemporary social context for the mythic personages of the poem, once it has shifted them from one kind of fable to another, the prose rounds itself off with an unexpected rhyme that marks its completion and signals a return to verse: "Piercing her to the brain. // Spelt out in brutal prose, all had been plain." The intrusion is somehow assimilated; the interruption has been, in effect, a scheduled one, in the same way that in Kafka's parable the leopards invading a temple come to be accepted as part of the ritual.

The tug-of-war between poetry and prose is on center stage in *The (Diblos) Notebook*. This attempt at a nouveau roman keeps wanting to slide into poetry, and we expect it to. Consider this representative example:

> How to describe the change? I use my body less. If I swim at all, it is closer to the shore. Now that I know what liquor does to my liver, I drink less more. I don't take people as seriously. I move from place to place. I no longer think of myself as having a home. (Orson: Home is where the mind is.) I read more (alas) & (alas again) I *write*.[21]

By making visible the "invisible" hand of the author, the *Notebook* mediates between alternative texts, shedding skins like a snake and retaining what it discards, albeit in canceled form. The erasure and substitution (e.g., "less more") make clear that the events of a novel, any novel, are expedient fictions, products of choice. The rhyme itself is funny because unexpected, perverse: we are, I think, meant to see that the logic of the psyche may fly in the face of all human reason or wisdom; it may conform instead to the logic of a rhyme.

3

If it is relatively easy to tabulate Merrill's literary debts, that is partially because he himself has kept scrupulous records. A consciously literary artist, for all that he wears his learning lightly, Merrill invites us to read his poems with poetry in mind, to examine parallels and precedents; his respect for tradition leads him to want to experiment with it. Like all authentically "new" poetry, Merrill's invents a past for itself or more than one; he squares the exigencies of formal verse with a contemporary idiom and "novel" material, and while doing so he directs the latter-day reader's attention to poets and writers who might otherwise, regrettably, seem foreign to our time. Merrill's attempts at invigorating what has already started to ossify, his effort to breathe new life into a form or a phrase that has fallen on evil days, not to mention his successful thefts from past masters, are exemplary at a time when we may have more poets, but we certainly have more ignorant poets, than ever before.

I have mentioned the lifelong influence of Marcel Proust; in the trilogy a far more apparent presence is that of W. H. Auden. The apocalyptic epic as a genre allows for huge chunks of personal history, and so it must have seemed especially attractive to Merrill as he entered mid-career—our contemporary euphemism for the middle of life's journey—preparing to come to terms with Auden's eclipsed generation. Here one must be careful to distinguish between the Auden who figures as a character in *Mirabell* and *Scripts* and the Auden who has served Merrill as a literary exemplar, a poetic father. As a familiar spirit, a historical personage filtered through Merrill's myth-making prism, a friend among the newly dead whose beneficent good cheer robs death of its terror if not of its sting, Auden is the wise guy and the wise man in one, no less sagacious for his foppery; it is his genius to convert seemingly contradictory impulses into complementary ones, to embody the spiritual and to sanctify the profane. This dream of Auden is likewise a dream of Merrill himself; both have a side in them for which Congreve's Mirabell furnishes an apt sobriquet. Auden is honored equally in strictly technical ways, for strictly technical reasons. In Auden's smithy Merrill had done his apprenticeship, after all. He learned to practice a strict economy of form and to play with language, to test his ingenuity and its flexibility at once; he had emulated the older poet's stylistic virtuosity and had borrowed some of his tricks. Merrill's right-angle rhymes ("leaves" with "lives," "washes" with "wishes"), for example: they derive from Wilfred Owen but almost certainly by way of Auden's *Paid on Both Sides*. Also on long-term loan from the Auden library are Merrill's uni-sex rhymes, alternating masculine and feminine endings—"change" paired off with "arrangement," "courier" with "your," "silver" with "chill." The delight Merrill takes in random collisions of verbal particles bespeaks a deep affinity with Auden—and with Nabokov as well. In Merrill's poetry as in *Lolita* and *Pale Fire*, creative pre-texts—an anagram here, a spoonerism there—are left like purloined letters in everyone's view, comical clues for the reader as sleuth to uncover.

Merrill has a weakness for the "hexagonal" (that is, "sick-sided") pun, but much of his paranomasia is founded on the conviction that words yield their choicest secrets through playful means, that linguistic "accidents" are meaningful and therefore not really ac-cidents at all, that language's special logic can lead to discoveries that seem "altogether too beautiful not to be true." When, in "The Will," appearing surprised at Ephraim's moral suasion, JM says "you think the Word by definition good," he is roundly reproved: "IF U DO NOT YR WORLD WILL BE UNDONE / & HEAVEN ITSELF TURN TO ONE GRINNING SKULL" (*DC*, p. 41). Ephraim is, of course, preaching to the zealously converted. From the start the trilogy opposes the immortal life of words against the fact of death: what establishes contact with the dead, and thus resuscitates them, is a board full of letters and numbers; and what else is the Ouija board if not a clear though audacious metaphor for language as the source of death-defying poetry?

The poet's faith in the power of language—"THE REVEALD MONO-THEISM OF TODAY," Mirabell calls it—does in fact inform his puns and wordplay; they are a function as much of his metaphysical or moral imagination as of his aestheticism and verbal hedonism. Take this extraordinary moment near the end of *Mirabell*, this parenthet-ical aside with power enough to capture the very essence of the volume:

It's the hour
When Hell (a syllable identified
In childhood as the German word for *bright*

—So that my father's cheerful "Go to Hell,"
Long unheard, and Vaughan's unbeatable
"They are all gone into a world of light"
Come, even now at times, to the same thing)—
The hour when Hell shall render what it owes.

[*M*, p. 180]

How much this passage beautifully says about childhood and in-
nocence; how much about the poet's native romanticism, his trust
in language as the great reconciler of opposites, his optimism. No-
tice too how the sci-fi comic book character we'd been hearing
about—"Von," in his Star Trek cape—has turned here into the
metaphysical poet, Henry Vaughan; and recall that the book aims
to synthesize elements of high culture and of low, to bring together
two far from ideal sorts of reader, "ONE ON HIS KNEES TO ART / THE
OTHER FACEDOWN OVER A COMIC BOOK." Finally, consider the pas-
sage as an example of what I have called Merrill's comic sublime:
haven't wit and wordplay made an imprecation sound ironically
"cheerful" indeed? "Whitebeard on Videotape," the poem separat-
ing "The Will" from "The Book of Ephraim" in *Divine Comedies*,
concludes with the reminder that "Along with being holy, life was
hell" (*DC*, p. 44). But Merrill's seasons actually run counter to
those of Rimbaud or Eliot; he has always believed heaven more
real than hell. Accordingly he finds *Paradiso* the most persuasive
volume in Dante's *Commedia*:

The resulting masterpiece takes years to write;
More, since the dogma of its day
Calls for a Purgatory, for a Hell,
Both of which Dante thereupon, from footage
Too dim or private to expose, invents.
His Heaven, though, as one cannot but sense,
Tercet by tercet, is pure Show and Tell.

[*DC*, p. 89]

There has always been a metaphysical dimension to Merrill's
wit. Like John Donne, Merrill is distinguished by his love of con-
ceit, of the baroque elaboration of a comparison or figure of speech,
as in this trilingual pun from "The Book of Ephraim":

To touch on these unspeakables you want
The spry nuances of a Bach courante

> Or brook that running slips into a shawl
> Of crystal noise—at last, the waterfall.
>
> [*DC*, p. 93]

The "Bach courante," or dance, metamorphoses into a running brook, or "Bach courante," *Bach* meaning "brook" in German, *courante* as the French for "running": thus, brook and dance act as surrogates for one another at the same time that they both define Merrill's "Unrelenting fluency." As Donne likens the legs of a compass to a pair of parting lovers, or identifies the sexual act with the exploration of the Americas, so the metaphysical Merrill invests a special significance in the doing of laundry ("The Mad Scene") or the solving of jigsaw puzzles ("Lost in Translation"). Such activities turn into rituals for the poet and as such serve an additional "metaphysical" purpose: they bear witness, they prompt self-examination, they become ways of disclosing, in brief and on a local level, larger mysteries of the cosmos.

With the conviction that the dramas of daily life participate in grand or mythic patterns, Merrill translates our cardinal winds into human terms—as "Nought," "Eased," "Sought," and "Waste" (*BE*, p. 73). Again one thinks of Donne and his anatomy of the universe. "I am a little world made cunningly," Donne writes in one of his *Holy Sonnets*, "Of elements and an angelic sprite," elements that must brave the assault of the elements:

> Pour new seas in mine eyes, that so I might
> Drown my world with my weeping earnestly,
> Or wash it if it must be drowned no more.
> But oh it must be burnt!

For Merrill, too, reality is elemental. The little world of the self, of earth and air composed, requires the destructive but holy powers of fire and water to intervene periodically. The envisioned angel in the window must endure a trial by water ("A Vision of the Garden"), and so must a mother's messages ("The Friend of the Fourth Decade"), while the houses of poetic tenancy inevitably undergo a fate of flames ("18 West 11th Street") before "OUR TRIALS BY FIRE YIELD TO THE TRIAL BY TEARS" (*M*, p. 154). "Log," the keynote poem of *Braving the Elements*, initiates the reader into the ritual blaze; a lyric of great delicacy, it likens itself to a burning log, made "less" by the very flames that cause "Dear light along the way to nothingness" (*BE*, p. 3). Writing, then, would seem to involve kindling the past, sending it up in smoke, and then recomposing it, a new "house" rising phoenixlike out of the ashes and sparks. Thus "18 West 11th Street" concludes with its "Original vacancy" recaptured, while "The Broken Home" survives its trial by air to end with "the unstiflement of the entire story" (*ND*, p. 30), a revealing pun, reinforcing the metaphoric identity shared by narrative and house. In effect the fate of Merrill's houses (lived in, abandoned, exploded, repossessed) is not merely described by such poems but enacted in them.

"The Will" offers a vanishing point for a number of the perspectival lines I have been drawing in this essay. One may fruitfully examine the poem in the context of Merrill's narrative aims; one may wander through the poem collecting evidence of the poet's fidelity to the Socratic axiom ("the unexamined life is not worth living") as modified by a reading of Freud; the poem may teach us how the flowers of poetry bloom from the wreckage of prose. Thematic continuities between "The Will" and earlier poems stare one in the face. At one point, for example, the poet suffers a figurative paralysis that brings to mind the "rigor vitae" of "The Thousand and Second Night"; like that poem, "The Will" is a "healing hieroglyph," a statement of resolution and independence in the Wordsworthian tradition, as well as a rejection of artifice, of the type of art that would paralyze experience. Stylistically, the poet's signature appears in the slant rhymes, the renewed clichés ("O dogwood days"), the way that language impels metaphysical conceit, as the title impels us to understand human volition in the terms of a legal document. From the point of view of form as well, "The Will" erects a bridge between Merrill's past and future selves. It introduces the telegraphic, uppercase line Merrill reserves for his otherworldly voices; in so doing it looks to the future—it is clearly an annunciatory poem, a harbinger of the benevolent "no accident" clause of *Mirabell*. As a series of sonnets, a poem composed of sonnets and not a sonnet sequence in the conventional sense, it as clearly seems to extend the past.

The use of sonnets as building blocks, linked yet separate, retaining their individual integrity yet flowing into a whole larger than the sum of its parts, qualifies as one of Merrill's most significant and original contributions to the treasure chest of poetic forms.[22] An inveterate sonneteer, Merrill has sought to adapt the form to the peculiar exigencies of his present, to tamper with the tradition and thus to renew it; as a result, as Kalstone notes, an entire Merrill volume can read "like a sonnet sequence following the curve of a love affair to its close."[23] As early as in "Three Sketches for Europa," Merrill had experimented in the direction of linked sonnets. The impulse is successfully realized in "The Broken Home" and in several poems in *The Fire Screen,* and by the time of "The Will" Merrill could confidently display his mastery of the form. More than anything else, it calls for a rigorous balancing act; the poem must be poised between the wish to "build in sonnets pretty rooms" and the urge to tear down the walls separating one from the other. Much of the poem's power derives from this tension between narrative fluidity and what sportscasters call "a break in the action." The conclusion of an individual sonnet acts at once as a climax and as a transition to the following sonnet in a way that suggests one of time's paradoxical properties: that the moment of completion and the moment of origin are one; that while completion is illusory, the illusion itself is meaningful.

Consider what happens when the first sonnet in "The Will" comes to a close:

> Now to pack
>
> This canvas tote-bag. I have wrapped in jeans
> With manuscript on either side for wadding
> Something I'm carrying to a . . . to a wedding. . .
>
> Then, wondering as always what it means
> And what else I'm forgetting,
> On my cold way. A car is waiting.
>
> [DC, p. 37]

The subtlety of the final rhyme is an exact measure of the extent of compromise in the sonnet's closure. The lines seem deliberately anticlimactic, even prosaic, serviceable for advancing the narrative.

But they demand, however subtly, to be read in a second way also, as concluding something. When read with this slight extra emphasis, the terminal phrases of the three lines gain in significance. The quest for "what it means" and the art of "forgetting" turn out to be two of the poem's major concerns; and as for that ominously waiting car, is it what it seems or not? Is it, as a matter of fact, a limousine—or a hearse? The poet has said he is on his way to a wedding, but could this ceremony follow hard upon a funeral? Perhaps he is somehow in Hamlet's predicament—perhaps, in some metaphoric sense, the funeral baked meats will coldly furnish forth the marriage tables. Could this be why the poet, a stanza earlier, hesitated before informing us that a wedding was his destination?

The constant give-and-take between formal means and narrative meanings allows for some startling effects. Sometimes the form gives way—two sonnets overlap, or one simply bisects another. At one point in the poem, the narrative is advanced by a purely formal maneuver: the sestet of the third sonnet in the series likens itself to the flight of a plane, while the space between an equivocal comma's temporary closure and the next sonnet's opening phrases enacts the landing:

> we have effortlessly risen
> Through on occasion to a brilliant
> Ice blue and white sestet
>
> Six lines six miles above, if not rhyme, reason.
> Its winged shadow tiny as an ant
> Keeps up far down, state after sunnier state,
>
> Or grown huge (have we landed?)
> Scatters into human shadows all
> Underfoot skittering through the terminal
> To greet, lulled, blinded,
>
> The mild, moist South. Che puro ciel . . .
>
> [DC, p. 38]

At other points it is the narrative that breaks apart, undergoing changes of tense and of point of view, moving rapidly from event to interpretation, stopping for a Ouija session, looking at itself being written. While the story seems to have to do with a wedding, it is in actuality a wedding *gift* that the plot revolves around, and the poem doesn't get to the church on time. The story is suspended, postponed, and never completed—until we realize that what seemed an interruption has become the story itself. Upon inspection, then, "The Will" resembles a diagrammed sentence in Proust; in both cases, the richness resides in ostensibly subordinate elements.

As "The Will" opens, we intercept the poet in "a living room" that keeps at bay "the dead of winter" outside; into the cold he will soon have to go, for this is a poem of spiritual rejuvenation and artistic rebirth, requiring a preliminary death—if only in metaphor. Enter two men and a woman "with a will." The scene eerily reverses the last tableau in "A Tenancy," the end poem of *Water Street*. There "my three friends" had come bearing gifts, welcoming the poet to his career as a host; here, like a dark version of that angelic trio, they are dressed in mourner's black. It is in effect a house-cooling party: what the lease was for "A Tenancy" the last will and testament is for the later poem. The poet prepares us for haunted happenings. Though familiar, the "living room" (with its hint of lebensraum) feels more than a little strange, reminding perhaps of Freud's contention that the "uncanny" ("unheimlich") is the homely in disguise, the demoniacal return of the domesticated ghost. Just as the room is "Somehow both David the Wise's and not his," so the will is both the poet's own (he does sign it) and not (it takes him by surprise). At a later moment, the poem will state the paradox more directly. It will decide that the human will can express itself inadvertently, that it necessarily takes time for one's consciousness to catch up with one's self. Now, taking leave of his mysterious visitors, the poet packs his bags; "In jeans / With manuscript on either side for wadding," he wraps the gift he has planned to bestow upon the bridal couple, a sculptured ibis whose "funerary chic" and handsome artifice "could stand for the giver"—for one of his defunct selves, that is, that the poem will leave behind.

After a parenthetical sonnet interrupts the narrative with a deliberate regression into the previous night's premonitory dream, a dream within the envelope of another, the poem makes way for a new theme, that of the "accidentally" self-inflicted wound:

I'm at an airport, waiting. The scar itches.
Carving, last month I nearly removed my thumb.
Where was my mind? Lapses like this become
Standard practice. Not all of them leave me in stitches.

[DC, p. 38]

The pun on "stitches" makes its wry point: there is a connection between laugh and scar, the latter being a sign at once of injury and of healing: the broken skin will mend with laughter as, with the help of high spirits, the poet will gain ample compensation for his losses. "What's done is done, dreamlike"; it has to happen and cannot be prevented. So it is far from an accident that the bag, "Gone underwater-weightless," is forgotten on the floor of the taxi taking the poet from airport to city. Nor, given the compulsion to repeat, does it mystify that again "Self-inflicted / Desolation a faint horselaugh jars."

Switching from "I" to "he," Merrill conducts "the prodigal" to his mother's house. It is here that, after joining his mother's friends—elderly "sirens" who "love their sweetly-sung bloodthirsty games"—at bridge, he discovers his loss. As often in Merrill's poetry, incidental details yield metaphoric energy, and so the game and their singing orchestrate this sestet:

He is sitting at the table, dealing,
When a first tentative wrong note
Is quickly taken up ("What is it, darling?")

By the whole orchestra in unison.
The unbid heart pounds in his throat—
The bag, the bird—left in the taxi—gone!

[DC, p. 40]

In a linkage like that between stanzas 7 and 8 of "Ode to a Nightingale," Merrill makes the last word of the sestet the keynote of the sonnet that follows:

Gone for good. In the first shock of
Knowing it he tries
To play the dummy, dreads to advertise,
"Drinks water" like a character in Chekhov.

[DC, p. 40]

The bag and its contents are "Gone for good" in both senses. Initial dismay and wonderment give way to relief at Ephraim's reassuring words, in a flash forward to the Ouija board months later:

U DID WELL JM TO DISINHERIT
YR SELF & FRIENDS OF THAT STONE BIRD

Why? Because its malevolent presence causes disaster to strike all who would possess it. What symbolic significance could it have for JM? The fate of its latest victim, the cabdriver's sister, explains "what it means": she is paralyzed. More "burden" than bird, the sculpture represents the sort of art that runs this danger, an art that has calcified, like Lot's wife, all natural force abated. The "old wall-eyed stone-blond / Ibis" is thus very like the "little tumblers finely etched" that we came across in "Charles on Fire." And JM, though tempted by "Exquisite / Peek-a-boo plumage" (*DC*, p. 48), must declare against it, must reject such time-arresting artifice in favor of the art of losing, of man unaccommodated and experience unadorned. He must renounce by an act of will what he had lost by a stroke of luck. *Felix culpa!* The lesson stands as a comic footnote to Kierkegaard's Knight of Faith. He who renounces, him we can save—only in Merrill's poem the renunciation is ex post facto. Since there are no accidents in the "overdetermined" realm of the psyche, the *passive* experience of forgetting can become a spiritual *action* (or an action instinct with spirit). By a mental lapse that somehow expresses his will, JM has—in Ephraim's precise phrase—managed to "DISINHERIT" himself and friends of the ibis and what it represents.

Ephraim's reassurance extends to the "missing bag's / Other significant cargo," the manuscript with which it had been packed. This is none other than the "mistaken / Enterprise" to whose loss "The Book of Ephraim" owes its existence: "Ephraim" substitutes for the missing manuscript just as, in *The Importance of Being Earnest*, the "real" Ernest Worthing arrives as the substitute for Miss Prism's lost three-volume novel. Indeed, "The Book of Ephraim" takes its place among those works of modern literature that seem, with greater or lesser irony, to prescribe the burning or abandoning of a manuscript as a necessary liberation.[24] The "GLUM PAGES" of JM's lost novel lacked the "GLORY" they wished to capture because,

Ephraim implies, the poet had relied on artifice; he is advised instead to go straight to the source, to "SET MY TEACHINGS DOWN." The connection between manuscript and stone ibis is now complete; they stand for one another. It is here, with his injunction to live and lose, to "LIVE MORE LIVE MOST" and "GIVE UP EVERYTHING EXCEPT THE GHOST," that Ephraim brings to mind Wordsworth's leech-gatherer: this is the timely utterance that heralds the intimations of immortality to come. Lest the point otherwise be lost on readers of *Divine Comedies,* the opening section of "Ephraim" contains this cross-reference to "The Will":

> Blind
> Promptings put at last the whole mistaken
> Enterprise to sleep in darkest Macon
> (Cf. "The Will"), and I alone was left
> To tell my story.
>
> [*DC,* p. 48]

"And I only am escaped alone to tell thee." So, quoting Job, Melville begins the epilogue to *Moby Dick.* "Because one did survive the wreck."

"The poem's logic," Merrill comments in *Scripts,* "Calls for the shattering of a glass" (p. 82). The logic of "The Will" calls for something similar, a breaking of form preparatory to, or coincident with, a redemptive epiphany. A bit of Proustian "foreshortening" finds the poet at his desk, suffering from "Paralysis," laboring fruitlessly on "drafts" of his experience, the formless "wastes and drifts / Of time."

> Then a lucky stroke unearths the weird
> Basalt passage of last winter,
> Tunneling black. The match struck as I enter
> Illuminates . . . My word!
>
> [*DC,* p. 42]

The knowing use of a cliché works wonders. As the direct object of "Illuminates," the exclamatory "word" completes a crucial thought; as an interjection, it breaks off the flow of words and brings the quatrain screeching to a halt. The imaginary tunnel with the real light in it has led to the climax of the poem, a flash of seeing that expresses itself as a formal disruption. For at this point the sonnet we thought we were reading stops, suspended after two quatrains, shattered by the advent of *another* sonnet. The latter, set off by parentheses, as though conscious of itself as an interpolation, bears glad tidings, a restorative vision brought about by the illumination of the poet's word:

> [(]Here was a manuscript. Here were
> Five catgut stitches laid in lusterware.
>
> And here in final state, where lost was found,
> The ibis sat. Another underground
>
> Chamber made ready. If this one was not
> Quite the profoundest or the most ornate,
>
> Give it time. The bric-a-brac
> Slumbered in bonds that of themselves would break
>
> One fine day, at any chance unsealing,
> To shining leaf and woken shades of feeling.)
>
> [*DC*, pp. 42–43]

Like a zigzag of stitches, this couplet sonnet enables the poem to recover from its self-inflicted wound. Only after this sonnet has run its course can the one it interrupted complete itself; only then can the poem attain the status of a "healing hieroglyph." For this pattern of interruption and postponed completion, Merrill had in mind a musical precedent. In Mozart's Piano Concerto in E Flat (K. 271) a rondo breaks off for the length of a minuet. But surely it is tempting also to see the interruption as a dramatic instance of Merrill's vessel-cracking art, his willingness to subject the forms he lives by to a ritual blaze. Through such displays of elemental bravery, Merrill achieves at last the exaltation that marks his great trilogy, an affirmation able to withstand the pressure of reality. So, at the end of "The Will," the dirty noise of a helicopter drowns out the vows of lovers and dying men, the sweet voices of doves and finches, but its shadow cannot "eclipse / The sunniness" below, the house no longer haunted (except for cozily familiar spirits), the "living room" illumined from within by words that have been put to a fiery test.

CHAPTER 2

On *Water Street*

J. D. McClatchy

Customarily, a collection of James Merrill's poems begins with a short lyric that anticipates by announcing them the concerns and tone of the whole book. The thematic departures and presiding patron of *The Country of a Thousand Years of Peace* are introduced in the opening title poem. "The Nightgown" in *Nights and Days,* "Log" in *Braving the Elements,* and "The Kimono" in *Divine Comedies* are each a conceit—as much an invocation of powers as a retrospective commentary on the act of writing itself—that sounds a keynote to be struck in important poems throughout the different books. *Water Street* is unusual in this regard for having no proleptic lyric. Instead, the book's longest and major poem, "An Urban Convalescence," comes first. Its pride of place is understandable; Merrill himself has called the poem "a turning point" in his career. In its grand way, then, it announces not only the preoccupations of *Water Street* but a decisive change in the poet's thinking about the emotional and technical capacities of verse.

If *Water Street* had been organized along the lines of his other collections, then Merrill might have placed the second poem, "From a Notebook," first in the book. Its very title points toward the volume's effective origins, and its figures for speech—the writer as Narcissus over his frozen pond or before a mirror's "dreamless oval," as steelshod skater tracing loops and spirals on the page's "fresh / Candor"—are no less eloquent for being familiar. But I suspect the more fitting prelude to *Water Street* would have been a poem that could double as its dedication—"For Proust." Like "From a Notebook," it too is a poem about writing, but an altogether more virtuosic and substantial one. The poem presumes to tell a story: one of Proust's midnight forays into the world to capture a detail for his novel, his rendezvous at the Ritz with a woman who might but never does hum "the little phrase," and his exhausted but enriched return to his study. But much more is illustrated by the poem than its exemplary anecdote. We might be alerted to this by the rare rhyme scheme (each quatrain's median couplet is an identical rhyme) that emphasizes the notion of repossession or by the evidence of a very Proustian foreshortening—whereby, for example, the conjured friend is at first "a child," then three stanzas and a conversation later has a white lock in her hair, and in the last stanza is replaced by, or transformed into, the "old, old woman" who tends him. "For Proust" is a deft portrait of, and tribute to, the novelist; it is also a summary of his novel's leading motifs and a succinct interpretation of the method of his *recherche*. The balance, in fact, between the writer's life and his art—what Merrill calls here "the painful sum of things"—is the poem's ballast. Throughout, the emphasis is on pain—on neurasthenia and anxiety, on betrayal and inadequacy—until that pain is strangely intensified by its conclusion:

> Back where you came from, up the strait stair, past
> All understanding, bearing the whole past,
> Your eyes grown wide and dark, eyes of a Jew,
>
> You make for one dim room without contour
> And station yourself there, beyond the pale
> Of cough or of gardenia, erect, pale.
> What happened is becoming literature.
>
> Feverish in time, if you suspend the task,
> An old, old woman shuffling in to draw
> Curtains, will read a line or two, withdraw.
> The world will have put on a thin gold mask.

[*WS*, p. 19]

His retreat is his great responsibility. By "bearing the whole past," he gives life to what is over, forgotten or misunderstood. "What happened"—that is, what he had experienced once and tried another time to understand—is given a continuous existence by and in his art. And that task, though fatal, redeems: the haggard life mask glows, first with fever, finally with immortality. "The thin gold mask," writes Richard Howard, "is not a defense against reality, nor a concealment from it; it is a funerary enduement which will withstand and redeem the wreckage of a life."[1] It is clever of Howard so to have merged—or to have allowed the final image to contain—both the artist and the world. Certainly the poem encourages such a reading. Proust enters his "one dim room" as if it were a tomb, so that his sacrifice—the sacrifice of himself into his novel—seems to merit the honor of a royal death mask. But it is the world, not the artist, that puts on the mask. On a literal level, the last line simply refers to the world beyond Proust's curtained window, a world then putting on the gold mask of dawn.[2] But more is implied. What is happening has become literature; image subsumes event. The world *will have* put on a rich finish—its outlines familiar but its appearance transfigured—when so portrayed by the artist and then so seen by his reader. The presence in this last stanza of the "old, old woman" is also suggestive. Again on a literal level, she is a conflation of Proust's servant Celeste Albaret, of his beloved mother, and of his grandmother. But she is, too, the world itself, that "ancient, ageless woman of the world" who presides over the close of "Ephraim." In a sense, then, it is she who puts on the thin gold mask, as earlier she had worn other masks: the conjured friend's, a child's, the loved one's. She has been both muse and material, and at the end it is the old woman who "will read a line or two." Are not an author's muse and his ideal reader two aspects of the same figure?

"For Proust," then, is as much a celebration of the natural yet mysterious sources of art as it is an evocation of the frail but god-like powers of the artist. Both those subjects are taken up in *Water Street*. And Proust himself, long Merrill's most deep-rooted influence, may be seen to have replaced Hans Lodeizen—the tutelary spirit of *The Country of a Thousand Years of Peace*—as the patron of this book. Hans was the Young Man taken out of time, cultivated but impersonal, a hero because a martyr, perfected because unfulfilled. Proust, on the other hand, is the more human figure and the more mature artistic model. Struggling against time in order to recover it, he is at once at the heart of the world and the perpetual outsider, the internal exile. Merrill seeks to live by Proust's great laws in *Water Street* and to adapt his novel's methods for poetry. Questions of scale and intimacy and intermittence, of the ability to create and to characterize the self, of the alchemical function of metaphor to change the lead of private experience into the gold of archetypal art—for all these questions and others Merrill sought an answering verse in this book. Where Proust sought his answers, in the primary worlds of childhood and the sensual life, so, too, does Merrill seek his. More than half the poems in the book are concerned with childhood, with family or domestic scenes. The specific and circumscribed settings of poems like "Getting Through" or "A Tenancy" are their new advantage. "The Water Hyacinth," for example, is addressed to his maternal grandmother (whose elegy is the following poem, "Annie Hill's Grave"), juxtaposing old memories of her and of hers with present realities of age and illness. The ingenuous tone with which the poem opens is secured from slackness by the strong affection in its direct address and by an easy and convincing naturalness that is new in Merrill's voice:

> When I was four or so
> I used to read aloud
> To you—I mean, recite
> Stories both of us knew
> By heart, the book held close
> To even then nearsighted
> Eyes. It was morning. You,
> Still in your nightgown
> Over cold tea, would nod
> Approval. Once I caught
> A gay note in your quiet:
> The book was upside down.
>
> [WS, p. 39]

From that point on, the poem deals with what else is now "upside down," time having overturned all but such memories. The poem increases in syntactical complexity as it broadens the scope of its concern. And to resolve the poem, Merrill combines his perspectives to focus on a remembered detail that is both historically exact and symbolically apt. The water hyacinth, imported at the turn of the century when she was honeymooning, later choked the St. John's River near his grandmother's native Jacksonville:

> A mauve and rootless guest
> Thirsty for life, afloat
> With you on the broad span
> It would in sixty years
> So vividly congest.
>
> [WS, p. 40]

Other of Proust's discoveries and maneuvers are present as well, either as compositional aids or emotional attitudes. There is a new attention to motivation, the use of involuntary memories, the deployment of interlocking images, a heightened awareness of the imperfection of the present and the transience of the past. They animate the best poems in *Water Street*—"An Urban Convalescence," "A Tenancy," and "Scenes of Childhood." But I would group the book with Merrill's early work because, while these three poems are superior to anything in his two previous books, and by their innovations help define the direction and force of his subsequent work, they are not matched by the remainder of the book. In comparison with *The Country of a Thousand Years of Peace*, this book may even seem a slighter one; there are fourteen fewer poems, and a narrower range. There is a delicacy at work in *Water Street* that gives several poems charm ("Five Old Favorites," "The Lawn Fete of Homunculus Artifex"), and a heartiness that gives others some bite ("Roger Clay's Proposal," "The Reconnaissance"), but neither quality makes any of those poems very significant. Not until *Nights and Days* can he sustain for the length of an entire book the originality and intensity that mark the three important poems in *Water Street*.

Leading off the book as it does, "An Urban Convalescence" occupies a position analogous to that of "Beyond the Alps" in Robert Lowell's *Life Studies*, a book published three years before *Water Street* and one whose crucial autobiographical emphasis may well have helped Merrill to fashion the circumstantial intimacy of his own poem. In both poems, life changes to landscape, as Lowell put it: both are trains of thought that end in Paris, Merrill's in memory, Lowell's in anticipation. "Beyond the Alps" is a pivotal poem in Lowell's work. It stands as a renunciation of his tortured and hieratic Catholic beliefs, preliminary to the secular cast of *Life Studies* with its pathetic portraits of impotence and madness. Though *Water Street* has none of the novelistic coherence of *Life Studies*, and certainly none of its anguish, "An Urban Convalescence" stands in a similar relation to Merrill's previous work. It too signals a rejection. More by its example than by any declaration, it abjures an earlier belief or mode, in this case the baroque preciosity, the feints and baffles of *First Poems* and *The Country of a Thousand Years of Peace*. The style of those books is gestural: taut or spiraling, all running colors and arrested development, preferring ecstasy to refinement, contradictions to continuities. The best of that style—its brio, its lavishness, its fondness for paradox—remains in *Water Street*. Its ornate excesses and riddles do not. Modest set pieces such as "To a Butterfly" or "The Parrot Fish" serve to remind one of how few such emblematic poems there actually are in the book and of how Merrill is now less content with intellectual conceits and more dependent on phenomenal details, vivid and familiar, than he was before.

To compare "Saint" or "The Charioteer of Delphi" in *The Country of a Thousand Years of Peace* with "Angel" in *Water Street* accentuates the difference. The former poems, metrically constrained, deal in extreme states of soul, in rapture, despair, havoc. The free verse of "Angel" is altogether more relaxed and genial and corresponds to the poem's witty amiability. Like the earlier poems, it too explores the themes of learning and mastery but takes up those themes in a context of the commonplace. It too measures the self against an idealized image, but far from lamenting the distance between them, it delights in their comic disparity. Like the statues of Sebastian and the charioteer, the guardian angel above the poet's desk—conceivably a postcard—has an iconic presence but is no martyr with whom the poet longs to identify himself. This angel, a sort of antimuse, is both ironic and unaware, self-important yet humorously miniaturized:

> Above my desk, whirring and self-important
> (Though not much larger than a hummingbird)
> In finely woven robes, school of Van Eyck,
> Hovers an evidently angelic visitor.
> He points one index finger out the window
> At winter snatching to its heart,
> To crystal vacancy, the misty
> Exhalations of houses and of people running home
> From the cold sun pounding on the sea;
> While with the other hand
> He indicates the piano
> Where the Sarabande No. 1 lies open
> At a passage I shall never master
> But which has already, and effortlessly, mastered me.

The angel's silent reproach makes him seem at first like Stevens's angel surrounded by paysans, the necessary angel of earth come to lead the poet to the promised land of reality. Inside, composing, mastered by another artist's music, the ephebe is directed to the world beyond his window—the world Proust transcended by absorbing. But the lexical ambiguity in the first line, whereby the poet's metonymous desk is itself "whirring and self-important," is the clue. The moral the angel next draws is only a projection, an "as if," of the poet's own frustration and self-doubt:

> He drops his jaw as if to say, or sing,
> 'Between the world God made
> And this music of Satie,
> Each glimpsed through veils, but whole,
> Radiant and willed,
> Demanding praise, demanding surrender,
> How can you sit there with your notebook?
> What do you think you are doing?'

[WS, p. 42]

The poet sees himself poised between the world and his art, cut off from the one, incapable of the other. The world having been described as a work of art (a "crystal vacancy," and the sun pounding on the sea as if on a piano note) and Satie's Sarabande given the divine status of mastery, they reinforce each other and, by their self-sufficiency, "Radiant and willed," combine to accuse the poet of precisely what he has not—or not yet, not until "Angel" is over—been able to create. At this point in the earlier two poems, the speaker would have turned disconsolately back in, or been stung into reminiscence. But Merrill is in a puckish mood here. A teasing decorum settles the score, as the poet turns back to his page. Neither his piano playing nor his writing are yet connected, or legato, he has said, but by the last line the completed poem serves to confound the angel's conscience and the poet's doubts:

> However he says nothing—wisely: I could mention
> Flaws in God's world, or Satie's; and for that matter
> How did he come by *his* taste for Satie?
> Half to tease him, I turn back to my page,
> Its phrases thus far clotted, unconnected.
> The tiny angel shakes his head.
> There is no smile on his round, hairless face.
> He does not want even these few lines written.
>
> [WS, p. 42]

Merrill's avoidance of melodrama in this poem, of emotional impasse or baroque expedients, is characteristic of *Water Street* as a whole and of a new bearing in his work to come. His poems now tend to insist on questioning their own assumptions, on tempering headstrong convictions with heartfelt reservations, on maintaining a revisionary attitude toward both experience and his feelings about that experience. The effect, for all the opportunities it gives the poet to vary a poem's pace and to manipulate a reader's responses, is one of emotional honesty, an openness that belies the very artistry used to achieve it. This quality becomes a hallmark of Merrill's best poems, which accommodate their own second guesses. A poem, though intricately worked, will sometimes seem a series of fresh starts, each more precise and more resonant than the last. As a man comfortable with the subtleties of imagery, the speaker of these poems is used to threading the maze of his thoughts, will not trust himself too readily and, because he can explain them, is not surprised by his mind's play or his language's darting eloquence. What I call here a poem's "emotional honesty" should not be mistaken for the frankness of the confessionalists. It may be, as Valéry noted, that a man knows too little of himself to reveal to us, in his "sincere" confessions, much more than we could easily have guessed without his telling us. *Water Street* is not itself autobiographical in any documentary sense. Unlike the sometimes flat transcripts of Ginsberg or Lowell, it does not serve up the raw events of Merrill's "outer" life or the overdetermined accidents of his emotional dealings. Nor does it even draw very specifically and consistently on his own biography, as "The Book of Ephraim" will later do. Yet there seems a candid intimacy to this book that is absent from his earlier work and is the distinction of his later. In an interview Merrill once shrugged off confessional poetry as "a literary convention like any other, the problem being to make it *sound* as if it were true."³ It is, in other words, a manner rather than the matter of a poem that confers its intimacy. But this is not only an affair of style: certain nuances of tone, adjustments of perspective, the forging of private experience in the hearth of myth and fable, pattern and drive. It is also a demand for a probity prior to the poetry, which the style must reinforce. Whatever Merrill may reserve from the reader, we feel he has not deceived himself. His most affecting poems, from *Water Street* on, succeed not because of how they expose or suppress the facts of his life but because they rely on an intellectual scrupulosity while searching out the truths of the heart.

2

Water Street begins, in "An Urban Convalescence," with a recovery. The title implies an illness that is never specified in the poem, as are the paralysis in "The Thousand and Second Night" or the virus in "A Fever." There may have been—probably was—an actual illness, but for the sake of the poem, it is more metaphoric than real, a spiritual condition rather than a physical ailment. From one point of view it can be seen as the Proustian creative malady. In this view the invalid and the artist share and feed on a hypersensitivity that is denied the "normal" man. And like the convalescent who seeks out reviving stimulants, the artist as *homme nerveux* seeks out—and is sought out by—new sensations that, however slight, stir old, ramifying memories, as they certainly do in this poem. But from another point of view we might see it less as an enabling difficulty than as a disabling facility. And I think Merrill names the problem, albeit covertly, in a turn of phrase so "facile" as to be distracting. "The sickness of our time" very nearly translates, after all, the *maladie du temps* that pervades the speaker's consciousness and the poem's impulses toward escape, stability, reassurance. Hampered by the existential horror of mortality, the sickness unto death that is time itself, the only convalescence possible involves a new understanding of his life that would allow the speaker to reconcile himself to loss and limitation.

That it is an urbane convalescence might be expected, but an *urban* one? We have great recuperative odes, from Coleridge to Ashbery, with rural or retired settings, and we are used by now to the sort of urban pastoral that Frank O'Hara perfected. But Merrill's poem—though an arcadian pattern can be perceived, with its garlands, tendril, fruit, roots, the Champs-Elysées themselves—deliberately leaves behind the pastoral world of natural resources and idealizing fictions, and seeks its remedy elsewhere. The poem begins outdoors:

> Out for a walk, after a week in bed,
> I find them tearing up part of my block
> And, chilled through, dazed and lonely, join the dozen
> In meek attitudes, watching a huge crane
> Fumble luxuriously in the filth of years.
> Her jaws dribble rubble. An old man
> Laughs and curses in her brain,
> Bringing to mind the close of *The White Goddess*.
>
> As usual in New York, everything is torn down
> Before you have had time to care for it.
> Head bowed, at the shrine of noise, let me try to recall
> What building stood here. Was there a building at all?
> I have lived on this same street for a decade.
>
> [WS, p. 3]

The opening is done in quick, broad strokes. Within a dozen lines the setting is vividly sketched in and the speaker's character outlined. He is delicate, disoriented, literate. The scene itself—which could hardly astonish a New Yorker but might startle a *penseroso* isolated a week with his own thoughts—is nearly grotesque. What

in the trade is called "construction work" is an image—one that
Lowell later used effectively in "For the Union Dead"—that serves
two purposes. On the one hand, it establishes the poem's premise
by symbolizing the uncaring ravages of time and of a discontented
civilization. That theme with its attendant images—of demolition
and fragmentation, of convulsive change and wasting—is quintes-
sentially the theme of modern poetry itself. If Merrill did not have
Baudelaire's "Le Cygne" in mind while writing "An Urban Conva-
lescence"—which is unlikely for one so well versed in French poet-
ry—then at least a reader might recall the earlier poem's lament
that "la forme d'une ville / Change plus vite, hélas! que le coeur
d'un mortel." Baudelaire goes on to contrast the shifting cityscape
with the permanence of private memories:

> Paris change! mais rien dans ma mélancolie
> N'a bougé! palais neufs, échafaudages, blocs,
> Vieux faubourgs, tout pour moi devient allégorie,
> Et mes chers souvenirs sont plus lourds que des rocs.

In Merrill's poem there are no *chers souvenirs* of New York. The
mad external destruction both reflects the speaker's illness and
mental confusion and is a projection of it. But at this point the
second meaning of the image is active, for Merrill's New York is
less Eliot's Unreal City than it is Baudelaire's *cité pleine de rêves*.
Who fumbles luxuriously in the filth of years but the dreamer or
the analysand? If not so pointed or clinical in its associations, then
the image of "construction work" does signal a turn inward, and if
not a conscious excavation of the self, then a willingness to permit
the operations of involuntary memories. This purposiveness on the
speaker's part is underscored by the religious imagery that domi-
nates the passage. He joins the apostolic "dozen / In meek atti-
tudes," his "Head bowed, at the shrine of noise." There is less
irony in those terms than there may seem at first, and the pattern
is continued through the rest of the poem, whose crisis-quest for-
mat would dictate such images. The speaker who sets out as a
flâneur soon enough becomes a passionate pilgrim—and therefore,
like the invalid, a type of the artist himself, a type familiar from
Wagner or from Henry James.

This realization leads us to yet another layer of references in these stanzas. The laughing, cursing old man in the crane brings to mind—to the speaker's mind—the close of *The White Goddess*, that cranky "historical" grammar of poetic myth by Robert Graves. Merrill may simply be referring to the book's discussion of the ties between the crane and Apollo, to whom the bird is sacred—even as it is also associated with the creation of the alphabet and, by extension, of poetic language. But the allusion may be more complicated. What also comes to mind is the Work of the Chariot. In his peroration, Graves harangues the modern world's mechanistic, patriarchal, and repressive order, its spokesman the left-handed satirist who curses—a word he derives, questionably, from the Latin *cursus*, "a running, especially the circular running of a chariot race," a *cursus contra solem*. The satirist is opposed to the bard, a recurrent figure in the history of poetry and the only true poet in Graves's reckoning. He is distinguished by his devotion to the White Goddess—who is about to appear in Merrill's poem, with "white gestures," in a cab. For Graves, she is the aboriginal Triple Goddess who is both enchantress and inspirer, Mother and Muse, the only theme of the true poet's song. And her son is Apollo, the poet-god-victim who celebrates her. In her guise as Moon, she appears as child (New Moon or Spring), as woman (Full Moon or Summer), as hag (Old Moon or Winter). Is it merely coincidental that these are the three apparitions of woman in Merrill's "For Proust"? I doubt it. There are a great many affinities between *The White Goddess* and Merrill's work in general—so many, in fact, that it would be impractical for me to pursue them here. Even if we ignore the intricate connections between Graves and Merrill, or between *The White Goddess* and "An Urban Convalescence," it is crucial to comprehend that the speaker thinks of what he sees *in terms of* a theory of poetry and is reminded of a book that seeks to answer a single question: how is the poet inspired? That is the question that Merrill's poem poses, too. When the speaker says, "I have lived on this same street for a decade," he means to be rueful about his inattentiveness. But Merrill himself means something more. A decade had passed between *First Poems* and *Water Street*, so that in an important sense he is referring to, and bringing into question, the kind of style and material he had "lived on" to date. The next stanzas disrupt the surface of his musing with a rush of ghostly memories:

> Wait. Yes. Vaguely a presence rises
> Some five floors high, of shabby stone
> —Or am I confusing it with another one
> In another part of town, or of the world?—
> And over its lintel into focus vaguely
> Misted with blood (my eyes are shut)
> A single garland sways, stone fruit, stone leaves,
> Which years of grit had etched until it thrust
> Roots down, even into the poor soil of my seeing.
> When did the garland become part of me?
> I ask myself, amused almost,
> Then shiver once from head to toe,
>
> Transfixed by a particular cheap engraving of garlands
> Bought for a few francs long ago,
> All calligraphic tendril and cross-hatched rondure,
> Ten years ago, and crumpled up to stanch
> Boughs dripping, whose white gestures filled a cab,
> And thought of neither then nor since.
> Also, to clasp them, the small, red-nailed hand
> Of no one I can place. Wait. No. Her name, her features
> Lie toppled underneath that year's fashions.
> The words she must have spoken, setting her face
> To fluttering like a veil, I cannot hear now,
> Let alone understand.
>
> [*WS*, pp. 3–4]

The lithe poetic line here is particularly effective. The stops and starts, the florid reverie, the mesh of associations, render perfectly a mind both consciously working to recall and being seized by memories beneath thought, the speaker's equilibrium having already been unsettled by his illness and by the racket. The first stanza here sets up a model of memory, and the second is an example of its involuntary force. While trying to summon up a whole, a detail appears—not the building, but an ornamental garland that may or may not have been carved on the building that might have stood there. Why that garland, and when did it "become part of me"? How is the phenomenal world internalized and spiritualized? How does the incidental sensation leave a memory trace that, later, is involuntarily recalled as the catalyst for still other memories? Proust says of the uneven paving stones: "the fortuitous and inevitable way in which the sensation had come about determined the truth of the past it resurrected and of the images it set in motion." So Merrill's poem proceeds fortuitously and inevitably, by a series of imagistic links—lintel dissolving to cheap engraving used to wrap a real bouquet given to the woman in a taxi a decade ago in another city on just such a day as this. . . . That he cannot remember who *she* is, that he dismisses her condescendingly as one of "that year's fashions," and that the whole scene has ominous overtones (it is "Misted with blood," the engraving is "crumbled to stanch" the flowers clasped in her "rednailed hand"), suggest that the memory is an especially painful and still injurious one. If this is what Freud called a screen memory, then the incident may be a substitute for something that happened much further back in time or more recently still (and so may be connected with his illness). But it is left deliberately, insistently vague—almost as if to suggest and include all those possibilities.

At a low point in *The Captive* Marcel comes to a realization: "Nothing assured me that the vagueness of such states was a sign of their profundity." And the same would be true of this poem as well unless we read it more metaphorically than pathologically. Marcel eventually triumphs by turning his memories into art. Art is also the real focus on the stanzas above. What he remembers, surely: the carving, the engraving, the cinematic girl. And the descriptive language, too, stresses the artificial: "calligraphic," "crosshatched rondure," "gestures," "fashions." More important, the memory assumes a mythic dimension. The woman is the embodiment of an idealized city, a dreamy Paris of *temps perdu*. Whether she is Graves's white goddess or a veiled figure more in the manner of Cocteau than of Keats, she is a muse. And even as she fades, she is Eurydice to this poet's Orpheus. In any case, it is a fugitive vision, a failed or incomplete memory. But it serves to remind him of the nature of memory itself, and of a life, a person, the past—which is what the next stanza portrays:

So that I am already on the stair,
As it were, of where I lived,
When the whole structure shudders at my tread
And soundlessly collapses, filling
The air with motes of stone.
Onto the still erect building next door
Are pressed levels and hues—
Pocked rose, streaked greens, brown whites.
Who drained the pousse-café?
Wires and pipes, snapped off the roots, quiver.

[WS, p. 4]

The memory of the woman that draws him deeper into the past only to undo it had demonstrated how private experience is shaped by myth—the lesson of art itself. The woman's resemblance to Eurydice tells us a great deal about the man who so remembers her. That strain continues here, if we imagine the speaker imagining himself as Orpheus climbing the stair of Hades, that realm of roots. Orpheus's music made the stones dance; here his "air" dances with "motes of stone." Later, having failed, he faces a Maenad-like "shrieking," his "eyes astream" like Orpheus's singing head. But this, perhaps, is to bring to the forefront what was only meant to be lurking. A specific myth is less important than the cast of mind. The first half of this poem works its way by suggestions, by overlapping and cumulative images and allusions that continually add meanings while resisting a single intention. The real street he "lived on" in the opening stanza, for instance, is here replaced by memory's imaginary house "where I lived." It is the fabled house of art, but rather than make that explicit, the poet characteristically shies away, and all is melted into air, into thin air. The motes of stone in his mind's eye become again the soil of his seeing, and exposed in that are its very roots—which, with a blink, become the wires and pipes of an actual dwelling and the fanciful cordial of its various stories. The initial question "Was there a building there at all?" has been answered by the revelations of memory, and the question now is "Who drained the pousse-café?" "Drain" means not just to empty but to drink or *approfondir*, and it is self-evidently the poet who has, without having realized it, taken in his own past, who heard then and understands now.

"Well, that is what life does." This next line, which clears the poem's throat before introducing a dwindling, moralizing coda to its first half, is typical of Merrill's manner. The poem began with a jolt, turned inward with a shudder, and has come back quivering. Now the catchphrase—the same sort of cliché or journalistic language the poet will later regret having to use—stabilizes the situation. But its shrug disguises a literal truth. That *is* what life does: destroys and restores, *aboutir à un livre:*

> Well, that is what life does. I stare
> A moment longer, so. And presently
> The massive volume of the world
> Closes again.
>
> Upon that book I swear
> To abide by what it teaches:
> Gospels of ugliness and waste,
> Of towering voids, of soiled gusts,
> Of a shrieking to be faced
> Full into, eyes astream with cold—
>
> With cold?
> All right then. With self-knowledge.
>
> [*WS*, pp. 4–5]

There is much about the design and tone of "An Urban Convalescence" that is reminiscent of Henry James—of "The Jolly Corner," say, or parts of *The American Scene*. Merrill's convalescent is one of James's poor sensitive gentlemen. The fateful "inner detachment" of John Marcher in "The Beast in the Jungle" comes strongly to mind in this connection. Marcher—whose very name links him with Merrill's walker—is blocked from life by his sense of "being kept for something rich and strange" and suffers, as Merrill's speaker does not, a terrible failure of human energy. Both men are ill, though: Marcher with his compulsive fantasy, Merrill's speaker with his own sort of inhibiting delicacy or inner detachment. Only when it is too late does Marcher read "the open page of his story," "the sounded void of his life": "This horror of waking—*this* was knowledge, knowledge under the breath of which the very tears in his eyes seemed to freeze. Through them, none the less, he tried to fix it and hold it; he kept it there before him so that he might feel the pain. That at least, belated and bitter, had something of the taste of life." Merrill's stanzas above, while similar to Marcher's realization, have none of its despair. They resolve *in time*, not only to face up to the world of brutal experience, but to acknowledge the "ugliness and waste," those oxymoronic "towering voids" and "soiled gusts" in his own life and character as well. It is on himself that he means to cast a cold, self-knowing eye.

If the poem had ended here, it would have seemed determined rather than conclusive, too abrupt and even forced. The poem's second half, however, extends and fulfills it. In *First Poems* the long poem "Variations and Elegy: White Stag, Black Bear" has a somewhat similar (though reversed) structure. After the six intricately metered variations, the more loosely written elegy is a resumption of the material already set out, but its fantasia tends to wander from, when it is not circling around, the initial terms of the poem. The concluding seven quatrains of "An Urban Convalescence," on the other hand, are an altogether more brilliant stroke. While nearly parodying details from the first half of the poem, they manage to recapitulate its narrative, in the process revealing its unsuspected delusions and depths. To begin with, the speaker moves indoors— or rather, back indoors: from exposure and commitment to enclosure and doubt, from what life teaches to what art questions. The quatrains themselves—the measured feet and rhymes to which the outdoor ramble has come—manifest the shift:

> Indoors at last, the pages of *Time* are apt
> To open, and the illustrated mayor of New York,
> Given a glimpse of how and where I work,
> To note yet one more house that can be scrapped.
>
> Unwillingly I picture
> My walls weathering in the general view.
> It is not even as though the new
> Buildings did very much for architecture.
>
> Suppose they did. The sickness of our time requires
> That these as well be blasted in their prime.
> You would think the simple fact of having lasted
> Threatened our cities like mysterious fires.

[WS, p. 5]

In an entirely different key, the poet is here reviving the crisis that confronted him at the start of the poem, but observation is replaced by a more intense speculation. The massive volume of the world is parodically reduced to the pages of a weekly newsmagazine—a change that signals others. Where the first part of the poem is concerned with volume, or space (even as absence), this part is concerned with time. The female figure in the first part, whose "red-nailed hand" is a token of her role as Nature, is supplanted here by "the illustrated mayor" or governing male figure of Art. The involuntary memory is now an unwilling picture, and the imagined threat—to shelter, security, self—is more immediate than it was before. What is threatened is both a house ("where I live") and a way of life ("how and where I work"). There is every reason to think that Merrill is contemplating the fate of his own poetry, imagining it potentially "scrapped," or "weathering in the general view" to be replaced by newer, inferior models. His aesthetic standards, part of a tradition that has "lasted," are what is undermined by the corrosive but faddish "sickness of our time." How forcefully the third stanza enacts that threat by wrenching the rhymes from their proper end positions!

Having imagined the threat from outside, but without being able to console himself with any phrase like "Well, that is what time does," he now focuses even more sharply inward—on the poem itself and on the way in which language can both reflect and cause a collapse from within:

> There are certain phrases which to use in a poem
> Is like rubbing silver with quicksilver. Bright
> But facile, the glamour deadens overnight.
> For instance, how 'the sickness of our time'
>
> Enhances, then debases, what I feel.
> At my desk I swallow in a glass of water
> No longer cordial, scarcely wet, a pill
> They had told me not to take until much later.
>
> [WS, p. 5]

It is a bitter pill he swallows—in a glass "No longer cordial" like the pousse-café drained earlier and "scarcely wet" with a poem's

representational energy. The pill he takes corresponds to his earlier
vow. In this case, the self-knowledge has to do not with his rela-
tion to experience but with his sense of art. At once a sedative and
a stimulant, the pill induces a reverie of the Parisian interlude and
its romance—the kind of dream that Pater called a finer memory,
raised a little above itself and above ordinary retrospect. The final
stanzas splice the two parts of the poem together in order to reach
a conclusion tempered by both experience and art—a conclusion
that proposes yet a new beginning:

> With the result that back into my imagination
> The city glides, like cities seen from the air,
> Mere smoke and sparkle to the passenger
> Having in mind another destination
>
> Which now is not that honey-slow descent
> Of the Champs-Elysées, her hand in his,
> But the dull need to make some kind of house
> Out of the life lived, out of the love spent.

[WS, p. 6]

Through the course of the poem, the city—whether as occasion or
as emblem, whether discursive New York or dreamy Paris—has
come to be identified with the speaker's own nature and his artistic
options. What now seems an amalgam of the two cities glides into
mind, this airborne passenger's train of thought, but it dissolves
into "Mere smoke and sparkle." The glamor of a distant (in time)
and idealized (in detail) Paris, he realizes, is an image for but not
the purpose of the poem—by the pronominal switch ("her hand in
his"), in fact, we see the memory depersonalized into an image. As
a "destination," such a sweet descent to the Blessed Fields, while it
may be a fate better than death, cannot finally satisfy one whose
happiness, as Merrill put it in a previous poem, is "bound up with
happenings." In one sense, the whole poem dramatizes a "recovery"
from just such a temptation to the attenuated "sophistications of
nostalgia." The underworld of memory is not the poet's home, and
the rubble of contemporary reality can provide no refuge. Neither
the present nor the past, then, is exclusively the subject of art; of
neither material will the poet seek to "make some kind of house"

or sense of himself. Rather, his "dull need" (a term with all the understatement of real and inescapable conviction) is for "the life lived," "the love spent." Those are very Proustian phrases—that one can have only what one no longer holds—but they also articulate a less rueful wisdom, and celebrate the sheltering presence of the past. In his remarks about "An Urban Convalescence," David Kalstone noted that in its research for durable images the poem itself comes to be—to have made—the "house," a "set of arrangements for survival," a new structure and tribute to what is "salvageable from the past."[4]

Kalstone's reading helps to clarify the poem's largest intentions, and to identify the terms of its importance in Merrill's career. This poet's abiding subjects have been present from his earliest work, but "An Urban Convalescence" introduces, by its format and resolve, new ways of containing them. This is not a poem of the Broken Home, whose theme is dispossession, but of the Missing House, whose theme is self-possession. "An Urban Convalescence" is perhaps the most poised of a number of such poems; there are more extreme versions at either end of his career, poems that also address the question of how art stabilizes the passage of time. The last of his *First Poems*, "The House" would be one in which "deed and structure" are one, but the poem abandons that task—"we who homeless toward such houses wend / May find we have dwelt elsewhere" (*FP*, p. 71)—for a sense of nature's vast maternal emptiness as a compensatory refuge. In *Braving the Elements*, "18 West 11th Street" confronts similar but explosive premises, and tries to restore to history's fragmented ruins the shape of its original dimensions. Similar to those two poems, but more successful than either, "An Urban Convalescence" seeks to free the poem from any constraints but those of the imagination itself, or from what Merrill calls with exquisite irony "the dull need." The poet works here to free himself of both the past and the present—the young woman in the cab and the old man in the crane—and to create for the poem its own moral and emotional standards. Such a convalescence is a paradoxical freedom, since it allows him a series of accommodations. By expanding the range of his voice and therefore of his consciousness, Merrill has been able to accommodate the past and the present, to accommodate the demands of Nature and Time within the confines of Art. For at the same time, he has sought to free the poem from stylistic bridles or pretenses. While myth may provide a bracing frame and autobiography the foreground of detail, neither dominates. Style, then, is an instrument of discovery and freedom, finally of reconciliation. The city that glides into the last stanzas—by now clearly seen as the infernal city of art's "material"—is abandoned in favor of "another destination" that the poet has "in mind." That "destination"—a word that neatly combines location and ambition—is the civilized domain of poetry itself, where a house and a life and a poem may come to stand for one another.

3

The poem as makeshift or eternal dwelling place, maze or monument, is a familiar, even a favorite one, of poets. *Water Street* makes use of that convention and of others. Throughout the book, poems take up the theme of art and love as sanctuaries. Death, too, is a fine and private place. In "Annie Hill's Grave," a casket "like a spaceship" bears her body to Necropolis, that "Land of our dreams" where she is reunited with her long dead husband who "lies in the next booth." In the rather eerie "Letter from Egypt," a boy's ancient golden tomb becomes a modern bridal pair's "first apartment." So, too, the glittering hotel's "packed public rooms" in "For Proust" are succeeded by the artist's own "one dim room without contour" in which the Ritz's fracas and fragrance will then be reimagined. There is, in all these poems, an easy correspondence between the timelessness of death and the immortality of art, between the space of a tomb and the expanse of the mind, effected by the poet's use of metaphors of liberating enclosure for both.

The tension between containment and release to be noted in such of Merrill's *First Poems* as "The Broken Bowl" whose "Spectrums, released, will speak / Of colder flowerings," is reworked in "Prism," a plaintive address by "a paperweight"—that is, by the crystal object and by the paper or burden of writing that weighs on the poet. The broken bowl's splinters had "cut structures in the air," made of the poem itself a "room for love's face." "Prism" is a less romantic, more perplexed account of artistic vocation. Like the prism itself, meaning to end up in "a maroon plush box, / Doze the old vaudeville out, of mind and object," the poet has instead

> lately taken up residence
> In a suite of chambers
> Windless, compact and sunny, ideal
> Lodging for the pituitary gland of Euclid
> If not for a "single gentleman (references)."
>
> [WS, p. 16]

It is all "playful inconveniences" there, sliding floors and invisible walls. Grown used to style's false insights and betrayals of outlook ("Those dagger-eyed insatiate performers"), only rarely is it given to poet or prism "to see clearly." When, in other words, the prism becomes a mirror, it sees the poet as he does not want to see himself—spent, "a body / Unshaven, flung on the sofa," his eyes reflecting "years of vacancy." The "pea-sized funhouse" (a phrase that conflates the prism, the poet's room, and that old vaudeville of mind and object) becomes a glinting allegory of art, both a type and a parody of the revolving gem of stars above. But it is an allegory in which the human is belittled and forsaken. Merrill uses the same sort of image, the maze of perspectives, for love in "Poem of Summer's End," where the disorientations of heat and travel, the distractions of the sexual appetite, provide mean sidelights on a relationship. The setting here is a shabby room in an Italian inn. The poet is shown his lover's face, first in an "instructing" gloom, then in a revealing beam of light. Each is an "image blind with use, a clue," and love itself is seen—from the inside—as "that slow maze / So freely entered."

In the journey Water Street itself makes, between "An Urban Convalescence"—which David Kalstone calls a separation, "a poem which dismantles a life in New York City where life is continually dismantling itself"[5]—and "A Tenancy," a conclusion that returns to the point of departure and settles the poet in a new house and renewed life, there are many excursions. Some are into the poet's past, others to foreign locales. On each, the question is that posed in "After Greece" (as it is in Elizabeth Bishop's "Questions of Travel"): "But where is home?" From "My country's warm, lit halls" of deceptive and entrapping familiarity, the poet seeks to escape, first by recalling a stay in Greece, then by dreaming of it:

> All through
> The countryside were old ideas
> Found lying open to the elements.
> Of the gods' houses only
> A minor premise here and there
> Would be balancing the heaven of fixed stars
> Upon a Doric capital.

> [*WS*, p. 12]

The dream that allows him to "flee" makes of it a passage, or street, down which he returns to a "home" identified with memories purified to essentials. Where "passage" means entry, and "stanza" is stopping place or room, Merrill is working in *Water Street* with a limited but enriching set of interacting images. They recur and culminate in the book's final poem, "A Tenancy."

The word "tenancy" can mean either the period of a lease or the occupancy itself. Merrill's poem deals with both, with the span of a life and the plan of a house, with time and space, time *as* space. The occasion of the poem is his new occupancy of a house in Stonington, on the street of the book's *title* in every sense. But the subject of the poem, like that of "An Urban Convalescence," is self-possession and art's accommodations. The poem owes more than its subject to "An Urban Convalescence." Its format—the long free-verse exposition that seems ruminative and improvisatory, tightening into crisp rhymed stanzas—not only follows the book's opening poem but seems quite intentionally to echo it, in order both to "frame" the book and to emphasize the continuities between the two poems. So, too, their plots are substantially the same: the initial casual detail (in "A Tenancy" it is "Something in the light") that prompts a deepening recollection; a depressed return through layers of time to the present moment; a further reverie that gradually emerges into a moralizing resolution. Even motifs of the earlier poem are repeated: the garland as emblem of time, the room as verse. But for all the notable similarities between the poems, there are important differences. Though its final lines are directed out toward a reader, are more "sociable" than those of "An Urban Convalescence," "A Tenancy" seems a more private, even elliptical one. To an extent, it is more overtly autobiographical than "An Urban Convalescence," which depends on generalized references and on mythical allusion, but the revelations (if that is what they are) are obscure. It is also more overtly a parable of Merrill's own poetic career but, while more difficult to decode, is less rich than "An Urban Convalescence."

The first sentence negotiates the exchange between present and past and returns the poem to a time (1946) when he had first begun writing seriously. Having been demobilized, he tries on his old civilian clothes. The peacetime world demands of him a different sort of service:

> Something in the light of this March afternoon
> Recalls that first and dazzling one
> Of 1946. I sat elated
> In my old clothes, in the first of several
> Furnished rooms, head cocked for the kind of sound
> That is recognized only when heard.
> A fresh snowfall muffled the road, unplowed
> To leave blanker and brighter
> The bright, blank page turned overnight.
>
> [WS, p. 51]

As the fable unfolds, this poetic room rented from Tradition is furnished with "ponderous *idées reçues*" and clichés like "the Real / Old-Fashioned Winter of my landlord's phrase." Gradually, "the more I looked," the objects in the room "grew shallower." This is a very idiosyncratic choice of words, especially in a stanza that starts (with "But") by signaling a change of mind. "Shallower" means not that the observer is, say, projecting his boredom onto the objects around him but that those objects—like the later "pebbles under water"—are growing diaphanous under his scrutiny, that they are revealed as themselves and are thereby able to reveal more than themselves. There is an influx of power, and "from within, ripples / Of heat." The "new radiance"—both willed and involuntary—rises to a pitch of memory and dream, the romantic sublime and literary allusion:

Brittle, sallow in the new radiance,
Time to set the last wreath floating out
Above the dead, to sweep up flowers. The dance
Had ended, it was light; the men looked tired
And awkward in their uniforms.
I sat, head thrown back, and with the dried stains
Of light on my own cheeks, proposed
This bargain with—say with the source of light:
That given a few years more
(Seven or ten or, what seemed vast, fifteen)
To spend in love, in a country not at war,
I would give in return
All I had. All? A little sun
Rose in my throat. The lease was drawn.

                                    [*WS*, p. 52]

The setting—the end of a victory celebration—is clear enough but
not illuminating unless we are to imagine the end of the poet's
battle with recalcitrant material and circumstance. His Faustian bar-
gain is more significant. He hesitates to call it diabolical, hesitates
to name it at all, and settles for a figure of speech: "—say with the
source of light." Merrill's diffidence in the face of the sublime is
entirely characteristic. Years later, in the very Faustian *Mirabell*
(section 8.6), this same "SOURCE OF LIGHT" is identified as "IMAGINA-
TIVE POWER" and is said to be "ROOTED IN THE LIVED LIFE." And so it
is here. The bargain struck, of course, is with himself. He finds the
light to see by—that is, his imaginative power—in the lived life,
in the same light that fills the room and is reflected from the
windowpane onto his face, like luminous tears. He asks then, for
a term of fifteen years, for love and peace, for emotional fulfillment
and stability, an *un*broken home. But the poem's "double seeing"
permits another interpretation. The span of time is that between
his dedication to his art and the publication of this very poem's
account of it. And in his asking for "love, in a country not at war,"
we can discern the subject of his first book and the title of his
second. In return, he offers "All I had" and wonders how much
that is or would be. I take the lump of a "little sun" that rises in
his throat—like a rainbow's compact—to be an effective symbol
both of the dawning of poetic song and also of the isolation and
sacrifice demanded by that gift. What the tired men in uniform

return to—homes, families, little sons—Merrill realizes he must renounce. His lease, drawn like a noose, is on what Yeats called the perfection of the work.

The single discrete line that returns the poem to the present—"I did not even feel the time expire"—also brings it to its crisis:

> I feel it though, today in this new room,
> Mine, with my things and thoughts, a view
> Of housetops, treetops, the walls bare.
> A changing light is deepening, is changing
> To a gilt ballroom chair a chair
> Bound to break under someone before long.
> I let the light change also me.
> The body that lived through that day
> And the sufficient love and relative peace
> Of those short years, is now not mine.
> Would it be called a soul?
> It knows at any rate,
> That when the light dies and the bell rings
> Its leaner veteran will rise to face
> Partners not recognized
> Until drunk young again and gowned in changing
> Flushes; and strains will rise,
> The bone-tipped baton beating, rapid, faint,
> From the street below, from my depressions—
>
> [WS, pp. 52–53]

These are difficult, elusive lines. They begin in a flat, assertive tone of self-possession: "Mine, my things and thoughts" have replaced the "ponderous *idées reçues*," even as the Latinate adjective and foreign phrase give way to plain speaking. Yet the "changing light" that is the poem's metaphor for the will to art is ambivalently celebrated, the nearly awkward inversions and the foreboding phrase "Bound to break" adding a markedly strained note. The tone of voice grows increasingly unsteady and sad. Even his ironic evaluation of his bargain and achievement—"sufficient time and relative peace"—is disclaimed. Of the body he no longer has—that is to say, of a life he has used up or outgrown—he asks "Would it be called a soul?" The best gloss of those puzzling lines is actually the poem that precedes "A Tenancy" in the book, the exquisite lyric "Swimming by Night." Its glimmering sketch of the poet as sorcerer's apprentice is one Merrill reuses several times in later work. In *The (Diblos) Notebook,* for instance, it is "the genie conjured up out of oneself";[6] and in "The Thousand and Second Night" it is given its most explicit definition: "The soul, which in infancy could not be told from the body, came with age to resemble *a body one no longer had,* whose transports went far beyond what passes, now, for sensation" (*ND,* p. 12). *Transport,* whether meant literally as metaphor itself or metaphorically as the move to a new house, is the subject of the poem, and it might be said that the Faust legend is paradoxically introduced in order to stress, not the speaker's eventual loss, but the poet's formidable soul-making. The last lines of this passage, which skillfully blend all the prior military and musical motifs, are a final transport to summary. Again, it is the "lived life" that dominates, but in its secondary, Proustian meaning of memory or re-cognition rather than as experience.

The final three stanzas are more self-consciously direct in spite of some lingering questions. There are lurking, unresolved connotations to the three friends, who seem at first to have come to claim the bargain's cost, or to suggest other visitors, from Job's comforters to the magi. And the gift of wine and the use of the word "host" recall, though to no certain end, the religious streak in "An Urban Convalescence." But these are minor considerations. Clearly these good-natured, metrically alert stanzas are intended to conclude the poem and its retrospect on a note of balanced determination:

> From the doorbell which rings.
> One foot asleep, I hop
> To let my three friends in. They stamp
> Themselves free of the spring's
> Last snow—or so we hope.
>
> One has brought violets in a pot;
> The second, wine; the best,
> His open, empty hand. Now in the room
> The sun is shining like a lamp.
> I put the flowers where I need them most
>
> And then, not asking why they come,
> Invite the visitors to sit.

If I am host at last
It is of little more than my own past.
May others be at home in it.

[WS, p. 53]

The amicability is evident at once. The dance that swirls through the earlier reverie is now parodied by the speaker's hopping and his friends' stamping. The muffling snowfall at the start of the poem has here melted into an easy image of renewal. And the synonymy of dwelling and art, of sheltering room and sustaining stanza, is memorably put in the lines "Now in the room / The sun is shining like a lamp," where by the comparison the "source of light" is domesticated to the poet's desk lamp. The last stanza settles the group in the room and the poet in his new house; it settles the poem and the entire book as well. Its open invitation, after all, points backward as well as forward, inviting the reader to reflect on the book's own conversion *from* artifice to experience and *of* that experience into a higher art. That has been accomplished not only by the evidence in the book of Merrill's appropriation of his own life but also by his recognition that imaginative power compensates for lost time and that the past can only be recovered by the presence of art. That is, both the subject and the technique of poetry are the "LIVED LIFE."

4

Two poems in *Water Street* lay parent figures to rest with equal parts of regret and relief. "Annie Hill's Grave" rather briskly buries Merrill's grandmother, and "The Smile" concerns an old man, associated with money, who "turned his face and died" (the poem's title refers to his bedside set of false teeth that are a mocking memento mori). These poems, by implication, raise a subject that others deal with overtly: the mixed feelings, the conscious yearnings and unconscious desires, of the child. More often than not, that child is given a typological rather than an autobiographical emphasis. The combination of unwitting innocence, instinctual aplomb, and sensible anarchy that characterizes a child's emotional life—at least in literature—is turned to advantage in several poems and usually with a portrait of the artist in mind. "The Lawn Fete of Homunculus Artifex" is a nervous and unconvincing example of this. "A Vision of the Garden" is a much better one. On a frosted windowpane the child draws a face through whose lines he beholds a winter garden so beautiful that the joyful sigh it elicits clouds over the vision. Thus in outline the story of the lost paradise is retold, and Merrill then draws the fitting conclusion (as he had in "The Doodler") by linking the child's inadvertent actions with the mature poet's "cold lines" of calculated craft and with his lover's face, recognized now at last. The inspiration and object of his art, in other words, are brought together and allow him to recapture the garden's original vision of transcendence. In such a poem—a brief and delicate lyric with considerable psychological, even philosophical ambitions—the figure of the child is doubly useful by bringing with it those associations it has been accumulating since Wordsworth's day. But what it gains in resonance it sometimes loses in immediacy. A poem like "The World and the Child," I think, is in its quieter way more impressive. Its astute control—and I should add that it is one of the few villanelles to include a convincing dramatic narrative—and the gradual amplification of its thematic terms (wisdom, love, pain) give it a haunting, nearly surreal quality, like certain songs by Mahler. What the child upstairs, "awake and wearied of," hears in the adult conversation downstairs is an accurate description of the poem itself: "mild variation, chilling theme." With no more than common experience and a few ordinary details—the click of a door, the hoot of an owl—Merrill succeeds in recreating the child's terrible loneliness and the world that is its cause and consolation.

This same disparity in technique and tone I have noted between the two short poems also sets apart the book's two longer poems that deal with the child. "Childlessness" is histrionic, lofty in conception but murky and perplexing to read. "Scenes of Childhood," on the other hand, with its clear succession of events and images, its shorter lines, its keen understanding of its own disclosures and equivocations, is a more conventional or straightforward poem and finally a superior one. This is largely a technical, not a thematic, unevenness: both poems deal with material that is profound and volatile. The evidently tortured emotional depths of "Childlessness" trouble its figural surface. Though there is, deliberately, little exposition, the plot is simple enough: the speaker is awakened by a winter storm, broods on his "childless" life in terms of the storm's abundant natural forces, then falls back into a nightmare of images impossible to construe except as a turmoil of unfixed guilt. How are we to read the first sentence, "The weather of this winter night, my dream-wife / Ranting and raining, wakes me"? That statement means he was asleep and was presumably dreaming before the action of the poem begins, and it therefore implies that a trace of the earlier dream (of the Family Life?) is shaping his now conscious sense of the scene. But that interpretation leaves too much unspoken. Part of the poet—the part, in fact, that wrote the poem—is married to Dream, that mysterious muse and queen of the night. That part of him is indifferent to the generative task. But another part is haunted by his grand refusal and has interiorized into his dream the endless cycle ("toddlers, holy dolls, dead ancestors") and a relentless guilt. For having fathered no children of his own, he feels condemned to remain ("In token of past servitude") his parents' child. Throughout the poem he tries, perceptibly or cryptically, to subvert that fate. By taking a maternal Nature as his "dream-wife," he ensures that his terrible arraignment will be in protective, nurturing hands. Later she is ambivalently called "the enchantress, masked as friend," and she unfurls bolts of a sunset whose exotic colors so remind one of art itself that when, at the end of the poem, the cloak "Has fallen onto the shoulders of my parents / Whom it is eating to the bone," the shirt of Nessus seems a son's crime as well as an artist's revenge.

The play of lights, the family romance, the emotional storm and stress, are all present again in "Scenes of Childhood." But "the primal / Figures" of the home movies replace the obscure, overwrought dream in "Childlessness," and there is, in this longer, more surely paced poem, a telling interplay between a rhetoric of conscious diagnosis and a diction of subconscious neurosis. The projector and screen—like Proust's magic lantern—are especially good images to contain these complexities. In fact, Merrill uses the film at key points all through his career—as technique (the newsreel rewound in "18 West 11th Street"), as subject (the work of

Maya Deren running throughout the trilogy), and as symbol. In "Scenes of Childhood" the film shows its viewers—the poet and his mother—to themselves, in both senses. The projected scenes of the past show them as they were thirty years before, and those scenes introjected reveal to the poet past connections and his present relationships. The screening itself heightens the tension. The literally explosive film becomes a sort of play within the play, a tiny Oedipal melodrama enacted *and* witnessed by its protagonists.

The poem's fifteen stanzas can be divided into two nearly equal sections. In the first eight stanzas, the poet and his mother are together, both in the room and in the film. In the next section, the poet is alone and meditating on those thoughts aroused by his heated encounter with himself and his past. The poem's sequence of encounter and meditation recalls that of "An Urban Convalescence"—though, of course, the pattern is one familiar from those great crisis poems by Wordsworth and Coleridge in which accident (a leech gatherer or lime tree bower) conspires with deep psychic currents to bring the poet to a new understanding. The opening four stanzas of "Scenes of Childhood" set the scene in a deliberate fashion—and for good reason. The film's jolting effect would have been diminished if it had started any earlier in the poem than it does. Merrill uses these preliminary lines, then, to create some anticipation. The tone here is fretted: the poet's eyes smart, his heart is ajar in the face of the buried life about to be revealed. He also introduces here several apparently incidental motifs whose significance will gradually emerge later in the poem. The most important of these are the interchangeable firefly and star—images for the whole dilemma, both artistic and human, of scale and perception. By the time the film itself comes to be described—and it is symbolically set in a pastoral world of nostalgia, an Edenic context of violation—it can move rapidly through its frames of reference. Appropriately, it begins with the presiding Fates—the three sisters who "Loom":

> With knowing smiles
> And beaded shrugs
>
> My mother and two aunts
> Loom on the screen. Their plucked

Brows pucker, their arms encircle
One another.
Their ashen lips move.
From the love seat's gloom
A quiet chuckle escapes
My white-haired mother

To see in that final light
A man's shadow mount
Her dress. And now she is
Advancing, sister-
less, but followed by
A fair child, or fury—
Myself at four, in tears.
I raise my fist,

Strike, she kneels down. The man's
Shadow afflicts us both.
Her voice behind me says
It might go slower.
I work the dials, the film jams.
Our headstrong old projector
Glares at the scene which promptly
Catches fire.

[WS, p. 21]

When one thinks of the tedious lengths to which this same old story has been drawn out by so many novelists (and innumerable psychologists), the passage is remarkable for its concision and suggestive power. Its latent content is all quite manifest. The erotic triangle, operatic violence, and mock apocalypse are superbly handled. It should not go unnoticed how Merrill inflects the climax by having the rhythm of the lines and the enjambments (perhaps by implication, the reel of film itself) wobble with their own intensity; and how he complicates the encounter by making his father—the cameraman, as his son is now—a type of the artist and by having his mother "chuckle" now to see herself "mounted" then.

This first section of the poem, its inventory of attachments and defiance so provocative but predictable, is really just a pretext for the poet's subsequent meditation—the primal figure, so to speak, on which he works a series of variations in the next seven stanzas. It is here, in an effort to frame the past by taking its mythic dimensions, that Merrill moves from history to imagination, from film to dream. By discovering, sometimes inadvertently, archetypal patterns his own life completes, the poet can liberate the self from its traumatic past by assimilating it into a timeless domain that is finally art itself. But there is a deep ambivalence in the act.

Alone, the screen or "field" of historical consciousness blacked out, he turns his attention to the "shining deeds" outside, some low and inconstant (fireflies), others "staying lit" (stars):

> There are nights we seem to ride
> With cross and crown
> Forth under them, through fumes,
> Coils, the whole rattling epic—
> Only to leap clear-eyed
> From eiderdown,
>
> Asleep to what we'd seen.
>
> [*WS*, p. 22]

This is the first instance of the poem's transformation of private life into mythic pattern. The epic of dreamwork is not merely a child's crusade or Wagnerian saga. In fact, he was asleep to what he had actually seen: the cross and crown are obvious male and female symbols, and the fumes and coils through which he rides are the serpentine auroras of Wallace Stevens's great meditation on fate:

> This is where the serpent lives, the bodiless.
> His head is air. Beneath his tip at night
> Eyes open and fix on us in every sky.[7]

Stevens's poem—which is not a model but a towering precedent and an aid to reading Merrill's poem—takes up ancestral themes and an infinite course, and in searching for "a time of innocence / As pure principle" for himself and his poetry, Stevens had returned to the figures of his parents, reading them into his own work. Merrill, too, is writing about origins, about the self's place in a larger scheme that can rouse feelings either of nostalgia or of terror. Throughout "Scenes of Childhood," the image of distant stars, and of the serpent or dragon shapes their constellations assume, is associated with the mother and with her powerful temptations. From "Medusa" in *First Poems* to the many references in "Ephraim," Merrill habitually links the *anima mundi* or ancient, ageless woman of the world with this polyvalent emblem. And as in "Auroras of Autumn," she is, immense and nearly transparent, "the purpose of the poem." The father, then, is linked with the opposing motif—those fireflies that were first mistaken "for stars, / For fates." Fireflies are functionally similar to the fire-breathing, draconic stars (those in the heavens and those in the film) but are inconsequential. And when they are described as "low, inconstant," it is possible that Merrill is passing judgment on his father's responsibility for the Broken Home. In lines that bring in yet another sort of lens or way of looking at things, Merrill remembers his father in such a way as to dismiss a rival:

> Father already fading—
> Who focused your life long
> Through little frames,
> Whose microscope, now deep
> In purple velvet, first
> Showed me the skulls of flies,
> The fur, the flames
>
> Etching the jaws—father:
> Shrunken to our true size.
>
> [WS, pp. 22–23]

The last line refers back to that moment, earlier in the poem, when fireflies were suddenly distinguished from stars. But something more is signaled. First, it is *our* true size: his the same as his father's. Second, our true size is life-size. As an adult accommodation with the past, these lines show some sympathy for and with the father. He stands guard, in this passage at least, against the encroaching, overwhelming power of the mother. Where she exaggerates and tempts to oblivion, he stabilizes and even comforts.

There follows from these mixed feelings a release or interlude. His mother distant, his father shrunken, the poet indulges in an idyll, a solitary wandering through a landscape of his own making: "Under fresh spells, cool web / And stinging song new-hatched /

Each day, all summer." But this is interrupted, first by an image, then by language itself. When "A minute galaxy" of insects "needles" the poet, the reader sees circling a conflation of the two parental images. Fleeing, the poet runs "breathing / In and out the sun / And air I am." At the very point of his inspiration, of his avowal that he is out of nature, he realizes he has been betrayed by the overdetermined possibilities of words, and the spell is undone by what first induced it. The "Inaugural *Damn*" melts into the primal mother (or *dam*), at first a figure upstairs, and then an *ouroboros* shedding the Milky Way itself and tempting all us poor humans to abjure our claims to identity:

> The son and heir! In the dark
> It makes me catch my breath
> And hear, from upstairs, hers—
> That faintest hiss
> And slither, as of life
> Escaping into space,
> Having led its characters
> To the abyss
>
> Of night. Immensely still
> The heavens glisten. One broad
> Path of vague stars is floating
> Off, a shed skin
> Of all whose fine cold eyes
> First told us, locked in ours:
> You are the heroes without name
> Or origin.

> [WS, pp. 23–24]

These concluding stanzas are among the most resplendent in all of *Water Street* and can stand beside Stevens's idiom of an innocent earth, where

> The stars are putting on their glittering belts.
> They throw around their shoulders cloaks that flash
> Like a great shadow's last embellishment.[8]

Stevens wanted true innocence as a pure principle both for the self-originated individual and for the poem of original power. The choking sense of dependence—that catches his poetic breath—is the burden of Merrill's lament here. To emphasize his dread of not having originated himself, the fall from that Edenic paradise of his artistic idyll recapitulates the jammed scenes of his childhood that had earlier caught fire. It is then that the poem undertakes its final struggle for freedom. The last stanza can be read several ways: interpretation is strained, I think, by the conflicting demands of closure and doubt. Is the power of Nature and the parent apotheosized, or are we meant to understand that the poet would shed his parent, shed the skin of common humanity? Does myth save us from the merely material, or do we make mock heroes of ourselves at the expense of true relationships? Both, perhaps. The poem has reached that extreme point where desire is identical with power. "Fine cold eye" is a chilling term for both the army of unalterable stars and the authority of parental priority. But why does Merrill shift from the first person he has used throughout the poem to the generalized plural ("us," "ours," "You") at the very moment when he wants to claim a distinction between dynasty and individuality? Because it is a common temptation, yes. Because in the face of the mother's power it links the poet again with his father, perhaps. But why do the heroic constellations call the child a hero without definition or derivation—that is, with absolute freedom? The lines would more properly be an admission made *by* the child *about* his parents. Yet the child, of course, was once a star—of the home movie and of his own dreams. And he can be a hero when in the anonymity of type he is no longer—or no longer considered—a Merrill. And further, as an artist, he can by his creative act entitle himself to power otherwise denied him as son and heir. Other poems in *Water Street* sought to house the past and to identify the enclosing shelter of memory with poetry itself. "Scenes of Childhood" is a more private and troubled attempt to do the same thing, substituting heroic status for security. More important, the poem introduces—in a more direct, if unsettled manner than any other poem in *Water Street*—a series of dilemmas Merrill will confront in later books with persistent anxiety but with increasing confidence.

CHAPTER 3

Lyric Knowledge in
The Fire Screen and
Braving the Elements

Samuel E. Schulman

"Who can ever praise enough / The world of his belief?" Auden asked himself in his poem "The Price." He meant the question to describe a temptation he felt, as a poet, trustingly to dwell in his own rich self-created world. It applies as well to an embarrassment that readers of James Merrill have felt since he began to publish his trilogy of long poems. The epic ambition, the elaboration of myth and memory of the occult trilogy, tempt us to let these works organize Merrill's career into a version of Vergil's or Dante's. His early works must then form a poetic apprenticeship dimly pointing the way toward the more capacious forms and inclusive themes of the trilogy. And from the vantage point of the trilogy we are to look back on the earlier lyrics in order to discern both its beginnings and Merrill's own unreadiness to undertake the task. The world of Merrill's belief in the trilogy evokes a more sophisticated response in his best and most faithful readers. They want, less hesitantly than Wordsworth did, to turn our attention from the "thing contemplated" to the "Mind contemplating"—the "transitory Being that beheld this Vision" (as Wordsworth describes his undertaking in *The Recluse*). We want to know the sources of Merrill's knowledge in the trilogy, the origins of the powers that spoke to him through the Ouija board, and for them we know to seek inward. We investigate the man and not the myth.

When Yeats questioned the "mysterious Instructors" who spoke to him through his wife they told him with bland professionalism, "We have come to bring you metaphors for poetry." Our impulse is to make a connection between the vision and the man who beheld it: to regard the vision as a projected and complicated refraction of the self. So Helen Vendler suggests when she speaks of Merrill's sessions with Ephraim and his successors as yielding "a voice recognizably his own but bearing a different name,"[1] placing him in a tradition of poets who interrogate the self as if it were an other as earnestly as Wordsworth questioned his leech gatherer or Dante his Vergil. The summoning of the shades is an act of poetic self-discovery. Vendler presents a portrait of Merrill at work that is presided over by a presence she has not invoked. Her portrayal places him, for me, in the tradition of Whitman; Merrill is a poet for whom the myth of reincarnation takes the place of Whitman's identification—shifting and troubled at times—with the lives and voices of other Americans as he moved among them afoot with his vision.

Other readers have felt the press of Merrill's identity in other ways. Vernon Shetley, looking back on the trilogy as a whole, shares Vendler's readiness to find the refractions of Merrill's poetic self in the form of his work. In Merrill's work with the Ouija board Shetley finds a kind of trumpery or disguise, as he puts it, an "expression of a perfectly solipsistic will, structured in such a way that it refuses to admit being a product of will at all."[2] Again the issue is raised: self or not-self? We must choose between Wordsworth and the leech gatherer who brings him the knowledge of himself as if it were "a leading from above," news from nowhere.

Merrill himself, at times, feels the conflict between his own integrity and the knowledge he must convey. The trilogy by virtue of its method of composition raises these questions of knowledge continually. His ghostly instructors may be beguiled by Merrill's voice, but they cannot be stopped. They have a mission that must be carried out sometimes at the expense of Merrill's identity as poet. "ON WITH THE WORK!" (M, p. 167) they cry in the face of the poet's occasional frustrations. "It's all by someone else," he complains. "Mirabell once said / He taps my word banks. I'd be happier / If *I* were tapping them. Or thought I were" (*M*, p. 168). In the first two volumes of the trilogy especially there is a tension between the poet's desire to write and the job of reporting he must do. More than the enlightenment they offer, it is their fertility of imagination, the power of the shades, that puts the poet's presence at risk. "Isn't it like a door / Shutting us off from living?" (*M*, p. 123). So David Jackson worries about their sessions, as if the fascination and intensity of the spiritual conversation might overwhelm their ordinary life. Merrill can only answer him by speaking of the price of knowledge, as Auden did—a cost paid inescapably by the self that knows, the poet who writes, the hero who acts. He cites Tolkien's heroes:

> They of course come through
> —It's what, in any Quest, the heroes do—
> But at the cost of being set apart,
> Emptied, diminished. Tolkien knew this. Art—
> The tale that all but shapes itself—survives
> By feeding on its personages' lives.
> The stripping process, sort of. What to say?
> Our lives led *to* this. It's the price we pay.
>
> [*M*, p. 124]

Merrill's undertaking of this "stripping process, sort of," is especially to be observed in the books of lyrics that precede the trilogy: *The Fire Screen* (1969) and *Braving the Elements* (1972). In these volumes he lets go the consolations of self and style, abandons the search for domesticity and contact, which characterize his earlier lyrics. And this process of letting go, this dispersal of the self, may be a precondition for the ecstasies of the trilogy and one of the sources of its knowledge. From his European exemplars—from Vergil and Spenser to Yeats and Proust—Merrill can be distinguished by the generous, even harrowing energy of his self-dispersal. He looks forward to no moment of revelation, confides to us no sense that his disguise or exile or dilettantism is merely a stage to pass through before he can throw off his weeds and appear to himself as wholly an artist. There is far more of Keats than of Proust in his Proustian ballad "Days of 1935." The little boy lies in bed wakeful and lonely, but his agonies need not attend upon the realization of a mature artistic vocation. To the imagination the boy proclaims "Already with thee!" and ventures like Madeline upon a premature elopement, "Trailing bedclothes like a bride / Timorous but happy." Yielding to fantasy's embrace in this way risks the self-undoing of Keats's lovers at the end of "The Eve of St. Agnes." "Captivity is beckoning" to the child who imagines his own kidnapping. He finds freedom by imagining his own fading-away into newspaper notoriety and false hope:

> The child. That population map's
> Blanknesses and dots were me!
> Mine, those swarming eyes and lips,
> Centers of industry
>
> Italics under which would say
> (And still do now and then, I fear)
> *Is This Child Alive Today?*
> *Last Hopes Disappear.*
>
> [BE, p. 14]

For all the period atmosphere of this poem, its weird combinations of the Runyonesque with the uncanniness of Goethe's Erlkönig, its most powerful moments are its own and show the child finding himself in his own disappearance. Proust's work, like Vergil's, reaches toward an increasing sense of presence and readiness, as if the completion of the self were identical with the realization of the work. Merrill moves in a different path, the path the flame reveals in "Log": "I gasped, and stumbled, and was less."

2

Such poetry—avoiding European conceptions of the poet's calling—is partly the result of an even more astonishing evasion of Merrill's native tradition, the American impulse to find what will suffice; "to convert the real world about him into an imagined world."[3] David Kalstone wants us to see Merrill as part of this tradition, as a poet who resembles Frost's young man who "thought he kept the universe alone." His beautiful idealizing essay on Merrill in *Five Tem-*

peraments speaks of a turn in his poetry "toward 'a local habitation and a name'" in *Water Street*, toward a poetry dominated by the "desire to stabilize memory" and by a "domesticating impulse" that imagines poems and memories as dwelling places.[4] This impulse is weaker in the later lyrics, where Merrill seems so often to flee from what is sufficient, from stability and self-definition. There are dwellings in *The Fire Screen* and *Braving the Elements* (including the spectacle of a house's self-destruction in "18 West 11th Street"), but they haven't the same charged life they possess in earlier volumes. Houses are not very important to a man who is in flight; one cannot be haunted by a house unless one haunts it oneself. When Merrill looks over his shoulder in these volumes he sees, typically, a kind of garment, the eloquent empty gestures of a suit of clothing. Clothing resembles us in its power to mimic our expressions, to reflect our vocabulary and our ways of seeing ourselves. Innocent of its wearer, a suit of clothes still has an odd half-life of its own; and this power Merrill uses as a trope for his own poetic style and for what is problematic for him in selfhood.

In the brief poem "More Enterprise" (*FS*, p. 15) Merrill offers a little parable of self-knowledge. Living in a Greek town, he has gradually distributed his wardrobe among friends and neighbors. Now it is only by a "scant wardrobe of gesture" that he can recognize himself. What had once seemed essential to him—his suit, his Italian shoes, and his vocabulary of self-possession ("The old strait swank / I came in")—all "struts the town on local heirs." In return he has acquired a new grammar of assent, the Greek's doubtful-looking headshake signifying Yes not No, which now possesses the poet in rather an uncomfortable way: "Into the grave I'll wear that Yes of theirs." What he has gained is less than knowledge or experience, and what he has exchanged for it is more than the inessential parings and curlicues of style. Merrill has allowed something of himself to the possession of others, a generous gesture that is difficult for him yet not regretted. (Compare it with Yeats's sardonic generosity in "A Coat.") Hereafter he will be less than he was: one sees him a bit perplexed as he walks away at the end, but his meaning is no longer in his control. His words say No, his gesture Yes. A more dramatic exchange of selfhood for garment takes place near the end of "18 West 11th Street" where the urban guerrilla who has just blown up the building that was Merrill's childhood home, and her own, emerges from the fallen walls for a moment before she disappears:

> The girl's
> Appearance now among us, as foreseen
>
> Naked, frail but fox-eyed, head to toe
> (Having passed through the mirror)
> Adorned with heavy shreds of ribbon
>
> Sluggish to bleed.
>
> [BE, p. 28]

Having unhoused herself, the girl now has only the ribbons on her back, ribbons of flesh which turn out to be (as they may have been for her) emblems of her ebbing life.

The theme of clothing runs through the two volumes, culminating in "Dreams about Clothes," the fantasy from which the phrase *Braving the Elements* is unexpectedly drawn. Why should this be? A more austere poet than Merrill, Alvin Feinman, uses the same image of clothing in a way that may help us understand. His major lyric "Preambles" meditates upon the tragic ineptitude of human knowledge and its unavoidable limits and follies. Its opening stanza:

> Vagrant, back, my scrutinies
> The candid deformations as with use
> A coat or trousers of one now dead
> Or as habit smacks of certitude[5]

The empty suit of clothing irrelevantly suggests the man who wore it, a suggestion no less powerful or comic for being innocent of intention. Feinman mocks the mental contrivances we rely on in our desire to rearrange experience, to absorb and order it in memory and art. Merrill's array of abandoned garments, stolen or distributed among the townspeople or absurdly living a life of their own, forms a counterpoint to the search for domestication of his earlier lyrics. In *Water Street* and *Nights and Days*, as Kalstone has shown us, Merrill imagines his poems as dwelling places—as he promises in "An Urban Convalescence" "to make some kind of house / Out of the life lived, out of the love spent." In the lyrics that anticipate the trilogy there is an equally strong impulse toward homelessness, flight, and the dispersal of the self. Merrill wants to rid himself of the habits that smack of certitude—of the claims to knowledge and self-possession he may have expressed in earlier works.

In *The Fire Screen* and *Braving the Elements* new houses become empty shells. For Merrill this sacrifice may be necessary to cultivate in himself another kind of vision, a different kind of knowledge (as I think it is not for Feinman). A pastoral landscape well suited to human imagination may not be the best place for visionary knowledge. For Wordsworth, a few miles above Tintern Abbey, a prospect of farms and fields would not suffice. He watched "wreaths of smoke," from the hearths of cottages in the wood,

> Sent up, in silence, from among the trees!
> With some uncertain notice, as might seem
> Of vagrant dwellers in the houseless woods,
> Or of some Hermit's cave, where by his fire
> The Hermit sits alone.

The shift is dramatic, almost violent. While watching over a domesticated, communal landscape Wordsworth has created an illusion of "houseless woods" as simple reminiscence yields in him to vision. In the poems of these later volumes Merrill moves himself out of doors, exposing himself in the houseless wilderness to the experience of loss, confusion, and dispossession.

3

As a volume, *The Fire Screen* is more extravagant in its gestures of disinheritance, and to the inherited myths of memory and experience offers a more rigorous refusal. As a book of love poems it rebukes the notion that a lover might possess another, or might himself be possessed by love, as he had been in the earlier poem "A Renewal": "When I next speak / Love buries itself in me, up to the hilt" (*CT*, p. 15). We can begin with a beginning. "An Abdication" is spoken by a deadpan Jehovah upon a "viewless throne" refusing the consolations of his own creation:

> First I looked at water. It was good.
> Blue oblongs glinted from afar. From close
> I saw it moving, hueless, clear
> Down to a point past which nothing was clear
> Or moving, and I had to close
> My eyes. The water had done little good.
>
> [FS, p. 26]

Each stanza like a sclerotic sestina repeats the dull chiasmus of disillusion: ABCCBA. The central self-rhyming "couplet" of each stanza spins away from the contrivings of nature, whether imagined in Stevensian terms ("moving, hueless, clear") or in those of Frost ("the poor, the hard, the real"). As the monarch of this world chooses intellection over sensation in the first three stanzas (he moves from *seeing* to *trying* to *realizing*) he begins to notice that his language offers very little control over the world he has created. In the second half of each stanza his own words come back to rebuke him, to temper the appropriating impulses of his vision. His series of predicative sentences (I looked, I tried, I realized) gives way to a sentence of which he is the object not subject. The result is a transformation:

> One dusk upon my viewless throne
> I realized the housecat's tyrant nature,
> Let her features small and grave
> Look past me as into their shallow grave.
> No animal could keep me from a nature
> Which existed to be overthrown.
>
> [FS, p. 26]

Happily deposed, the speaker shifts his burden of consciousness to another's brow. No longer the god of his little world, he need not worry how Adam might withstand nature's "proffered apple." Instead he is like Athena faced by a wiser Paris about to choose wisdom over beauty. "My cousin's eye / Lights on a rust-red, featherweight / Crown of thoughts." The act at the end of the poem—lifting the crown from himself and placing it "smartly" on another's brow—is partly a rite of passage. But it is also a grateful undoing of the self, a flight from what one sees, knows, and feels—the sum of which it is hard to distinguish from identity itself.

In other poems of *The Fire Screen* Merrill is at work transforming the domestic impulses of earlier poems into nightmares, making homes into houseless woods. "Flying from Byzantium" is such a poem. Singular in its range of tone and mood it consists of three variations of the mad-song stanza intoned by a grieving poet. Leaving Athens and a shared life, he thinks of the things he will not think of. He offers a collection of souvenirs, of random thoughts he hopes will lead him toward forgetting: no monuments of unaging intellect here but a "last unfocused Kodachrome," linen left forever at the laundromat, a house cat abandoned to a grisly fate, his lover's eyes not only lost but lost to mind: "If only / I thought that I would look in them again!"

The corollary holds true as well. The lover's eyes lost sight of means also the destruction of the poet. The last line might be translated "If only I thought that I would be seen by them again!" Yeats found in the imaginary destination of his journey toward Byzantium a compensation for ebbing power. Merrill lacks not merely a destination but a traveler: "I loved you, I am leaving. / Another world awaits me? I forget." *Amavi ergo non sum*: by the end of the first section Merrill's existence is again predicated by someone else's act of mind, as it was in "An Abdication." Saying farewell at the gate, soaring over Athens, his incantation of love depends on the will of another:

> You, you whose animal I am,
> My senses' mage and pentagram,
> Look, listen, miles above you
> I love you still, I love you . . .
> Then get in line to board the long slow tram.
>
> [*FS*, p. 29]

Merrill gives the place at the center to what is abandoned, not to the agent of change.

In the middle section of the poem, aboard the plane, Merrill endures a grimly demulcent dialogue with "the man in the moon," whose hoarse and weirdly modulating voice forces the poet to sit still and listen to a most peculiar exhortation:

> ["]So up from your vain divan,
> The one on which you wane.

> I've shown you how to shine—
> Show me the moon in man!"
>
> [FS, p. 30]

Astonishingly, it is one of the old ruses of Browning that we hear now, or the Tennyson of *Maud*: ebullient, emotional, with the extravagant and self-conscious enthusiasm of one of their more unbalanced heroes. And yet Merrill has only to rearrange the rhyme scheme in order to transform this stanza into the candid melody of *In Memoriam*, and this he does in the last section of the poem:

> "Mother, I was vain, headstrong,
> Help me, I am coming back."
> He put his lips along a crack,
> Inhaled the vague, compliant song.
>
> [FS, p. 3]

So his Victorian hero sings when he returns to earth, chastened and subdued but still resolute: "And yet / Dauntless the slug-horn to my lips I set," as Browing's Childe Roland proclaims. Merrill, to our surprise, is no longer to be identified with this penitent. At the end the poet is elsewhere, far from the sanctimonious hysteria of the lover abasing himself before a demanding muse:

> "That I may be born again
> Lead the black fly to my flesh."
> Far off a young scribe turned a fresh
> Page, hesitated, dipped his pen.
>
> [FS, p. 31]

The dreamer, lover, and slightly insufferable romantic poet veers off from the scribe, who writes the poem with scarcely a sign of inspiration or fellow feeling save in his slight hesitation. Merrill seems indifferent to the process of loss and fragmentation that this lover has just undergone, and comes close to mocking him when he declares himself recovered and sane, at the end of the second section: "North winds neighed, / A blaze of silver blues / Flooded the scene, no sign / That either heart had been hurt." This comes close to the insouciant gaudiness of Stevens's nature (at a moment when it is unconnected to the imagination, if not posing a threat to it). Merrill's hero shares none of the stubborn loyalty to their own special ordeal of his models in *Maud* and "Childe Roland to the Dark Tower Came." He seems rather an embarrassment to the coolly observing scribe at the end of the poem. The coldness of the landscape to which the lover returns when his plane lands is not so severe an ordeal as Merrill's self-distancing from the sources of his own art in this poem.

The brief poem that follows, "Last Words," makes plain the distance between the two figures of lover and poet whom we have just observed. There is the "I" of the poem's first two sentences, whose knowledge and eloquence is a grand efflorescence of being loved:

> My life, your light green eyes
> Have lit on me with joy.
> There's nothing I don't know
> Or shall not know again,
> Over and over again.

[FS, p. 32]

This love produces in him a power of sympathetic imagination that is evoked in Whitmanian terms (though such a response—a feeling that this faculty has been augmented and set free by being loved— was hardly a Whitmanian invention). Still, the process continues: he is the "dog that dies / In the deep street of Troy"; "dims with pain"; becomes the "stinging flies," the "bent head of the boy." But the process comes to a chilly end with the last sentence: "Part [of me] looks into your light / And lives to tell you so." The poet's rhetoric of sympathy yields suddenly to one of power, and he is as far from joy, and perhaps from love, as the scribe at the end of "Flying from Byzantium." He lives not in being loved, not in order to feel or to see, but only to tell. And it is the power to tell that the poem celebrates. One must free oneself from such an experience, of course, in order to speak of it.

Much of *The Fire Screen* is given over to these reports of loves lost. But the pain of which Merrill makes his truest subject is not the same pain one feels when one loses a loved one to time or to distance or to some other betrayal. Merrill separates not merely from those he loved but from the self that loves. He offers a variety of such separations in this book. There is the sophisticated regret of "Remora," spoken by a lover who feels superior and perhaps betrayed, claiming to see "in spite / Of being littler, a degree or two / Further than those one is attracted to." To his doomed affairs he drags not merely the body he calls his corpse but, clinging to it, "a slight / Tormented self, live, dapper, black-and-white" (p. 36). The more ambitious poems pursue separation and self-dispersal with more fury. In "Mornings in a New House" (pp. 40–41) Merrill's abiding theme of domestication surfaces in the aftermath of a ruined love affair: "And still at dawn the fire is lit / By whom a cold man hardly cares." The flame illuminates a fire screen decorated long ago by the poet's mother with an embroidered domestic scene, a house with a smoking chimney surrounded by birds and flowery trees. Here again I dissent from Kalstone, who makes of the fire screen an allegory of passion subdued by the art that absorbs and organizes it. Kalstone's reading is persuasive here because it is so loyal to the idealizing tendencies of Merrill's earlier lyrics—a loyalty that the poem itself cannot maintain. The last stanzas show the crewel-work house on the fire screen loosening itself from the grip of the here and now, of the passion—burning or burnt out—that so threatened the poet in the first half of the poem. No "interpretation of life," the pictured house draws the poet away from experience. Its "deep indoors" life excludes the world rather than organizing it. Merrill guesses that his mother, when she had worked this design ("to dwarf a house, *her* mother's"), had dimly foreknown his own existence, rehearsing it with her china doll. And now

> He stands there wondering until red
> Infraradiance, wave on wave,
> So enters each plume-petal's crazy weave,
> Each worsted brick of the homestead,
>
> That once more, deep indoors, blood's drawn,
> The tiny needlewoman cries,
> And to some faintest creaking shut of eyes
> His pleasure and the doll's are one.

Is the house, the real house in which the poet stands, getting any warmer? It does not matter. The imagined house has substituted itself completely. It makes the real superfluous. The same can be said of Merrill's life. His mother's foreknowing has made him, in a way, less: merely to be lacks the warmth and color of having been imagined. We feel the shock of the last two lines partly because they offer us a perspective that is not the poet's yet can be placed quite precisely: "to some faintest creaking shut of eyes / His pleasure and the doll's are one." These lines stand apart from the pulling and hauling of the adverbs and prepositions which, uncharacteristically for Merrill, so dominate the poem: "And still . . . By whom . . . Next . . . More or less . . . This done . . . Now between . . . until red . . . so enters . . . that once more . . ." The effect is paradoxically to make the poem's experience seem less under the control of the poet, less shaped by him. This is also the unexpected result of another odd feature, the way the last sentence spreads itself languidly over four stanzas, a sentence whose subject is "he." The poet's lack of presence betrays itself when he makes an attempt by grammar to enforce his power. Escaping the grip of the human will, which ought to govern it, the sentence cedes power to a mere effigy of the poet. Can we find human consolation in the mimetic powers of art? Not in this unwelcoming house.

4

In the long tragicomic ballad "Summer People," the last and most singular poem of this volume, we can trace Merrill's growing resistance to the obligations of his earlier lyrics. Merrill uses a highly artificial form to refuse the Proustian contrivances of art and the transforming powers of memory. It is an exercise in the literary-magical, a pseudo-ballad that reads as if E. F. Benson were to rewrite "The Ancient Mariner," in which the part of the albatross is taken by a spoiled house cat. Still, its theme is Merrill's own: can one ever be settled, at home, in a house, a season, a self? Its answers are grim and funny, in their self-mockery resembling Frost's

"Answer": "But Islands of the Bléssed, bless you son, / I never came across a bléssed one."

To a summer resort long settled into cozy and predictable social arrangements comes a mysterious and charismatic stranger named Jack Frost, the Prospero of this cell. It is a small world where people know one another much too well, and his advent enchants them all. It disturbs them, too. He fixes up the old church into a whimsical folly where he entertains his new friends with delightful lavishness. Something about all this activity is upsetting: he seems to promise even more than he supplies. His enchantments leave one unsettled and thirsty for more. So his first apparition, to the elderly novelist Margaret:

> A young man spoke to Margaret
> At a party: "Don't be bored.
> I've read your books, I like your looks"—
> Then vanished in the horde.
>
> [FS, p. 58]

Exactly what one could wish to hear about one's work, one's self, one's prospects for enjoyment! To a vaguely dissatisfied modern woman Jack offers a version of election. But how might one feel *after* hearing this? How does one respond? What has Jack promised?

Part of his charm, and of his danger, is that his dazzling residence in the town does not end with the summer. The others depart with the change of the first leaf, but Jack settles in past his proper season. Manuel the Portuguese grocer sees him in mid-winter:

> Whole nights, a tower window
> Threw light upon the storm.
> "Jack's sure artistic," Manuel said,
> "But how does he keep warm?"
>
> [FS, p. 61]

Jack, like the other people of the poem, cherishes a private idea of paradise. Most of these Edens will not survive in the open air (and we know from this that they are true paradises). Manuel has a vision of the town economy maintained forever on the largess of the summer people, as if laundry and baby-sitting money were enough to ward off the Chemical Plant that threatens in the future.

Margaret has "her novels laid in Europe / That she wrote in a garden chair"; Jane's art offers her access to an idealized domestic scene:

> Jane, speaking of pictures,
> Had started one of Grimes
> Drugged on Jack's lap. Those sessions
> Made for the merriest times.
>
> [FS, p. 63]

Ken, Jack's aging houseboy, yearns for the Japanese home to which he can never return:

> "Dear Jack-san, now am ord,
> Dream of my Kyushu virrage
> Where nobody catch cord."
>
> "Together, Ken, we'll go there,
> But for the moment stay.
> What would I do without you?"
> Ken bowed and turned away.
>
> [FS, p. 61]

Jack's ideal order is more dangerous than those of Jane and Ken because he brings it to pass. He makes summer a season not only perfect in itself but a rebuke to the ordinary lives of his friends. His summers are works of art, "High-water marks of humor / And humankindness," which banish discord at cards or charades. "Their faces bright with pleasure might / Not have displeased Franz Hals." It is no wonder that they return from their winter lives with little private dissatisfactions: "Their exile had been tiresome, / Each now confessed to Jack."

Jack's creative power serves above all to convince the others that their own ideals of a life elsewhere are incomplete—without him. He persuades them by his glorious example to outstay their proper season in the town, to abandon their own paradises and join him in his. Each year they stay longer: Christmas, Lent, and finally all winter long. And at the moment of Jack's triumph in teasing them out of themselves, tempting them to be more than summer people, Merrill as author steps into the poem. He confesses, while describing their slippery blisses, to a similar feeling of being a bit dizzy and uneasy, not quite at home. He fears that in the ballad form itself he has found a false and delusive tenderness, a domestication he must not risk:

> Logs burned, the sparks flew upward.
> The whiteness when they woke
> Struck them as of a genius
> Positively baroque,
>
> Invention's breast and plumage,
> Flights of the midnight Swan . . .
> The facts are in Margaret's journal
> To be published when she's gone.
>
> I should perhaps have trusted
> To dry-eyed prose like hers.
> The meter grows misleading,
> Given my characters.
>
> For figures in a ballad
> Lend themselves to acts
> Passionate and simple.
> A bride weeps. A tree cracks.

[FS, p. 64]

Of course things fall apart. The friends lose patience with one another in the cold winter light ("I mean you're gaga, Mother." / "And you, my child, are fat."). Margaret is clawed by Grimes one day and, unforgiving, has him put to death. And Jack, visited in dreams by Grimes's spirit crying vengeance, leaves the village forever. Without him, the images of paradise, the yearnings for home, become not only false but fatal. A premature spring flowering in Jack's garden helps to kill his abandoned houseboy:

> In the November mildness
> Rose delicate green spears—
> Spring flowers Ken had planted.
> His small eyes filled with tears:
>
> They were coming up too early!

[FS, pp. 71–72]

He goes inside and embarks on a fatal drunk. "Rong rife!" he toasts Nora and next day dies. Another day the small-scale para-

dise of the village itself departs forever. Manuel reports that the
Chemical Plant is coming to the harbor:

> ["]Fact is, the Plant got voted in.
> I call it a downright
> Pity you summer people
> Didn't care enough to fight."
>
> [FS, p. 69]

Nora protests: she has stayed over the winter, she is not just a
summer person! But to submit to Jack's enchantment is not to
transform oneself in real life. Consoling oneself with false para-
dises leads all the characters to neglect the things that do matter
and do exist in their lives.

Reflecting after Ken's funeral, Margaret idly proposes "That Jack
was a delusion / Of the whole community. . . . He had us all be-
guiled." The truth is that the community was a delusion of Jack's
and partly his invention. Like other artists (Nora is rereading Jane
Austen) Jack has the dangerous power to impose himself on the
world of fact, determining and shaping it to his own ends. As
Merrill says in the wonderful "Matinees":

> The point thereafter was to arrange for one's
> Own chills and fever, passions and betrayals,
> Chiefly in order to make song of them.
>
> [FS, p. 50]

The particular difficulty of *The Fire Screen* is that in it Merrill's art
begins to resist this version of art's powers and consolations and
yet is so lavish in the expense of its own powers. Uncomfortable in
his identification with figures like Jack, Merrill makes his character
flee from his cell, to the Jungfrau and Tibet—"Higher Things."
Such flights away from Byzantium are not a final solution.

5

In *Braving the Elements* Merrill avoids both extremes: Jack's super-
saturation of his world with his own presence and his impulse
toward escape and flight. The poet offers poems about the self but
without the anxious grasping toward identity of Lowell or Berry-

man, whose self-exposures grizzle the embers of a onetime life. The bravado of his title might suggest a plotting of his own life against other forces, powers that oppose him from without, but I think it is otherwise. The elements are his own, parts of himself, and his bravery is a willingness to see himself dissolved into elements, cast into other voices, represented by other styles and people. Take the most sharply focused poem of the volume, "After the Fire," which offers the clearest way of access to personal experience (*BE*, pp. 4–7). With its themes of return, of the changes wrought by time in surfaces not substances, it ought to be a poem of recognition in Proust's mode.

There has been a fire in Merrill's Greek house. Returning to inspect the changes he had ordered for its restoration, he discovers that the real changes have been in the people he knew there. There is his housekeeper Kleo—"how thin, how old!"—and her old mother, whose senility has brought with it a "terrible gift of hindsight," by means of which she proclaims to the town the buried lives of her daughter and grandson. Is Proust sufficient to the task? One thinks of Marcel's return to Paris after the war when he discovers all his friends have grown old. At the Guermanteses' party he finds in the alterations in the faces of those he remembers an inescapable reference to *himself*: "I became aware as I had never been before—by an inevitable inference from the metamorphoses which had taken place in all the people around me—of the time which had passed for them, a notion which brought with it the overwhelming revelation that it had passed also for me."[6] Merrill has memories of his own that surface in the poem, memories of loves felt and spent: "My eyes brim with past evenings in this hall, / . . . candles minutely / Guttering in the love-blinded gaze." But he avoids Proust's intensity of self-reference (an intensity that reaches an apocalyptic pitch when Marcel contemplates his own mortality a few sentences later). To the onrushing signs of change and deterioration in those he loves Merrill responds with something different from Proust's eruption of self-consciousness.

We can discern the outlines of his response in what might, in a different poet, be a conventional irony. He tells us about the fire: "The smoke cleared / On no real damage, yet I'd wanted changes."

Of course there is damage all around him, damage to his friends
and to his own past life. Merrill means us to attend to the verb of
sight, "to clear," and to the notion of revelation by means of vision
that it implies. For every mention of eyes or seeing in the poem
bears a terrible entail of blindness and loss; every mode of vision is
a trope for the inability to see. The first such moment, shaped by
the unsteady perceptions of the new arrival, is merely an error:

> Now Kleo's eyes begin to stream in earnest—
> Tears of joy? Ah, troubles too, I fear.
> Her old mother has gone off the deep end.

Even a momentary gap of misunderstanding, in so knowing a poet
as this, jolts us. His mistake furnishes a connection between Mer-
rill and the other people in the poem that will become more impor-
tant as the poem progresses.

More tears fall: Kleo's weeping as she endures her mother's
taunting stands for a reply, or a confession, that she represses:

> A strange car stops outside?
> She cackles *Here's the client! Paint your face,*
> *Putana!* to her daughter moistening
> With tears the shirt she irons. Or locks her out
> On her return from watering, with tears,
> My terrace garden. (I will see tomorrow
> The white oleander burst from its pot in the rains.)

The tears of unexpressed rage mingled with self-accusation, imitat-
ing partly the daylong weeping of Tennyson's Mariana, must be
matched with the tears in Merrill's eyes in his sentimental visit to
the remodeled house. Instead of seeing what is there, he imagines
the old faces glimmering through the doors, hears old voices that
still call to him. This is another way of being blind:

> My eyes brim with past evenings in this hall,
> Gravy-spattered cloth, candles minutely
> Guttering in the love-blinded gaze.
> The walls' original oldfashioned colors,
> Cendre de rose, warm flaking ivory—
> Colors last seen as by that lover's ghost
> Stumbling downstairs wound in a sheet of flame—

> Are hidden now forever but not lost
> Beneath this quiet sensible light gray.

The Greek house as a remembered setting for memories—
memories of a particularly glamorous and dramatic sort—is the
idealized center of the poem. The period decor, the candlelight, the
moving phrase borrowed from Donne which is much closer to
sentiment than Merrill's usual precision is—all of these elements
form part of an unflinching look at a love-blinded gaze. The ideal-
ized past, hidden primly by a coat of paint, is in absurd contrast to
the detonations of truth set off by the blind yiayia's "terrible hind-
sight." Placed crazily in the same verse paragraph, she hasn't
Merrill's quiet aestheticized command of the past. Her fits are "vi-
sions that possess her" and bring to her genuine revelations, be-
lated knowledge of her family's weaknesses.

The two ways of seeing inevitably clash. Merrill's memorial
virtuosity, all charm and confidence, confronts the silent rigidity
of the old woman:

> Next day I visit them. Red-eyed Kleo
> Lets me in. Beyond her, bedclothes disarrayed,
> The little leaden oven-rosy witch
> Fastens her unrecognizing glare
> Onto the lightest line that I can spin.
> "It's me, yiayia! Together let us plumb
> Depths long dry"—

But their encounter is overwhelmed by a torrent of sleazy café
French from the grandson Panayioti, attired in the poet's clothes,
which he salvaged from the fire. And in this moment, even in this
figure, the poet recognizes the loss of his own former self as he
had idealized it. Now he is dissolved and dissolute, distributed not
only in the remnants of his wardrobe but in memory as well. We
can guess the authenticity of this recognition because it happens
slowly and with pain. Merrill has exchanged his self-assured know-
ingness for something more like the yiayia's unrecognizing glare:

> I seem to know that crimson robe,
> And on his big fat feet—my slippers, ruined.
> . . . Meanwhile

Other translated objects one by one
Peep from hiding: teapot, towel, transistor.
Upon the sideboard an old me
Scissored from its glossy tavern scene—
I know that bare arm too, flung round my shoulder—
Buckles against a ruby glass ashtray.
. . . . .
Life like the bandit Somethingopoulos
Gives to others what it takes from us.

Wrenched away from his possession, these objects strike his gaze with a force more like life itself. Without the detachment—achieved by indirection, allusion, elaborated similitude—of his earlier vision of his lover "stumbling downstairs wound in a sheet of flame," the poet manages for the first time to see the past as we live it. It is glancing, fragmentary, in sudden motion: "I know that bare arm too, flung around my shoulder." The experience of recognition brings with it no elaboration of the poet's self-knowledge unless it is the knowledge that his identity is not to be willed or controlled. The gay Stevensian couplet at the end of the passage cannot disguise Merrill's sense of dismay and dislocation.

In the end, not just the poet's memory but his identity attends upon the vision of other people. To unravel the mystery of the fire is not the real problem (its solution is simple enough). The poem ends by giving back to Merrill his own name:

But the room brightens, the yiayia shrieks my name—
It's Tzimi! He's returned!
—And with that she returns to human form,
The snuffed-out candle-ends grow tall and shine,
Dead flames encircle us, which cannot harm,
The tables spread, she croons, and I
Am kneeling pressed to her old burning frame.

The poet's identity reconstitutes itself only in the crucible-like imagination of the "oven-rosy witch." He learns to recognize a self *dissolved*, scattered in objects detached from him in meaningless and violent fashion, restored to him by the accidental perceptions, the weaknesses and excesses of others. (Even Panayioti's gift to him is a cast off: un "Zoli foulard qui me va pas du tout.") I would guess that the Merrill of *Water Street* might make this poem center on the house, ruined and now restored. But the poet of *Braving the Elements* submits himself to the chancy and merciless perceptions of other people. To a remarkable degree he gives up the burnished and comforting gaze of the memorialist, forsakes his earlier desire for resolution: "to make some kind of house / Out of the life lived, the love spent."

Another poem of this volume, "In Monument Valley" (*BE*, p. 10), strikes a similar attitude toward the consolations of memory. It is Merrill's "Ozymandias," a monument to the notion of monuments. He begins by remembering the last time he rode horseback years ago. Located firmly in time and place, at Shoup's farm in June during a lull in the war, the poem shows us unity. Man and horse are one in intention, direction, destination. The poet displays a strength of willed determination put almost magically to work on this ride, and the effect, in the evening half-light, echoes that fantastic series of directional signals in the first section of "Out of the Cradle Endlessly Rocking":

> Stillnesses were swarming inward from the evening star
> Or outward from the buoyant sorrel mare
>
> Who moved as if not displeased by the weight upon her.
> Meadows received us, heady with unseen lilac,
> Brief, polyphonic lives abounded everywhere.
> With one accord we circled the small lake.

The imagination in youth imputes life, will, and sense wherever it can conceive of a response to it. And everything in nature has an answer, fully voiced, to the presence of the young poet. He is welcomed, made to feel at home.

Now it is different. "Yet here I sit among the crazy shapes things take." The mature poet is somewhere in the desert of the American West, where if nature is not so responsive to the human will, the imagination is even less eager to cast itself out of doors. The names of places here seem to dictate to the poet, each according to its own powers: "The 'Three Sisters' howl. 'Hell's Gate' yawns wide." And to an idle poet sitting in an air-conditioned car comes a ragged horse, native to the wilderness, barely recognizable: "Tottering still half in trust, half in fear of man— / Dear god, a horse." Like Wordsworth's decrepit leech gatherer in "Resolution and Independence," it seems a creature of the boundary regions between life and death. To the poet such an apparition is a dreadful intimation of failing powers, the fear that kills, and must like an angry god be propitiated. Wordsworth sacrifices more and more to the attempt. For him, making contact with the old man requires a terrible expense of attention and even dignity. "How is it that you live, and what is it you do?" Merrill's reaction to the horse is an immediate but less persistent. He offers the apple core he has been munching on, sees it refused by the horse, rolls up his window, and drives off. The resolute "one accord" between man and the beast at Shoup's farm is gone, and in its place Merrill inscribes an obscure and foreign-sounding epitaph:

> About the ancient bond between her kind and mine
> Little more to speak of can be done.
>
> [BE, p. 10]

Merrill seldom puts together such conventional phrases without making them sing for him and letting them be enriched by their context. Such is not the case here. This impoverished inscription might be gathered together with others that appear in the poems of *Braving the Elements*—like

> The peaks turn baseless as the fear
> That you will tell me what I live to hear
>
> [BE, p. 32]

and

> Only read aloud
> Do the words stay with me, through
> Whose roots those flat clear vowels flow
>
> To mirror, surfacing, the things they mean
>
> [BE, p. 30]

from "In Nine Sleep Valley," parts 5 and 1; and, from "Under Mars": "Though such as we have made them what they are." [BE, p. 40] Such lines—flat, monosyllabic, yet hard to fathom, pushing themselves toward tautology or toward closed, circular systems of belief—sullenly mock the meanings they bear. They evoke relationships between cause and effect, knowledge and action, desire and contact (such as the relationship remembered in the opening scene of "In Monument Valley"), only to show that they have vanished, "turned baseless."

The difficulties here are partly a matter of the grim far-western landscapes in which Merrill chooses to set these poems. Kalstone calls them "love poems played out against dwarfing panoramas and the geological erosions of a non-human world,"[7] and it is hardly surprising that in them there is none of the search for home and recognizable identity of Merrill's earlier lyrics. But even in the hinterlands the poet seeks extremes that will challenge self-identity. Repeatedly he offers himself up to the sacrifice. To observe these ceremonies is partly to share in them, as Merrill remarks with deadpan horror in "Banks of a Stream Where Creatures Bathe":

> I can't compete.
> Giving of my very
> Self, I've seen you
> Clouded by the gift.
>
> [BE, p. 38]

Or in the lines of "Under Mars" that adhere so faintly to one another:

> Paring nobody's orchard to the bone
> Cut both ways the pond believes
>
> And boulders' heavy sighs appear
> Out of mown meadows and inside a head
>
> Laid on the block you half erase
> Chiefly to yourself antagonist
>
> [BE, p. 40]

—so faintly that they mimic the poet's submission to self-division. His submissiveness in this poem is so extreme that he accords everything in the landscape the privileges of consciousness *except* the creative imagination. This he puts at the mercy of croaking "frog-footmen" of the campsite, croaking deities "Of empty sleeve and battle star / Who wither at a glance us gentlefolk / Though such as we have made them what they are."

In an even more difficult poem, "Yam," he offers a landscape itself carefully and methodically destroyed for the pastoral impulse, as if to cut off this avenue of escape or refuge for himself. The antipastoral in "Yam" alludes to the already forlorn mythologies of Milton's Nativity Ode and Keats's "Ode to Psyche" but in a different mode. Merrill discovers not a devotional attitude (however empty) but an altitude that forces the departure of all devotion, of the inspired sense of the poet's calling. "Go now by upward stages," he orders,

> Where an imaginary line is being
> Drawn past which you do not melt, you suffer
>
> Pure form's utter discontent, white waste
> And wintry grazing, flocks of white
> But with no shepherd-sage, no flute, no phrases;
> Parchment frozen, howling pricksong, mute
>
> Periods that flash and stun—
>
> [BE, p. 41]

A momentary hesitation before the enjambment yields "an imaginary line *is* being," which is helpful as a gloss on the poem. The tone may approach the sublime, but the message is troubling enough for a calmer poet. The physical self remains (its traces are on the cold hillside in the last stanza, mute testimony of feces lying "on snow in dark ideogram"), but the landscape arrogates the power of voice traditionally claimed by the "shepherd-sage," the poet. He remains a mute witness to the usurpation, with no voice or hideous hum, no grove or virgin choir to aid him.

If there is willfulness in these poems it displays itself by such acts of self-dissolution. The only other poet I know of so concerned with the dissolution of his poetic identity is Tennyson; and in this volume Merrill sometimes resembles Tennyson's character Tithonus, looking on the influx of love and inspiration with horror, with impatience awaiting their departure. The poet's climb in "Yam" above the timberline—a gradus supra Parnassum—forces Tithonus's pose upon him: he looks back on his own path with, I think, a forced detachment mingled with real yearning:

> Hit on the head, who brought you to this pass?
> Valleys far below are spouting
> Baby slogans and green gripes of spring,
>
> Clogged pools, the floating yen. . . .
>
> [p. 41]

The phrasing here suggests Stevens, bidding relieved farewell to "spring's infuriations" at the beginning of "Credences of Summer." Stevens is grateful for his release; the Merrill of "Yam" feels a bit stunned. But in another poem, Merrill provides a closer approximation yet to Tithonus's attitude.

For Tithonus, identity is inseparable from Eos's love for him, now long unwanted. Here he begs for a release from love that will bring with it release from self:

> Yet hold me not for ever in thine East;
> How can my nature longer mix with thine?
> . . . . .
> Release me, and restore me to the ground.
> Thou seëst all things, thou wilt see my grave;
> Thou wilt renew thy beauty morn by morn,
> I earth in earth forget these empty courts,
> And thee returning on thy silver wheels.

"The Black Mesa" borrows these tones and cadences to address the flatlands around him, lamenting more softly the form in which he has been cast. In the last stanza he speaks of the old, fated struggle between lowland and upland as an eternal, uncomfortable love:

> Sieges like that come late and end
> Soon. And are we friends now? Funny friends.
> Glaringly over years you knit
> A wild green lap robe I shake off in tears.
> I steal past him who next reclaims you, keep
> Our hushed appointments, grain by grain . . .
> Dust of my dust, when will it all be plain?
>
> [BE, p. 42]

As the tableland crumbles into the plain, the mesa establishes their essential identity with an echo of Tithonus's cry that he is different; he is not "morn by morn" but "earth in earth." The mesa is another lover like Tithonus, abandoned not by his mistress but by love itself: "By way of you a thousand human / Frailties found in me their last refuge."

Merrill refuses here the often consoling rigors of a particular notion of poetic identity—one that makes the self something to be shaped by its vocation. He also questions the imperial fiction that the self by being *knows* something. In the beginning the mesa's knowledge is overbearing, if anachronistic: he sees the flatland not as a mistress but as an empty page, the perfect site for his ruminating inscriptions. For his own identity the trope of "character" as writing instrument will suffice:

> So much is parchment where I gloom,
> Character still sharp enough to prick
> Into the hide my igneous
> Old spells and canticles of doom.
> The things that shape a person!
>
> [BE, p. 42]

The last phrase, uttered so conventionally, might tend to make us accustomed to a stone that responds were it not for the more demanding kinds of knowledge that succeed his tired repertoire of spells and curses. Though he can impose his messages on empty space, the poet even as rock is susceptible to seduction, to the deprivations of style and sexuality that make the blood drum. To adopt Auden as gloss: "There is no love; / There are only the various envies, all of them sad." Merrill goes on in the central stanzas to remind us of the love of Paphnutius for Thaïs—how "The desert father falls for the land's lie— / That 'grande horizontale.'" But the grand seduction in France's story is not the desert father's surrender to Thaïs's sensuality but the reverse. The grandest lie of all is Paphnutius's preaching—the power that defines him—that seduces Thaïs away from him and spirits her into the embrace of a God he had with his words created for her. So the priest is forced, like the mesa itself, continually to exchange one kind of knowledge (of the spirit, and of the imagination that confides it) for Thaïs's knowledge of the flesh, the experience of desire and loss. The way out of this exchange Merrill discovers in lyrics like these, which anticipate the submissions he undertakes in the trilogy. His solution is the difficult one of learning to relinquish knowledge, to diffuse identity, to yield to the power of other voices and names. *Braving the Elements* is an exercise in making *beaux abandons*, learning a lyricism based on the power of his voice not simply to enchant (the ambiguous power of Jack Frost in "Summer People") but to make enchantment do the work of self-dissolution.

CHAPTER 4

Persisting Figures:
The Poet's Story
and How We Read It

David Kalstone

First, a fable from Wordsworth. The poet, among throngs of people in the overflowing streets of London, loses individual shapes in a vision of their common origin and fate. Then

> Amid the moving pageant, 'twas my chance
> Abruptly to be smitten with the view
> Of a blind beggar, who, with upright face,
> Stood propped against a wall, upon his chest
> Wearing a written paper, to explain
> The story of the man, and who he was.
> My mind did at this spectacle turn round
> As with the might of waters, and it seemed
> To me that in this label was a type,
> Or emblem, of the utmost that we know,
> Both of ourselves and of the universe;
> And, on the shape of the unmoving man,
> His fixed face and sightless eyes, I looked,
> As if admonished from another world.

> [*The Prelude*, 1805 ed., VII, ll. 610–623]

Anyone who sits down to write will understand the force of this admonition and will have more than mixed feelings about it. The spectacle—and specter—of the blind beggar bearing the curt, written story of his life and otherwise expressionless, is both a rebuke and a prompting to autobiography. Wordsworth chose to stress the former, the element of rebuke. But the strength of his metaphor ("My mind did . . . turn round / As with the might of waters") suggests far more. The more we know of the history of his auto-biographical writing—his obsessive revisions, his refusal to publish a finished version of *The Prelude*—the more we sense his need to elaborate, to keep fluid the written image of the self. In copious writing, never quite ready for the printer, he satisfied the desire to escape the "fixed face and sightless eyes" of the blind beggar propped against a wall, wearing, like a shroud, the final story of his life.

Since Wordsworth—and under similar pressures—self-repre-sentation in poetry has taken unpredictable and extended forms, especially the hybrids that have emerged in American poetry of the twentieth century. It is now clear that ours is the century for poems that are rich and astonishing autobiographical mutants: not simply long poems, but sequences, even mosaics of prose and verse such as William Carlos Williams's *Paterson*. One thinks of the polyvocal collage of Pound's *Cantos* and Olson's *Maximus*; John Berryman's self-examination in the form of a dialogue with the first American woman poet, *Homage to Mistress Bradstreet*, then his overflowing series of *Dream Songs*; Robert Lowell's literal rewriting of earlier poems in the collection called *History*, loose sonnets that he re-garded as a single poem; Elizabeth Bishop's subtler rewriting of her earlier works in ways that refigure them, make them seem part of a larger, more idiosyncratic autobiographical performance. Most re-cently, James Merrill's trilogy of "divine comedies"—self-revisions in the form of interviews on the Ouija board—has insinuated itself into this company and, as every new member of a family does, helps us see these strange works bathed in a shifted and revealing light, the new arrival different enough so that the *family* traits etch themselves all the more clearly.

No one would claim that all the works I have mentioned (or others that might be mentioned) are of equal value, but it is clear from even a short list that they share certain characteristics. They are emerging works, written and published over a period of time, as were *Paterson*, the *Cantos, Four Quartets*, Merrill's trilogy, Berryman's *Dream Songs*. In that respect such poems bear a family relationship to those of Whitman, who kept shuffling and reshuffling his verse, adding and subtracting to make the single long constructed *Leaves of Grass* coterminous with his life. Some of these works represent public revisions of the author's verse—Lowell's *History*, for example—in which the act of revising and the nature of the poet's changes become themselves part of the autobiography. Many of these modern hybrids, by their very form or sometimes apparent lack of it, forcibly remind us that self-representation in recent long poems has by and large cut loose from the straightforward narrative basis, from the myth of assured growth, implied in Wordsworth's *Prelude*. And of course it has long since been deprived of the beautiful articulation of Dante's definite spiritual stages.

The long poems of this century grow out of lyric modes. Many of them (the *Dream Songs, History*) are lyric sequences. Others (*Four Quartets, Paterson*, Merrill's "divine comedies") have lyrics embedded within them. Still others depend upon a poet's earlier work in shorter forms, his manipulation of the signs and symbols discovered through his lyrics, a process familiar in Yeats. If we are to read the poet's story, we must be aware of its lyric beginnings, often in poems obscure and on the surface impersonal. We must attend as well to the *emerging* nature of poetic autobiographies, the self-revisions not so easily available in larger prose structures. What writer of fiction has the luxury to engage in public revision of his work after it appears, as Lowell did when he transformed his *Notebooks* into *History*? The energy of many poetic autobiographies lies in the way shorter lyrics move toward larger structures. It may have been easy to overlook this tendency in the 1960s, when confessional poems made an appeal based on bursts of self-disclosure. But an even more pervasive obstacle is raised by our reading habits of the fifties and sixties: the excessive reverence in which since 1945 we have held the short perfect lyric as the dominant unit of poetic expression. Our preference has made for more carefully wrought poetry, certainly—and for closer readers, too. But it has also led to a new kind of carelessness: the trivializing and splintered attention some critics give, as if books of poems were only bundles of single poems to be sorted and graded like fruit. The implication is that modern poetry is a kind of dwarf art, a bonsai. Splintered criticism—a preoccupation with lyric perfection—as well as the more obvious appeal of confessional poetry have to some extent obscured the radical views of identity with which recent poets have themselves been struggling. A large part of the structuralists' comments about the problematic relation of writing to identity has long been anticipated by writers themselves, though not always explicitly. As for their audiences, we are learning to read the poet's autobiography not simply in surface bursts of self-disclosure but in his acts of transformation—in the way his shorter works grow, are gathered, are refigured in constructions uniquely, idiosyncratically his own.

What often baffles the contemporary reader is the lapse of narrative. We miss even the interior continuity of classic prose autobiographies such as John Stuart Mill's. The long poem governed by a *single* voice is seldom the form chosen for extended twentieth-century efforts, nor do our long poems necessarily sustain the illusion of development implied in the subtitle of *The Prelude*: "The Growth of the Poet's Mind." But if Wordsworth is our first and classic model for poetic autobiography, his own difficulties with his poem foreshadow the stumbling blocks of modernism. For him *The Recluse* was his "life work"; he never considered *The Prelude* of 1805–1806 as complete, never devoted himself to finishing it, and went through a series of delaying revisions, so that only after his death was it finally published and given its title by his wife. Or, as Richard Onorato puts it, "*The Prelude* came between the poet and his 'great' work and extended itself until it became the expression of a dominant intention to get hold of oneself."[1] What interests the most acute modern critics of the poem is the strain that that intention produced. Wordsworth rooted his fable of the poet's growth in his childhood experience of nature, the very nature haunted by the loss of his parents in early youth—a loss scarcely acknowledged in his poem. The fiction of an emerging and integral poetic character only barely conceals the turbulence one feels in Wordsworth's images of inspiration and poetic power. *The Prelude* projected a necessary fable of identity and composure, but often at the cost of forcibly reidentifying the parentless landscapes of Words-worth's childhood with benevolent sources of imaginative strength. Both Richard Onorato and Harold Bloom have pursued these ques-tions of poetry and repression; they remind us that however much *The Prelude* overtly insists on a myth of triumphant identity, every-thing about its imagery and the history of its publication—the de-lays, the hesitations—suggests instability and doubt.[2] Modern verse autobiographies have insisted less on the presentation of a *single* identity, on myths of assured growth, have been less embarrassed by the impulse to revise, and indeed have absorbed the element of instability into the very form of the work—something Wordsworth could never do.

The most extreme, sometimes baffling, but often compelling expression of this dilemma in recent American poetry comes in the work of John Ashbery. Ashbery has made a career of uncertainty, of multiplying beams of awareness, and has caused a great deal of discomfort among his readers for doing so. Ashbery's characteristic melancholy grows from what he sees as the difficulty, the impos-sibility of representing the self on the printed page.

> It becomes plain that we cannot interpret everything, we must be selective, and so the tale we are telling begins little by little to leave reality behind. It is no longer so much our description of the way things happen to us as our private song, sung in the wilderness, nor can we leave off singing, for that would be to retreat to the death of childhood, to the mere acceptance and dull living of all that is thrust upon us, a living death in a word; we must reg-ister our appraisal of the moving world that is around us, but our song is leading us on now, farther and farther into that wilderness and away from the shrouded but familiar forms that were its first inspiration.[3]

For him

> All diaries are alike, clear and cold, with
> The outlook for continued cold. They are placed
> Horizontal, parallel to the earth,
> Like the unencumbering dead. Just time to reread this
> And the past slips through your fingers, wishing
> you were there.[4]

Time is represented as a terrifying hourglass in which the present does not really exist:

> the sands are hissing
> As they approach the beginning of the big slide
> Into what happened. This past
> Is now here.[5]

It is only in the simplifying representations of memory, a film of ourselves, that we retain the illusion of a single or stable identity. "These windows on the past enable us to see enough to stay on an even keel in the razor's-edge present which is really a no-time, continually straying over the border into the positive past and the negative future whose movements alone define it. Unfortunately we have to live in it. We are appalled at this."[6]

This mosaic of quotations from Ashbery's work suggests the reasons for some of his desperate measures, his attempts to multiply voices on the page. His recent "Litany" sets two independent poems in columns against one another and, as if it were written in a three-dimensional script, encourages us to overhear overlapping facets of identity in simultaneous speech. Ashbery's is only the most extreme example of contemporary attempts to find a notation that adequately represents the facets of the self. It is to these explorations, to these hybrid works, that James Merrill's trilogy is intimately related.

These are obviously dangerous ways of telling the poet's story. As Helen Vendler suggests, such poems are "replay[s] in slow motion of all the eclectic litter and learning that crowds [the poet's] mind: unburdening himself, he discharges, in an art relatively random by contrast to that of his earlier years, portions of everything he knows." She goes on: "The jumble that is any fifty-year-old memory poses for a reader the problem of other minds; the encyclopedic modern poem, from the *Cantos* on, presses the question almost intolerably."[7] If Merrill escapes this danger, it is not so much by avoiding what Vendler calls the "jumble" as by exposing it critically. His otherworldly voices, in what we can now see as the repeated, revising sweeps of three grand movements, force him to watch his past compose, decompose, then reassemble in three successive lights: the human play of "Ephraim," the cold biological

structures of *Mirabell,* and the transmogrified virtues and vices of
Scripts for the Pageant. Above all, the voices force him to interrogate
his earlier poetry, his shorter works, and to act out tensions be-
tween abbreviated utterance, the closed and often frustrated world
of the lyric, on one hand, and, on the other, the larger emerging
vision of his recent long poems. Every poetic generation has its
own version of the exchange between briefer and more expansive
works. Ours seems to have an exaggerated psychological intensity:
under the pressure of the apparently random, long poems often
show us how the illusion of identity gathers. The ways in which
poets go beyond—and utilize the discoveries of—their lyrics tells
us a great deal about the formation, or deformation, of identity.

Merrill's generation came of age after World War II and per-
fected a certain kind of emblematic lyric in which the poem as-
sumes an almost impersonal, objective authority. Such poems pre-
sented objects or incidents—the Parrot, the Pelican, the Weed,
the Death of a Toad—things of this world, through whose limits
are glimpsed, only glimpsed, a larger truth: Ceremony, Mind, the
World without Objects is a Sensible Emptiness. To be more specific:
a poem I enjoyed a great deal when I was first reading contem-
porary poetry was by Richard Wilbur. It is called "Mind":

> Mind in its purest play is like some bat
> That beats about in caverns all alone,
> Contriving by a kind of senseless wit
> Not to conclude against a wall of stone.
>
> It has no need to falter or explore;
> Darkly it knows what obstacles are there,
> And so may weave and flitter, dip and soar
> In perfect courses through the blackest air.
>
> And has this simile a like perfection?
> The mind is like a bat. Precisely. Save
> That in the very happiest intellection
> A graceful error may correct the cave.[8]

Wilbur's poem has all the virtues of fifties poetry: wit, elegance,
formal control. Within a lyric's short space, the modulations of a
single voice control paradoxes and win for a mysterious subject—

the mind's movement in darkness—a sociable acquiescence. The puns—"senseless wit," "conclude against a wall of stone"—remove, through an exercise of mind, much of the blankness that threatens it. (A more fearful version of the problem is Frost's "All Revelation.")

Wilbur's poem came back to me as I was reading James Merrill's *Mirabell*. The "bats of the mind" reappear there, not necessarily as an allusion to Wilbur, but drawn from the common stock of images that gives us "batty" as an adjective. Merrill's bats appear, not as images in the 1950s sense—objects contemplated and distanced in a lyric—but, unlikely as it may sound, as dramatic characters. They are intruders who force their way into his poem and deliver speeches, not only in a different verse measure (syllabics, fourteen to a line), but in a different typography, the persistent uppercase sections that are one of the odd features of the trilogy. As readers of Merrill's "Book of Ephraim"—the predecessor of *Mirabell*—will know, the plot of these book-length poems revolves around transmissions received as from another world on the Ouija board. Merrill has referred to "the saving absurdity of the board," a phrase that both suggests and dispels some of the embarrassments of receiving his material in this way. What he means by "saving absurdity" is that such transcriptions permit disparate voices on the page, some of them nonhuman. The method accommodates inconsistencies; it represents clashing planes of consciousness without ever claiming over them the authority of any single human presence as the lyric does. The speaker in this poem—he is called JM—at first resists conflict. He is appalled by the bat voices, appalled at their intrusion, appalled at finding them constituents of the human mind—and fascinated by their history. They are heard as voices outside the sociable range of human discourse—peremptory, bearing fearful news. Readers of "The Book of Ephraim" will remember it as the book in which Merrill began communication with the world of the dead, shadows of the past that live on and in fact shape and define the collection of responses we call the self. "The Book of Ephraim" is a much more populated book than *Mirabell*. It overflows with remembered friends and lovers, the living and the dead seen in the light of the ways they enriched the poet's memory and imagination.

In *Mirabell* the world of the dead is presented in less comforting ways. The deaths of dear ones are everywhere, but now the powers of extinction are introduced center stage, and the bat figures are their ambassadors. They introduce the potentially inhuman aspects of mind and power, the dwarfing vistas of chemical and biological force; "brains with wings," someone calls them. These are the Books of Number in a very real sense. The bats are identified by numerical formulas instead of human names. They claim to speak from within the atom and demand the poet's "word banks" so that they can tell their long tale of attempts to perfect matter through scientific control (in something called the Research Lab). At first this mission repels JM, but gradually it initiates him into a mesmerizing vision of life seen as chemical, biological, and mathematical process, potentially manipulable by the human mind and teasing humans out of thought with its vision of perfection and perfectibility.

Mirabell's bats may be said to represent the same forces that Wilbur depicted in his lyric poem and that Merrill himself called up in an earlier short poem, "Hour Glass." And yet they are a far cry from the similar figures in these lyric poems. The *Mirabell* bats enter as independent voices, not rapidly assimilated and interpreted by a lyric speaker. Instead, they are experienced adversaries and instructors whose clashing voices cast an odd light on the traditional speaker of short lyric poems; they call into question Merrill's own earlier and related lyrics—and indeed, the lyric training of his generation.

We are accustomed to thinking of earlier poems of this generation as peculiarly impersonal or detached, static, taking place in a timeless or eternal present. Yet the poets themselves, looking back at those apparently objective lyrics, have come to see them in surprising lights. Adrienne Rich, thinking of one of her mannerly early poems, remarked, "In those years formalism was part of the strategy—like asbestos gloves, it allowed me to handle material I couldn't pick up bare-handed."[9] James Merrill expressed similar thoughts about his own *First Poems*:

> These early versions of desire
> We come upon some nights instead of sleep

Blaze tinily, like fire deep
In windowglass far from the fire.

Light years away, their light, their heat
Are almost zero to the sense. We'd fed
Feelings genuine but dead
With language quick but counterfeit.

Remembered as by Jack the Ripper,
Between the burning and the pane
A self lost young falls open in its plain
Brown wrapper.[10]

It is odd and suggestive that two quite incompatible poets should recall work that appears impersonal on the page in images of fire—a fire resisted by gloves in Rich's metaphor or, in Merrill's, reflected as "fire deep / In windowglass far from the fire." Both writers understand the emblems in their early lyrics as being *exposed*—images of desire, only perhaps with hindsight understood.

Proust—one of Merrill's masters—tells the story of his old servant Françoise who would sigh with envy when she heard of people visiting the cathedrals of Milan or Rheims or Arras. Yet in all the time she lived in Paris she had never once been to Notre Dame. Indeed, remarks Marcel, why should she be expected to? Paris was the city of her daily life and hence one in which it would be difficult for the old servant to "situate the objects of her dreams." The last phrase is the instructive one. So much of a writer's life is given over to locating and relocating an object, an incident of his youth or dreams in order to unfold its meaning by properly situating this object of desire. The only true or essential book, Proust says, does not have to be "invented by a great writer—for it exists already inside him—but it has to be translated by him." Proust likens it to deciphering hieroglyphs, the symbols within, so that "the function and task of a writer are those of a translator." This statement is as true of poetry as it is of prose. One of the self-portraits that Merrill allows himself in *First Poems* is of "a young man / With his comic hat on, waiting in the middle / Of many things for his painter to come and make / Most of them plausible."

It takes a long career to make the resonant objects of a writer's youth legible and "plausible." The lyric poem was valuable for

Merrill and for other young poets of his generation because it helped identify objects of desire. Only repeated encounters enabled Merrill to interrogate those early and mysterious images so close to the unspeakable and to give them a new and refigured place. It is precisely in these acts of refiguring that he performs his most telling acts of self-representation. In the relatively depopulated *Mirabell*—depopulated by comparison with "Ephraim"—Merrill came most to understand this. The strange sci-fi world of *Mirabell* is an auto-biographical theater as well because of what it re-imagines in Merrill's work and because of the way it accomplishes transformations. *Mirabell* exposes the instability of what we regard as our most private signs. It suggests the continuing pressure under which—in the act of imagining an identity—we interpret and reinterpret such symbols. Three examples should begin to make this clear.

Mirabell, as everyone must now know, is a figure from another world, a bat who becomes a peacock. The stanzas in which that peacock first gloriously manifests itself are written in a verse form that sends us back to one of Merrill's *First Poems,* "The Peacock." Those *First Poems* are particularly strange and occluded. Many are spoken as if by a solitary child staring with wonder and bafflement at elusive natural emblems: seashells, periwinkles, a prematurely hatched robin's egg. "The Peacock" treats its exotic subject ruefully, as if to veil the pleasures that draw the poet to its brocaded tail, its zodiac of eyes, and the black, green, blue, and gold of its plumage. Lest the poem reveal too much of the feeling behind this attraction—luxuriant and literary at once—it is sheathed in a moral armor, transparent but brittle, identifying beauty with vanity and awkwardness. The young Merrill praises those who have "perfect beauty," which is "merit in word, emotion, deed," and so do not grieve, as the speaker does, when exotic "beauty passes." The poem presents a blurred icon of an early self, mistrustful of its desires.

Peacocks reappear several times in Merrill's verse but most astonishingly in *Mirabell,* where four human witnesses participate in the metamorphosis of one of the imperialist scientific bats into a gorgeous plumed creature. JM and his lifetime friend David Jackson are "accompanied" regularly on the Ouija board by two recently dead friends, the poet W. H. Auden and a Greek lady, Maria Mitsotáki, both of whose voices and figures have become vital parts of Merrill's consciousness. In life and in memory these two stand for admired qualities: Auden's poetic style, his curiosity and humane literacy; Maria's natural wit and courage and attentive friendship. Together they form—Auden and Maria—a kind of natural parentage of loving intelligence for JM and DJ.

Enter then, after these four have protested the peremptory crudeness of some of the bat speakers, a gentler bat, 741, whose opening gambit is to cast in front of them on the board a set of punctuation marks as if to humanize, add nuance to, the communications. His conversations with the humans, dead and alive, produce a strange effect. Their language transforms this numbered messenger. As he reveals to them the secrets of the experimental world, he becomes aware that one of *their* secrets is being revealed to him:

B4 OUR MEETINGS I WAS NOTHING   NO TIME PASSD   BUT NOW
YR TOUCH LIKE A LAMP HAS SHOWN ME TO MYSELF & I AM
ME: 741! I HAVE ENTERD A GREAT WORLD   I AM FILLD
WITH   IS IT MANNERS?

[*M*, p. 61]

The exchanges with human speakers have the power to differentiate, to confer identity and eventually a name. Before their eyes (so to speak: it is reported by Wystan and Maria on the board) the bat turns into a peacock. This is a charming and comic tribute to the power of human language ("SHOWN ME TO MYSELF"), which clothes and ornaments matter. An even stranger moment follows. "WE ARE IN A FOLD OF ENERGY / WE 5," the new peacock announces. He means that the attuned imaginations of Maria, Wystan, DJ, and JM can be said to have called forth 741 and to have transformed him into a peacock. And that transformation is celebrated in a lyric that recalls the moment in Marvell's "The Garden" when the freed mind is likened to the preening bird that "waves in its plumes the various light." The *Mirabell* lyric, in the very same stanza Merrill used for "The Peacock" in *First Poems,* celebrates the "gift of tongues at matter's core," the power of human language to name the peacock's colors, to create histories and a friendship like that of the four humans who among them make this poem. But the lyric also suggests that the triumphs of human speech are physically entwined with the charring and decomposing forces of the world of matter, the bats' world:

> The stored wit flickers out, the spine erodes
> And pain in lightning raids
> Strikes at the tree; now charred, now sleeved in sleet,
> Miming itself to sunset, the tough rind
> Compact enough, we trust, of royal reds
> And marble slabs of meat
> Not wholly to be undermined
>
> As milkweed, gnat, and fumes of vinegar
> Chafe in molecular
> Bondage, or dance in and out of it—
> Midnight's least material affairs
> Reconciling to glow faint and far
> Each atom the sun split,
> Whose heirs we are who are the air's.

[M, p. 66]

Those last puns seal both the triumphs and the limits of our verbal power.

The peacock lyric, in form and content, makes its bow to Merrill's *First Poems*. It presents another icon of the poetic self, its beauty and vanity, but without any of the earlier poem's ruefulness and uncertainty, without its self-derogating tone. A refiguring has taken place of a sort that becomes characteristic and liberating in Merrill's trilogy: the once exotic and secretive image becomes naturalized, a viable part of self-presentation, given full dramatic place in these longer poems and inevitably linked with decomposition and the impersonal processes of change.

A second example. In an early poem, "The Octopus," the rich imagery of gems is introduced in a sinister context, the promise of richness curiously turned in upon itself. The poem equates a dreamer's emotional seizure, a rapt vision, with the long grasping arms of an octopus in an aquarium. On the threshold of vision, the dreamer, like the sleeping octopus, is awakened, to one of those

infrequent moments when it is lured into action by hints of meaning
outside the glassy walls of its tank.

> There are many monsters that a glassen surface
> Restrains. And none more sinister
> Than vision asleep in the eye's tight translucence.
> Rarely it seeks now to unloose
> Its diamonds.
>
> [CT, p. 3]

What is disquieting about this poem is the ensuing sense of be-
trayal, essentially self-betrayal and guilt. The mind's awakening is
a frenzied arousal. Its bejeweled intuitions are identified both with
the greed of the ungainly octopus trying to encompass desired
objects and with its sinister and beautiful dance.

> His hands move clumsily in the first conventional
> Gestures of assent.
> He is willing to undergo the volition and fervor
> Of many fleshlike arms, observe
> These in their holiness of indirection
> Destroy, adore, evolve, reject—
> Till on glass rigid with his own seizure
> At length the sucking jewels freeze.
>
> [CT, p. 3]

The final image and the pun of the penultimate line tell the story.
Richness is not associated with the profusion of the universe out-
side but instead with some ingrown unappeasable hunger of the
poet dreamer. It is experienced with no sense of fulfilled pleasure
but instead as frustration, encoded anger, and paralysis. As with
the peacock's plumage in another early poem, the jewels of "The
Octopus" are presented as a hoarded beauty locked in an ungainly
frame rather than as signs of receptivity to the pervasive and gen-
erous presence of color and energy in the world.

These emblematic jewels are refigured frequently in Merrill's
poems but most fully in *Mirabell*. In an astonishing segment, their
dazzle is linked to danger and anxiety. JM is in Boston with his
friend David Jackson, who is to undergo surgery. But in the opening
moments of this section one hardly knows where one is. First, in a

sonnet, Merrill introduces the actress Sarah Bernhardt and afterward performs an even stranger modulation:

> She stood (wrote Jules Renard of the divine
> Sarah) in one place, letting the stair unwind
> Her profiles, eerily descending wand
> Of the still center, or its weathervane.
> Gone, she endured. Globes lit the banister's
> Counterspiraling ascents of bronze
> As in remembrance Lalique's cabochons
> Waxed and waned upon that brow of hers
>
> Like this pale purple atom (phosphorus)
> Periodic among satellites,
> Messengers, sugar chains and residues
> —*Her* memories of past performance? Cues?—
> Whereby the curtain on a triple thud
> Has risen. It's the theatre in our blood.
>
> 22.vii.   Boston Museum of Science.
> Studying a model (2.5
> Cm. per angstrom) of the DNA
> Molecule—a single turn blown up
> Tall as a child. My ignorance reduced
> To jotting down—red, blue, black, yellow, white—
> Colors of the bit-player beads, the carbons
> And nitrogens all interlinked, on pins
> But letter-perfect, purines, pyrimidines,
> Minute intelligences that indwell
> The chromosome and educate the cell . . .
> Even grossly simplified, as here,
> It's too much. Who by reference to this
> 3-D Metro map's infernal skeins
> And lattices could hope to find his way?
> Yet, strange to say, that's just what everyone
> On Earth is promptly known for having done.
>
> Noon.   In the hospital across the river
> David is wheeled up from surgery,
> Helped into bed—still numb from the waist down.
> Gaps in his sorry gown don't quite conceal
> Streaks of dim, white-bandaged red. His gaze
> Lights on a face within mine. . . .

[*M*, pp. 109–110]

We begin with a writer's memory of Bernhardt's motionless profile, unwound, as it were, by a spiral staircase. Then suddenly, as if a veil had fallen away, the bejeweled theatrical presence is compared to the DNA molecule, that is, to a model of it with colored knobs in the Boston Museum of Science. The presence of Bernhardt is felt as if imprinted with that pattern at the basis of human life. The most exotically theatrical, individual, willful, calculated, and idiosyncratic figure is identified with the most common, impersonal, and indwelling chemical force. The conflation, on one hand, hints at human triumphs through an emblem of human will in performance: "the theatre in our blood," as one speaks of theatrical families. On the other hand, the phrase calls up that "theatre in our blood" which reduces us to mere stages for chemically determined dramas, the genetic patterns that pulse through undreamed-of life spans. It is only then that the poem modulates to DJ after his operation, in a scene that is thereby invested with both of these perspectives on human life: the tenderness and vulnerability of human names and identities, and then the eerie superhuman sense of a gaze that "lights on a face within mine," as the two friends seem to speak beyond themselves.

Moving from lyric to autobiographical scene, Merrill has refigured elements from his earlier poems in a way that both accommodates and dwarfs the ego. Unlike the self-enclosed jeweled consciousness of "The Octopus," the refigured image in *Mirabell opens* the poet to experience, to a sense of the richness of human language as well as of the beauty of nonhuman physical forces, "the gift of tongues at matter's core." Death and extinction are never very far from the surface of this poem: the death of DJ's parents; Maria's radiation treatments and her death from cancer. Yet *Mirabell* stresses, to an even greater extent than "Ephraim" did, that language is the body of the dead—what they have left behind to be absorbed and developed by the living.

The retrieval of images is, for Merrill, a liberating process and is, in a sense, the subject of his autobiography, as it was of Proust's. The small examples I have cited, along with many others, contribute to a larger pattern that I can begin to suggest by citing two final passages, again, one from early work, one from later.

The poem "Childlessness" dates from 1962. In it the speaker's childlessness and unnamed homosexuality make him feel a traitor to a personified nature, which he imagines as his "dream wife." Only in the middle of the poem and only for a moment is she friendly to the poet, an enchantress who clothes him in "entire bolts of voluminous pistachio, / Saffron, and rose." The transitions are rapid and decisive:

> But in my garden
> Nothing is planted. Neither
> Is that glimmering window mine.
> I lie and think about the rain,
> How it has been drawn up from the impure ocean,
> From gardens lightly, deliberately tainted;
> How it falls back, time after time,
> Through poisons visible at sunset
> When the enchantress, masked as friend, unfurls
> Entire bolts of voluminous pistachio,
> Saffron, and rose.
> These, as I fall back to sleep,
> And other slow colors clothe me, glide
> To rest, then burst along my limbs like buds,
> Like bombs from the navigator's vantage,
> Waking me, lulling me. Later I am shown
> The erased metropolis reassembled
> On sampans, freighted each
> With toddlers, holy dolls, dead ancestors.
> One tiny monkey puzzles over fruit.
>
> [WS, p. 28]

Once again, as with other early poems we have looked at, the poet experiences an unsettled relation to his surroundings. That tiny monkey puzzling over fruit is a cousin to the ungainly peacock and the sinister octopus. He witnesses—and is part of—a community miniaturized by art in which the world's gifts and profusion are encountered only ruefully ("toddlers, holy dolls, dead ancestors"). The vision begins with more promise: sunset colors first clothe, then permeate the poet as pulsing energy-opening buds. They rapidly become bombs responsible for the miniature Dunkirk beneath him. By the end of the poem the coat of many colors has become a shirt of Nessus for his parents, whom, as he says, "it is eating to the bone." The swift transformations—dream wife into enchantress into scourge; buds into bombs—deflect any resolution, confound meaning. What was briefly a mantle of creativity, a sign of pleasurable participation in nature, is sloughed off guiltily as the sign of a hoarder's pleasure.

There is a similar and central passage in Book 7 of *Mirabell*. JM is about to telephone his mother, and then, instead, and without the antagonism felt in "Childlessness," starts thinking about Nature and Art, the world's profuse body and the witty patterns mind makes of it:

> Once out of nature, a mercurial
> Inch, look back! Sea, jungle, alpine snow,
> Buff desert far below
> Alternate by "turns" as in a music hall.
> So distanced, it could be the way
> Of our own world, as the fops in Congreve knew
> With their strut and plumage—ah! mightn't Mirabell do
> For our peacock's name?—and flowery word play
>
> Based on her wee wild orchid in bumblebee
> Motley, her anthology pieces that led
> Back through such juicy red
> Volumes to seed. All this is eminently me.
>
> [M, p. 138]

If there is a conflict of mind and nature, there is also an enchanting interpenetration:

> She answers with a tug of the old magnet,
> Making me look up from where I sit.
> Cocked to those infinite
> Spangled thinnesses whose weave gosling and cygnet
> Have learned already in the shell,
> The mind's ear registers her vocalise.
> Flagstad herself had no such notes as these
> Of lashing hail and rapturous farewell.
>
> [M, p. 139]

Such language fuses—in a pun—exposure to nature, the lashing hail, with the pleasures of the art it recalls, the hail and farewell of the great Wagnerian Flagstad's "vocalise." The lashing hail, which in "Childlessness" is linked only to guilt and a punishing Nature, is here inseparable from both the ecstasy of art and the encoded biological signals that "gosling and cygnet / Have learned already in the shell."

This is also the passage in which the metamorphosed 741 receives his name and is identified with the poet's own cocky dandyism—a sign of how many changes of tone this lyric embedded in narrative can comfortably include. In the space of fifty-six lines, Merrill can encompass his doublemindedness—the mind's pattern making, its attraction to nature's rich randomness, its lightning discomfiture with each activity. He can affectionately and satirically glance at the peacock artist and can still express the fallible and vulnerable fears for his own mother, all hinging on the commonplace question of a telephone call.

These examples of Merrill's refigurings, transformations of early images, involve, perhaps disconcertingly, the acknowledgment of an antagonistic component, nonhuman, in the exercise of human creativity. Merrill's earlier poems, as if fearing that discovery, as if fearing coldness or lack of intimacy, treated the imaginative act guardedly, ruefully, and with a certain frustrated yearning. Its symbols seemed too private to share or explore. But "The Book of Ephraim" and *Mirabell* show us that, however personal such material may be in origin—those exotic images of peacocks and jewels, the idiosyncratic feelings of being separate in sexuality or the child of a broken home—it can become more than a matter of shame or secrecy. The private symbols become part of a dialogue with the world in which we learn that such objects of desire are only signs borrowed from more enduring and inexorable alphabets. So, for example, Merrill's story has to be told in a form that makes it seem as if a sometimes painful physical adjustment of language had been forced upon him: uppercase speakers, lowercase speakers, lyrics, dialogues. In *Mirabell* he is challenged by emissaries of the chemical and biological bases of life, bombarded by voices of extinction using *his* words and *his* pages. The poem's divided form suggests how, in the face of such things, we create and maintain the illusion of personality and identity.

Mirabell has allowed Merrill to retain much of his eccentricity, lightning wit, and elite preoccupations. But the poem also acts as a daunting corrective by linking these idiosyncrasies to the organic bases of life. As the second book of Merrill's trilogy, it has some, but only some, of the purgative function of Dante's purgatorial cantos: *Mirabell* takes an abrasive view of the human self-indulgences of "The Book of Ephraim." But it is also a dialogue, and human voices make their mischievous and disarming returns. It is, I think, a major critical mistake to take the "system" of these poems as absolute or the large allusion to Dante as indicating a definitive moral progression. Ultimately Merrill's trilogy is more Ovidian than Dantesque.

The classical world gave a generic sanction to the poet's movement from shorter to longer works, from pastoral to georgic to epic; to this Dante added the further religious sanction behind the movement from profane sonnets to Divine Comedy. In our less structured moral world, the sanction is *only* psychological and the movement is from private or lyric images to some larger autobiographical fiction, one to which it almost seems the poet has been driven. What is most honest and most troubling about Merrill's trilogy is that there is no final truth revealed: individual revelations keep changing their shapes, and symbols of such personal origin demand constant reinterpretation. In the trilogy one order of spirit replaces another. From one angle the poems assert great faith in our human ability to envision and analyze our origins. Then, suddenly, one looks at the poems again, and they seem desperate attempts to make something authoritative of what must remain stubbornly private. The poems reveal the frailty of language as much as its power, and *Mirabell* is the key book—for that reason a disturbing one—in exposing the chasms under the eroding bridges of human speech.

But Merrill has prepared us for that from the very start. In "Ephraim" he quotes Heinrich Zimmer: *"The powers have to be consulted again directly—again, again and again. Our primary task is to learn, not so much what they are said to have said, as how to approach them, evoke fresh speech from them, and understand that speech. In the face of such an assignment, we must all remain dilettantes, whether we like it or not"* (DC, p. 106).

CHAPTER 5

Merrill and Dante

Rachel Jacoff

We have become used to the idea that any allusion to the systematic nature of Dante's vision would do no more than confess the impossibility of its recreation in our own time. Dante's totalizing syncretism is the very emblem of what a modern poet, qua modernist, dare not attempt except in ironic or nostalgic admission of its otherness. Thus, despite the Dantean epigraph to "The Book of Ephraim," and despite its otherworldly donnée, one initially felt the differences rather than the affinities between Dante's *Comedy* and Merrill's *Divine Comedies*. The shift from singular to plural in the volume's title virtually invited awareness of Merrill's playful distance from Dante. His astonishing freedom and flexibility of tone gave Merrill a dazzling range of registers with which to sweeten the solemn, to sanctify the silly. Since there are, I believe, no precedents for a funny philosophical poem, it took readers some time to realize what Merrill was up to. Now that his trilogy is completed, it is clear that Merrill has attempted nothing less than a Dantesque project of his own. This undertaking is something that neither twentieth-century literary history nor Merrill's own earlier career as a lyric poet could have prepared us for.

The few but strategic allusions to the *Comedy* in the trilogy are all to the *Paradiso*, Merrill's preferred cantica. Where other poets may be drawn to the powerful characterizations of the *Inferno* or to the scenes of lyric aspiration and tenderness in the *Purgatorio*, Merrill is fascinated by the *Paradiso*'s more abstract, impersonal beauty. In the central M section of "Ephraim," Maya's transfiguring dream

145

is glossed by Ephraim as a consequence of the return of a dead soul to its deathplace, temporarily allowing the live soul that it replaces to glimpse heaven.

> This dream, he blandly adds, is a low budget
> Remake—imagine—of the *Paradiso*.
> Not otherwise its poet toured the spheres
> While Someone very highly placed up there,
> Donning his bonnet, in and out through that
> Now famous nose haled the cool Tuscan night.
> The resulting masterpiece takes years to write;
> More, since the dogma of its day
> Calls for a Purgatory, for a Hell,
> Both of which Dante thereupon, from footage
> Too dim or private to expose, invents.
> His Heaven, though, as one cannot but sense,
> Tercet by tercet, is pure Show and Tell.
>
> [*DC*, p. 89]

However fanciful this deadpan explanation—it will be called a "satellite truth" when a second version of Dante's inspiration is offered in *Mirabell*—it does put the emphasis where Merrill himself feels it, on the primacy of the *Paradiso*.

And within the *Paradiso*, the quintessential passage for Merrill is Dante's vision in Canto XXVIII, a vision he recalls in *Mirabell* and discusses at some length in a recent essay on Dante.[1] In Canto XXVIII Dante is in the ninth sphere, the Primum Mobile, the borderline between the material world (since it is the last of the spheres orbiting the earth) and the spiritual tenth sphere, the empyrean of pure light and love. Dante sees a point of infinite brightness surrounded by rapidly whirling concentric circles representing the nine angelic hierarchies, each of which is in turn responsible for the motion of the nine spheres through which Dante has just passed. What puzzles Dante is the apparently inverse or asymmetrical relation between the two systems, the model and the copy, *l'essemplo e l'essemplare*. The inverse ratio between size and priority is restored to symmetry by the introduction of the dimension of speed: in the heavenly "mode" the smallest circle, the one closest to the point, is the fastest, while in the "copy," the largest circle, although furthest from the center (the earth), is also the fastest. This complex pas-

sage has recently been discussed by physicists who see it as pro-
phetically intuiting post-Einsteinian concepts of the universe.[2] Mer-
rill, with a sure instinct for the convergence of the mystic's vision
with the scientist's, is drawn to it as an instance of the homologous
coincidence of micro and macrocosmic structure.

> IN DANTE THE VISION WAS STARLIKE   AS HE LOOKED INTO
> THE ATOM'S EYE HE SAW THE POTENTIAL OF PARADISE
>   JM: Ah. This refers
>   To that uncanny shining tininess
>   Ringed with decelerating zones of light
>   (*Paradiso* XXVIII) on which, says Beatrice,
>   The heavens and all nature are dependent.
>
> [*M*, p. 38]

In his essay on Dante, Merrill spells out this double vision more
fully: "We may picture it partly as a model of electrons whirling
round the atomic nucleus—in our day, the point on which all na-
ture and its destruction depend; partly as an abstracted solar sys-
tem." Merrill's poem repeatedly reverses its own binocular vision
to affirm a similar homologous design:

>   Microscopic particles on one hand,
>   And on the other, Majesties, your Grand
>   Design outspiraling past all detail.
>
> [*S*, p. 196]

Dante's vision in Canto XXVIII is more abstract than the christo-
logical vision at the end of the poem, but this "timeless and dimen-
sionless point" that governs both the "heavenly and natural uni-
verses" is the one that Merrill sees as the source of the poem's
authenticity: "The vision as reported sets the mind reeling. What
must it have been to experience?"[3] Given the power of this Dan-
tesque vision for Merrill, we should not be surprised to read the last
"human" words of *Scripts*: "Up, far up, O whirling point of light."

This particular passage in Dante speaks to Merrill partly be-
cause of its concentricity, as does a surprisingly similar passage
from chapter 27 of *Middlemarch*, to which Merrill alludes in sections
N and Y of "Ephraim." Eliot speaks of the power of a lighted
candle to create the illusion of concentric circles on a randomly
scratched pier glass:

> Your pier-glass or extensive surface of polished steel made to be rubbed by a housemaid, will be minutely and multitudinously scratched in all directions; but place now against it a lighted candle as a centre of illumination, and lo! the scratches will seem to arrange themselves in a fine series of concentric circles round that little sun. It is demonstrable that the scratches are going everywhere impartially, and it is only your candle which produces the flattering illusion of a concentric arrangement, its light falling with an exclusive optical selection.

In Eliot's version, the coherence of the concentric is illusory, a parable for the dangers of subjectivity and egoism. The mirror and the lamp, those two traditional figures for fiction, conspire to make a figure of order. What is the very form of the divine design in Dante is, for Eliot, an image of the fictive quality inherent in any human perspective. The difference between Eliot's and Dante's concentric structures is the difference between casting the light and seeing it, between creating order and discovering it. Merrill's own poem wavers between these two ideas of order, suspicious of its own subjectivity and yet escaping from such fears in moments of "joy of the unbaited hook," moments when design reveals itself ineluctably. The poet's role as scribe, his necessary collaboration with DJ, the dialogue between the board's capitals and the poet's regular print—all these suggest ways out of the limits of subjectivity and solitary revelation. Merrill's version of the sublime is immensely sociable. Insight is celebrated communally and conversationally, culminating in grand choral fetes.

The problem of subjectivity is related to the poem's search for "a way of telling that inspires belief," a stance toward revelation that grants it an objective validity. Dante, at the opening of the *Comedy*, establishes his credentials precisely by calling them into doubt: "I am not Aeneas, not St. Paul. Neither I nor anyone else thinks me worthy of such an experience." This disclaimer allows Vergil to formulate Dante's journey as a manifestation of Divine Grace. The providential quality of the journey is subsequently attributed to the poem that records it as well. In the center of the *Paradiso*, Dante's ancestor Cacciaguida defines the poem as Dante's postexilic mission and reward, and Dante refers to it twice as a sacred poem, "'l poema sacro / al quale ha posto mano e cielo e terra" (XXV, 1–2). Like Dante (*Par.* X, 27), Merrill casts himself in the role of scribe. He includes a whole variety of possible attitudes toward the poem's matter in his and DJ's reported reactions to it. But however skeptical, witty, or even defensive their attitudes may be, the cumulative effect is a capitulation to the authenticity of the material.

This device works partly because Merrill's poem retains a provisional and metaphorical attitude toward its own "information," just as Dante's poem treats its own cosmology analogically. In both poets, physical and metaphysical facts have an interlocking identity. Dante, for example, moralizes the various landscapes of the poem. In the *Inferno* the settings are a facet of characterization, just as the physical forms of the punishments are literal versions of the spiritual errors they embody. In the *Paradiso*, Dante gives the astronomical characteristics of the various planetary spheres a metaphorical relationship to the souls found within them. Merrill achieves a similar freedom by treating scientific concepts metaphorically while interpreting a variety of creation and destruction myths in scientific terms. This procedure invites us to think of science and story as mutually illuminating. It is celebrated at the end of *Mirabell* as the poem's key lesson:

> THE ELDER FACTS IN LIVERY OF FABLE
> HAVE JOINED THE DANCE   FOR FACT IS IS IS FABLE:
> THIS IS OUR GIFT FROM MIRABELL. . .
>
> [*M*, p. 169]

Fact and fiction overlap in mutually enhancing ways in the poem's content as well as in its autobiographical references. Both "the world's poem and the poem's world" require incessant translation.

> Hadn't—from books, from living—
> The profusion dawned on us, of "languages"
> Any one of which, to who could read it,
> Lit up the system it conceived?—bird-flight,
> Hallucinogen, chorale and horoscope:
> Each its own world, hypnotic, many-sided
> Facet of the universal gem.
>
> [*DC*, p. 75]

Each of these "languages" speaks, as does each of the facts and fables the poem incorporates, of its own particular version of the "Grand Design": "These overlapping pandemonia: / Birdlife, leaf-play, rockface, waterglow / Lending us their being" (M, p. 181). Each of the fables points to a truth none of them alone can adequately represent. If myth is a religion we do not believe in, then Merrill's is a religion of myths, each of which yields up its portion of a larger truth in retelling and translation. The great poem (one of the nine short poems that precede "Ephraim" in *Divine Comedies*) "Lost in Translation" addresses the issue of coexisting versions of a truth beyond any provisional expression of itself. In that poem Merrill paraphrases Rilke's translation of Valéry's "Palme." The image that informs all three versions is that of a tree tapping a deep and secret wellspring of unseen authority. Merrill's trilogy assumes such a source for its branching and interlocking versions, a Platonic unity behind evident multiplicity.

As a variety of facts and fables are translated into one another, so, too, the characters themselves turn out to be versions of one another or of some archetypal principle. There are, as the poem acknowledges (M, p. 128), a host of characters whose names begin with M, as does the poet's own. The three great female figures of the poem—Maya, Maria, and Mimí—are avatars of the eternal feminine in various forms. Maria is always in black, Mimí in white, and Maya moves from one to the other both in her paradisiacal dream and in her film apotheosis in *Scripts*. There are a variety of "artistic" figures whose work reflects facets of the poet's own; not only the literary figures, but musical and artistic heroes are invoked and celebrated. As the minor characters in a Shakespeare play illuminate aspects of the hero, so many of the poem's characters seem to dramatize an aspect of the poet's own character. In Dante, too, we often have the sense that encounters are forms of self-confrontation for the poet. Particularly in the memorable sinners of the *Inferno* we see Dante embodying one of his own tendencies in extreme form, and so these episodes have a double charge of sympathy and judgment.

A further set of interrelated identities arises from the poem's exploitation of the notion of reincarnation. In "Ephraim" the idea of reincarnation is linked to the theme of prior or buried selves. The poem relates these prior selves to a series of prior versions of art: the *Tempesta*'s X-ray original script, the lost manuscript of JM's novel, which intermittently appears embedded in the poem, the transcripts of the Ouija board conversations that are nearly burned in Z—all those "priorities" that lie beneath the surface and give it nuance and resonance. As the trilogy progresses, the revelations of reincarnation accelerate and proliferate, so that there is an increasing sense of slippage. At one point in *Scripts*, JM calls attention to the "shrinking" of the cast:

> Is the cast
> Much smaller than we'd thought? Does our quick-change
> Michael double as—DJ: Ephraim?
>
> [*S*, p. 123]

The poem accelerates its doublings and unmaskings as "Everything merges and reflects" and seems both to relish and to regret such "mergers"; but it insists on their validity even when such a claim threatens to tip the emotional balance, as it surely does when Maria, around whom so much of the poem's human power and pathos is constellated, is revealed to be Plato in drag, all set for a new incarnation as a child in Bombay. It is as if Dante had saved Vergil after all. Maria's fate, like Vergil's, had seemed the tragedy within the comedy, a haunting reminder of all that cannot be finally reconciled within the poem's affirmative ethos.

The doublings and identities between characters represent one of the poem's many plots of "coincidence." The linguistic version of this energy is manifest in the discovery of hidden identity, a discovery that leads to puns and wordplay of all sorts. The puns delight us as if they were a kind of secret subplot filled with its own surprising correspondences. They are especially effective when a word is clearly placed in one set of conventional associations and is suddenly unveiled in another context. We might think of the way Merrill's discussion of *The Rake's Progress* in *Scripts* turns into a meditation on paradise, with an "ALL STAR REVIVAL OF THE RAKE / AS A GARDEN TOOL" (*S*, p. 226). Or the beautiful close of *Mirabell*, which depends on "opening up" Wittgenstein's famous dictum:

> The world was everything that was the case?
> Open the case. Lift out the fabulous
> Necklace, in form a spiral molecule
> Whose sparklings outmaneuver time, space, us.
>
> [M, p. 180]

Or the lovely play on ABBA as the Hebrew name for father and as one of the poet's favorite rhyme schemes. The pun, and the spoonerism, a related source of comic energy in the poem, exemplify the poem's playful rage to uncover similarities in the fleeting world of appearance. The pun both embodies this rage for correspondences and is its reverse image, since it actually uncovers differences in apparently similar forms. The *Oxford English Dictionary* (which Merrill has called "the collective unconscious of the race") gives the putative etymology of the word "pun" as the Italian *puntiglio*, or "fine point," a wonderfully suggestive possibility in this particular connection, given, as we have seen, Dante's partiality to points and Merrill's own.

Aside from specific allusions to the figure of Dante and to passages in the *Comedy*, the most important evidence of Merrill's reading of Dante comes, as we might expect it to, in his use of Dante's rhyme scheme. And how brilliantly he utilizes Dante's terza rima, rhyming sometimes unobtrusively and at other times improbably. Merrill links the three parts of the trilogy by placing, in each of them, a near-climactic sequence in this privileged form. The first and third of the sequences are set in Venice and are linked thematically to each other and to the central paradisiacal dream sequence in M. (Maya's dream is recalled and is given its apotheosis in the terza rima sequence of *Scripts*, where it is "rerun" as her film and a kind of "resurrection"). The second of the three terza rima sequences contains Robert Morse's "elegy" and is linked to the Venetian theme of the other two by mention of "Maria's Himmelfahrt," the subject of the great Titian painting in the church of the Frari. The masterstroke is the ending of each of the three sequences on the word "stars," the very word (*stelle*) that Dante uses to rhyme his three cantiche with one another.

Furthermore, the poem that introduces the middle section of *Scripts*, "Samos," is written in the verse form that Dante invented, the canzone stanza, sometimes (and inaccurately) called a double sestina. This hypnotic poem exploits the limits of the difficult form triumphantly, the five repeated rhyme words ringing changes on the four elements (land, air, water, light) and implying the five senses by the use of the fifth word, "sense." All the "V work" of equivalencies spelled out across the length of the poem is condensed in fugal density here. (The pervasive importance of the number five, V, in its multiple permutations reminds one of Sir Thomas Browne's *Garden of Cyrus* rather than of Dante's triune numerology.) Merrill makes one minor change in the Dantesque form; while Dante's *congedo* (last stanza) brings the rhyme words back in simple retrogression, using the central rhyme word twice (hence, a six-line final stanza), Merrill uses each rhyme word only once in the last stanza and in the order of their first occurrence in the poem's opening stanza. The final stanza thus reiterates the centrality of the "five" to the poem's theme and suggests that Merrill has uncovered the ethos of the form that Dante had loved for its sheer technical virtuosity, its "novità."[4]

If Dante provides Merrill with certain privileged rhyme schemes and verse forms, images, and a precedent of poetic authority, he also suggests a challenge:

> Everything in Dante knew its place.
> In this guidebook of yours, how do you tell
> Up from down? Is Heaven's interface
>
> What your new friends tactfully don't call Hell?
>
> [M, p. 162]

This objection, posed by RM (and in terza rima, no less!) is one that the poem never fully answers. It is not possible to tell "up from down" because Dante's vertical and hierarchical structure is finally antithetical to Merrill's more horizontal and concentric vision. The movement of Dante's poem is linear, or, more accurately, spiral. Merrill's is circular, in keeping with its cyclical sense of individual and cosmic history. The cyclical turns of historical time are connected to the very structure of the atom, its plus and minus charges both necessary to life:

> When we suppose that history's great worm
> Turns and turns as it does because of twin

> Forces balanced and alert within
> Any least atom, are we getting warm?
>
> [S, p. 196]

Hell may be "Heaven's interface," but it is inseparable from it, as Merrill hints in a marvelous bilingual pun:

> It's the hour
> When Hell (a syllable identified
> In childhood as the German word for *bright*
> —So that my father's cheerful "Go to Hell,"
> Long unheard, and Vaughan's unbeatable
> "They are all gone into a world of light"
> Come, even now at times, to the same thing)—
> The hour when Hell shall render what it owes.
>
> [M, p. 180]

Dante's compartmentalizing imagination is alien to Merrill's propensity for turning things on their heads, identifying doubles, uncovering equivalencies. The circular structure of the poem virtually demands that its epilogue end on the opening words of "Ephraim," recalling the form of "the great wordsmith Joyce / Forging a snake that swallows its own tail."

In both Dante and Merrill the poet's relation to his literary past must be seen doubly; there is the question of his literary predecessors, and there is the question of his own earlier work. Dante dramatizes the issue of literary influence in a variety of ways: by actual encounters with other poets, by discussions of poetic practice, by literary allusion, and by direct comparison, as in his "competition" with Ovid and Lucan in the metamorphosis of the thieves in *Inferno* XXV. Above all, he explores the problematics of influence in the complex role given to Vergil. Merrill, too, summons up the tutelary figures of his own poetic development: Auden (who is given the largest speaking role among such figures), Proust, Stevens, Blake, Yeats, and Pope are all duly saluted. The selective audience to which the poet will read the completed trilogy at the end of the epilogue is a veritable alphabet of literary influence.

Merrill's poem takes up the issue of influence most directly at the close of *Mirabell*, where JM laments being a vehicle of others' voices:

And maddening—it's all by someone else!
And in your voice, Wystan, or in Mirabell's.
· · · · ·
Here I go again, a vehicle
In this cosmic carpool. Mirabell once said
He taps my word banks. I'd be happier
If *I* were tapping them. Or thought I were.

[*M*, pp. 167–168]

This complaint provokes a capacious response from WHA, a lengthy paean to the nourishing value of tradition.

THINK WHAT A MINOR
PART THE SELF PLAYS IN A WORK OF ART
COMPARED TO THOSE GREAT GIVENS   THE ROSEBRICK MANOR
ALL TOPIARY FORMS & METRICAL
MOAT ARIPPLE!
· · · · ·
IS NOT ARCADIA TO DWELL AMONG
GREENWOOD PERSPECTIVES OF THE MOTHER TONGUE[. . . ?]

[*M*, p. 168]

The poet's cultivation of other voices, other visions is part of the poem's theme as well as its procedure. It is the literary form of its human sense of community and yet another link the poem forges between the living and the dead. In his appearance at the end of *Scripts*, Yeats tells the poet, "You have refashioned us by fashioning this." And he mimes the point by speaking in a series of Yeatsian images.

In addition to placing itself with respect to literary influences, the trilogy also takes a retrospective look at Merrill's own earlier poetry; the early poems are given prophetic value as they are validated by the new and richer context of the trilogy. Phrases and images from several early poems are recalled, as are whole poems. One of Mirabell's discourses occasions the following set of poetic recalls:

JM: He's read *First Poems*!
"Transfigured Bird"—the title caught his eye.
DJ: Should I have bought that new gray suit?
YET YOU BOTH RIGHTLY AVOID GREEN ROOMS
JM: "The Emerald"—I give it back.

[*M*, p. 122]

We are reminded of another key earlier poem, "The Broken Home," at the end of the epilogue where the fictional space of the fare- well fete is transformed from a schoolroom to the ballroom of that earlier poem. In "The Broken Home" a reverse transformation had taken place; the ballroom of the poet's childhood home had been turned into a schoolroom by its new owners.

This sense of a poetic career in continuous redefinition is one that the greatest writers give us; the totemic people and objects and poems of the past are revisited and rewritten. Dante's career manifests this ongoing redefinition from the start, his first book, the *Vita Nuova*, presenting itself as a collection and rereading of earlier poems. The *Comedy* incorporates ideas and lines from Dante's earlier poems, but usually it does so to show the distance that Dante has come from them. Thus the two citations to the Odes of the *Convivo* occur in contexts in the *Comedy* that are palinodic.[5] The palinodic energy of these incorporations is related to what I have called the linear movement of Dante's poem, its sense of progress. In Merrill's trilogy, on the contrary, the earlier poems form, like Ephraim's theory about Dante, a "satellite truth," a version that orbits larger truths and is validated by them and time.

"Lost and Found" would be a fine alternative title for the tril- ogy, given its Proustian energies. "The Will," a preparatory poem to "The Book of Ephraim," chronicles a series of losses that are the prelude to an unwilled dreamlike discovery of restoration. The tomblike setting of the poem's opening scene is transfigured in its closing dream dip into the underground-unconscious in which all is intact, awaiting release. The totemic lost Ibis of the poem be- comes in a pun (I-*bis*, the second I, or reconstituted self) an image of the recourses (memory, dream, the unconscious, and the other- world) against the death of the originary self. Loss and death are the pretext of recovery and restoration, and of the text itself.

Death is, of course, one of the great themes of the trilogy, both the source of its cast (what Merrill at one point calls "ill-got gains") and the motive of its Orphic endeavor. The poem resurrects the voices of the poet's friends, giving them an ongoing existence, open at once to future change and to revisionary readings of their own pasts. The idea of post-mortem friendships between friends of the poet who had not known each other in life is an especially delightful and fruitful notion. (Dante uses a similar idea in the Statius-Vergil encounter when Vergil explains to Statius that he has loved him ever since Juvenal arrived in Limbo bringing word of Statius's affection for Vergil.) At times the world of the dead seems more open-ended than the world of the living:

> DJ: It's almost as if *we* were dead
> And signalling to dear ones in the world.
>
> [*S*, p. 79]

In Maya's apotheosis, "Her darks print out as bright, her dyings live. . . . We are the ghosts, hers the ongoing party." The poem defines heaven as "a machine for making the dead available to life," and its own restorative energies work to just such an end. Yet the poem includes the reality of loss and grief, and the possibility that its fictions are simply that:

> DJ: I know,
> I hated that. Loss *is* loss. JM: Though
> Hasn't the Board helped us at all to see
> Losses recouped?
> . . . . .
> our own otherwise
> Dumb grief is given words. DJ: Or lies?
>
> [*S*, p.53]

Despite the honesty of such an admission, the poem is affirmative both in individual and in cosmic terms, promising the survival of the species as well as of individuals we have come to know. At the end of *Scripts*, each of the major figures is granted his wish: Ephraim is given his senses, Feeling is restored to grace, and Mirabell to nature, united at the last with the enchanting Uni to form a Pegasan image:

> And should elsewhere
> Broad wings revolve a horselike form into
> One Creature upward-shining brief as dew,
> Swifter than bubbles in wine, through evening air
>
> Up, far up, O whirling point of Light—:
>
> [*S*, p. 235]

The epilogue conjoins the worlds of the living and the dead with unique poignance as JM begins to read the poem aloud to his newly arrived grief-crazed friend:

> And my worst fear—that, written for the dead,
> This poem leaves a living reader cold—
>
> [*CLS*, "Coda"]

But by now it hardly seems possible for the reader to keep the two realms separate. Ephraim's definition of heaven as "the surround of the living" has been so fully incarnated that the poem has brought heaven to earth, just as its promise will be the ultimate transformation of earth into heaven. Dante looks forward to a Paradise from whose height one would see the earth as a "little threshing floor." For Merrill the earth itself will become a Paradise.

Merrill's poem inhabits what Rilke calls *"the great unity,"* an "unboundaried" realm shared by the living, the dead, and those yet to come:

> Death is the *side of life* that is turned away from us: we must try to achieve the fullest consciousness of our existence, which is at home in *the two unseparated realms, inexhaustibly nourished by both.* . . . We, of this earth and this today, are not for a moment hedged by the world of time, nor bound within it: we are incessantly flowing over and over to those who preceded us and to those who apparently come after us.[6]

The trilogy attempts what no other poem of our time has dared: to acknowledge the fragmentary, provisional, kaleidoscopic nature of contemporary knowledge and belief and to incorporate such awareness in a poetic structure that does justice to "the pressure of reality" (*DC*, p. 110) without succumbing to it. And it does so on a scale that invites comparison with the very grandest poems of our tradition.

CHAPTER 6

The Divine Translation:
Elegiac Aspects of
The Changing Light at Sandover

Peter Sacks

BUT MORTALITY ALLOWS FOR THE DIVINE TRANSLATION
—*Mirabell*

In a downcast century whose poems of major length—*The Waste-land, The Bridge, Paterson, The Cantos, History, The Dream Songs*— have almost all suffered from the very darkness and fragmentation they have tried to overcome, how is it that James Merrill has suc-ceeded in writing a long poem (more than 15,000 lines) that is, above all, triumphantly consoling? Unquestionably, *The Changing Light at Sandover* does confront pain and sorrow, the death of friends and parents, the extinction of cultures, even the threat of global ruin. But Merrill's astonishing achievement is to have transfigured the experience of loss and fear to one of celebration and to have moved, in a series of arduous revelations, beyond the stances of resignation or fractured yearning to one of magnificent confidence. In doing so, he has become our greatest poet of serious and far-reaching solace, a poet whose inspired defense against a dark view of mortality and fate burns brightly, "the way good solace seethes."

That last phrase comes from Wallace Stevens's elegy "The Owl in the Sarcophagus," and I suggest that *one* among several ways to read Merrill's poem is as an elegy writ very large, as a multiple elegy of epic proportions. While such an approach cannot exhaust the poem's totality, it may nonetheless offer a perspective on certain organizing themes and motifs of the work as well as on essential features of its narrative structure and momentum. So, too, such an approach brings us close to the sources of the poem's distinctive power of consolation.

An elegy is a poem of mourning and consolation, in which, to quote Merrill himself,

> Those ghastly graveyard facts become a dance
> Of slow acceptance; our own otherwise
> Dumb grief is given words. DJ: Or lies?

[S, p. 53]

David Jackson's rejoinder, an instance of *The Changing Light*'s persistent questioning of its own fabulous nature, points here to the fact that most elegies necessarily depend on "lies" or rather on certain kinds of almost mythological figuration. After all, an elegy seeks to create a believable fiction that returns the dead to us in some transfigured version of themselves, be it as a flower, a star, a reborn infant, or a genius of the shore. Each of these versions derives, however implicitly, from the figure of a renascent god, to whom the dead are figuratively assimilated and who represents some principle or project that employs rather than suffers the passage of time and that grandly includes death as a necessary element of its career. In a successful elegy, the living come to recognize their role within that overarching career, involving as it does a close alliance with the dead.

Borrowing a definition of heaven from WHA (Merrill's Auden), we may see the elegy itself as a "MACHINE WHICH MAKES THE DEAD AVAILABLE TO LIFE" (M, p. 166). No less, perhaps, it makes the living available to death. To write or read such a poem is to enter the enlarged space that the dead apparently create for the living, a realm compounded of their mourned absence from this world, and of their new, imagined dwelling places.[1] Indeed, an elegy should work between those two regions, rather in the way Merrill conjures both "sides" of the mirror and the Ouija board. By virtue of imagination, memory, love, *devotion,* the living seem to look or listen, with refined senses, into a region in which figures for the dead continue to exist. And where else but within that region and within those moments of devotion should they also seem to encounter those other imaginary beings, which they assume to be divine—familiar spirits, angels, God? As Merrill has written in "A Dedication" for the dead Hans Lodeizen, "These are the moments, if ever, an angel steps / Into the mind" (*CT*, p. 83). In its course, therefore, an elegy has the effect not only of elevating the dead but also of raising the living, of orienting and refining them toward a compensatory gift of poetic power, of hitherto concealed knowledge, or of their portion of divinity.

By thus celebrating the dead, the living come to rehearse their own immortality. The motif of resurrection may, therefore, govern their *own* experience of almost alchemical refinement, of stripping to divine densities. Greatly elaborated, this is perhaps the essential theme of the trilogy. Merrill and Jackson are drawn, largely by their continuing devotion to the dead (Jackson has spoken of his parents, for example, as having been taken up "like bait, to focus attention away from the preoccupations of the day and onto the dictée from the other world")[2] into a region of consciousness in which they communicate not only with the dead but also with progressively higher attendant and supervisory powers, Ephraim, Mirabell, the Archangels. The series of communications is structured precisely as an ascent, a graduated course of lessons, in which the living, aided and protected by the affectionate mediations of the dead, learn increasingly about the nature and history of creation, the forces of chaos and evil, and particularly about the deathless "v WORK" that strives for survival and for the possibility of paradise on earth.

Among other things, V represents *vie,* life; also the number five, associated with the human senses and with the V work's immortal paragons, the Five, of whom more later; also, in the chiasmic emblem for man (*S*, p. 192), "TWO ARMS REACHING UP WARD," stretching "TOWARD REASON AND LIGHT." The V work, strives to "make sense of things," a project of conversion, not merely cognition. Furthermore, in its accompanying work on the process of perfecting human life and on assuring the "march toward Paradise," the V work depends on a constant reincarnation and improvement of human souls. As such, it makes sense of death itself and provides precisely the kind of overarching and immortalizing "career" that any genuine consolation requires.

Now, these elements—devotion to the dead, initiatory instruction, sensory and visionary refinement, reincarnation and apotheosis—all relate to the original sources of elegy, the ritualistic celebrations of death and rebirth associated with such deities as Osiris, Adonis, Dionysus, Persephone. The ceremonious enactments, originally of martyrdom and vegetal return, in the course of history gradually took on more elevated reference, modulating through Orphic and Pythagorean interpretations to become ascetic rites of intellectual ascent, guaranteeing spiritual resurrection. As is well known, Plato inherited much of this legacy, revealed not only in elements of his beliefs but also in his dialectical rites of philosophical self-purification and of continuing spiritual elevation. It is interesting to notice how thoroughly Merrill celebrates not only the figure of Plato—one of the immortal Five and represented by the beloved Muse Maria Mitsotáki—but also Plato's Academy, the only Academy, as we are told in the closing moments of the poem. Have not all the lessons and "seminars" in Merrill's poem been activities of this Academy and of its antecedent cults of divine death and rebirth?

It is not surprising, therefore, to learn at the very outset of the poem, in section A of "The Book of Ephraim," that the poet

> had, from the start, a theme
> Whose steady light shone back, it seemed, from every
> Least detail exposed to it. I came
> To see it as an old, exalted one:
> The incarnation and withdrawal of
> A god.
>
> [DC, p. 47]

The entirety of The Changing Light reveals how fully this theme involves not only "incarnation and withdrawal" but also reincarnation, a sequence to which Merrill assimilates a series of deaths and rebirths, from the desperate immolation of Simpson at the outset to the epilogue's superb account of the rebirth of Robert Morse. Indeed, by concentrating on this elegiac structure of the poem, one recognizes most deeply the appropriateness and splendor of that exact trajectory, and one notices how many of the poem's concerns converge on that final reincarnation.

Before exploring how Merrill has extended and revised this traditional thematic development, we should remark on related innovative aspects of the poem, such as the means of its astonishing vividness and drama. Much of the drama, with its dazzling masques and pageantry, derives from the poem's already mentioned affinity to the ritual Mysteries of rebirth, with their unfolding arcana and their highly theatrical ceremonies of purification, of procreative renewal and spiritual ascent. The actual vividness of presentation, the manner in which we seem to see and hear the dead, to be among them and to witness their transfiguration—this is an achievement in many ways unmatched since Dante. In Merrill's case we owe that dramatic intensity largely to the media of the mirror and the Ouija board, the means by which Merrill and Jackson communicate visually and verbally with the spirit world. We may regard these as instruments, metonymic emblems perhaps, of the mind's eye and the inner ear. They are the tools of inspiration: through them, the material of visionary poetry reaches the poet and his psychic comedium, who thus find their place among such inspired scribes as Homer, Dante, Milton, Blake, and Yeats.

More specifically, the mirror and board relate to distinctly elegiac aspects of Merrill's vision. Together they form the "fair field" of the following beautiful lines:

WE MET ON THIS FAIR FIELD & SEEM BY ITS EASE TO BE
IN CONVERSE   YET WE ARE ALL THE DEAD & YOU THE LIVING.
THAT U DO NOT DOUBT US IS WONDER ENOUGH   THAT OTHERS
DO IS NONE . . .
. . . . .
FOR WHO LIVING
WELCOMES THE DEAD?
[M, pp. 163–164]

The mirror has of course been a recurrent motif not only in Merrill's earlier poetry but in the work of poets ranging from Spenser to Auden. As such, it has represented the artistic or poetic realm of composition, reflection, and speculation. In *The Changing Light* the mirror in addition becomes not only the point of contact between the living and the dead but the threshold between them and the "glassy foyer" through which Mercury-Hermes, messenger of the gods and transporter of souls (*M*, p. 152), ushers his charges. As though by the alchemical refinement that the entire poem celebrates, that "foyer" is created by the element mercury, which transmutes the black backing of egoism ("the screen / Of self which forms between God and His creature") into a permeable medium through which we not only "look *beyond* ourselves" but also, as in the case of Robert Morse, penetrate to heaven and to continuing contact with our friends on earth:

> NEXT I STEPPED BAREASS
> THRU SAND & WATER OF YR MIRROR GLASS
> & SURFACED WHERE 2 OLD & 3 NEW CHUMS
> WELCOMED ME, SKINS GLISTENING WITH LIGHT
> NO BRUSH COULD EVER RENDER
>
> [*S*, p. 216]

Mercury is also quick- or living-silver; and silver, we discover, is Merrill's defining mineral (*M*, p. 48). We begin to surmise the connection between the divine messenger, the alchemical element, the means of communication between the living and the dead and, of course, the language of the scribe. In a sense, Mercury is poetic language. And thus it is that after conferring on poetic techniques, WHA and JM are approved by the Archangel Michael in these words:

> IS THAT NOT THE DEAREST OF OUR FATHER'S HOPES?
> MAN USING HIS MOST DELICATE MACHINE, MINING LEAD &
> PRODUCING QUICKSILVER?
>
> [*S*, p. 64]

The connection between the Ouija board and language is even more obvious, but once again the essentially elegiac and redemptive aspects are worth stressing. As with the mirror, such associations derive not only from the board's function in the poem but from the images carefully associated with it. For example, the letters of the board are arranged in an arc or "covenant / With whom it would concern" (*DC*, p. 49). The covenantal rainbow arc of course signifies literal survival and spiritual salvation; but to extend the association by pun and metaphor, the board is also referred to as the "ARK," "THE LIFE RAFT LANGUAGE" (*M*, p. 25). More fully:

THE STAGE WE ARE ON IS LIKE ALL STAGES A HALF ARC
THUS THE LEGEND OF NOAH   THIS HALF MOON SHIP BORE THE DUST
GOD B SAVED OVER FROM THE FALL & ITS PARTICLES WERE
FORMULAS   ATOMIC STRUCTURES   COMMUNICANTS OF LIFE
THAT WAS GOD B'S METHOD & WE, APPROACHING U HANDS CUPPD
WITH LESSONS, HELPD U TO CONSTRUCT A METHOD OF YR OWN.
2 BY 2 WE HAVE ENTERD YR MINDS & NOW YEARS LATER
THE COMMUNICATION IS AFLOAT OVER A DROWND WORLD.
WE ARE NOT ALAS TO BRING U TO OUR ARARAT   WE
ARE TO BRING U TO THE MEANINGS U NEED   MUCH AS THE ARK
BROUGHT NOAH TO THE PEAKS & SLOPES OF A NEW WORLD.

[*M*, p. 159]

In the arc or ark of a survivor's language, the residue of a fallen world enters for preservation and rebirth. Like the mirror, the board is thus not only a redemptive field on which losses are recouped (*S*, p. 53) but the great transporting vehicle of language itself. Yet further, the ark imagery summons up the repository for the holy text of the Torah as well as the sacred chest by which the ancient Hebrews used to represent the presence of God among them.

So, too, the board, like an elegy perhaps, provides an "anchor point of heaven," a point at which the dead can moor themselves to the devotion of the living, and vice versa. This image of mooring is crucial to the poem, for as we are told, it was precisely a hubristic breaking free from their stone anchorages that brought on the fall of the dark angels and the destruction of their world. Merrill's task is thus, in part, to renovate the earthly anchor points and to restore the cables that connect them with the heavenly world. And with this mention of anchoring stones and cables, it is intriguing that the very first Ouija board communicant to visit Jackson and Merrill, "before Ephraim, before Stonington," had the name Cabel (Caleb?) Stone. As Mirabell later explains (*M*, p. 171), this seventeenth-century New Englander acted as a preliminary testing voice. And although DJ and JM were not yet ready to have their raft made fast "TO THE SHORES OF THE DEAD," the glow of their communication was sufficient to ensure future contact and to set in motion "THE SELECTION & TRAINING OF THE COMMUNICANT." This brings us to Ephraim and to the beginning of the poem.

Immediately, in the opening lines, the struggle is joined against Time and against that "ancient foe," the deadline—the "grave deadline," as Auden had punned in his "New Year's Letter." This issue of the deadline, coupled with a subsequent reference to The Book of A Thousand and One Evenings, suggests how intently the poem will seek to "press back" against the passage of time and against the imminence of death. As is true of many elegies, the defense is at first conducted largely by memory, the dominant mode in "Ephraim." But as the trilogy unfolds, it will pursue a characteristically elegiac movement from memory to prophecy, from an evocation of the past to an adumbration of the future or of a timeless present.

Interestingly enough, Ephraim is preceded by his representative, Simpson, whose appearance here, at the outset of the poem, is perfectly appropriate in several respects. As "a feeble nature / All but bestial," he is a suitably low first rung on the poem's ladder of ascent to Ephraim and, beyond, to Michael. Also, by "reliving" his death, he serves to blur the very distinction between life and death, forcing us to question the nature of that threshold, as we shall do throughout the poem. Moreover, not only does his experience prefigure that of JM in section L, but his particular death, by fire, is a horrible variant of what may yet come to represent the purgative stripping by which we die into a more essential state. Finally, his words "HELLP O SAV ME" are the first words from the other world. They come almost as a dramatic cry from the dead to the living, a cry for salvation, a naked appeal as direct and primitive as any that an elegist might hear. It is the initiating cry, and burden, of the poem.

Of course, to claim that this cry, as well as all the subsequent dictée in the poem, does in fact originate from the spirit world, is already to accept the poem's most crucial fable. If, on the other hand, we puzzle skeptically over the "actual" origin of this language, we would have to explore the very wellsprings of the poet's motive and inspiration. Perhaps the opening cry is that of the poet himself. Perhaps the spirit world and its voices dwell only within a somewhat occult region of the mind, making its own irrepressible request—the request that Gabriel insists "IS NOTHING LESS (OR MORE) THAN IMMORTALITY / JM: Since when? Not a request we made. / ONE THAT ALL MORTALS MAKE" (S, p. 32). JM's apparent innocence suggests how this request indeed originates within some less than conscious area of need, suggests in fact that the very relationship between the voices in the above dialogue, as, too, the relation between lowercase and uppercase throughout the poem, may be the relation between differing levels of consciousness. The dictée is thus one of desire or need or, more precisely, of an unconscious resistance to death, a call for immortality.[3]

In this light, it is especially fascinating to come upon the following particular references to Stevens and Jung in sections S and U of "Ephraim":

> Stevens imagined the imagination
> And God as one; the imagination, also,
> As that which presses back, in parlous times,
> Against "the pressure of reality."
>
> [DC, p. 110]

> Jung says—or if he doesn't, all but does—
> That God and the Unconscious are one.
>
> [p. 118]

We may thus hazard an entity, God-the-imagination-the-unconscious, somehow exerting a countervailing pressure against the obliviating power of "reality," time, death. Indeed, as we shall see, the supreme tenth sense of God is employed precisely in singing the song of continuing resistance: "I AND MINE HOLD IT BACK AND WE SURVIVE" (S, p. 78).

To reinforce our sense of how intimately the subconscious inspiration of this poem relates to the fear and pain of loss, we may explore Merrill's beautiful passages regarding the human-divine faculty of the imagination, otherwise called the "source-of-life," "S/O/L." This faculty, which most distinguishes humankind, even from the angels,

IS ROOTED IN THE LIVED LIFE   ONLY MAN RECEIVES GOD B'S
MAIN MAGIC: IMAGINATIVE POWER   THE APECHILD FIRST
HAD TO IMAGINE THE THIRSTQUENCHING VIRTUE OF WATER

& GOD ALONE CD PRODUCE THAT IMAGE. HIS ANIMAL
STEPBROTHER BLITHELY FORESOOK THE TEAT FOR THE WATER HOLE,
BUT BASIC MAN'S 1ST STEPS WERE TAKEN IN HIS MIND   THERE4
WE KNEW HE HAD COME FROM THE S/O/L

[M, p. 157]

The source of the image-making power is thus rooted in experi-
ence, where loss and mortality are urgent, and its occasions are
described in terms that refer them to an archetypal and recurrent
loss—perhaps our primary experience of loss and substitution. We
may speculate that such a loss was of the enveloping source of
nourishment that we once took to have been part of ourselves
before we fell into a sense of separate and mortal selfhood—the
loss, in other words, not simply of the mother, but of the entire
unifying matrix which she represents. It is in that moment of orig-
inal bereavement that man had to imagine, had to begin the play of
substitutions, of detours to the water hole—repeated acts of mourn-
ing that mark his entire life as most truly human. With each loss he
recapitulates that act of imagining some version of thirst-quenching
water, the liquid balm of consolation, which after all originated "AS
A TEAR IN GOD'S EYE" (S, p. 20). This consoling liquid, the "meed of
some melodious tear" is also, we are told, the element of the Arch-
angel Emmanuel:

THEN GOD SAID: 'TWIN ELIAS, EMMANUEL, YOU THE CALM ONE,
    GIVE MY CHILD BALM FOR SORROW'
& SO THROUGHOUT MAN'S FAREWELLS TO LIFE MY TEARS BATHE THE
    CLENCHED FACE, FLOW & ASSUAGE.

[S, p. 65]

Mortal losses thus kindle and renew The Changing Light's very
source of life, and their effects are precisely timed. For example,
whereas Maria Mitsotáki and Auden become the two most impor-
tant protagonists among the dead during the last two books of the
trilogy, they are also present earlier, respectively marking the be-
ginning and end of "Ephraim." Auden is contacted "during one
of our last conversations," and while the full extent of Maria's
role as original mediator between the poet and the spirit world is
not revealed until the epilogue, her death is mentioned early in
"Ephraim" as being coincident with the beginning of the poem

("Dead / In these last months of the dictatorship"). As JM makes
even clearer later in the poem: "She died the same week I began /
Ephraim—four years ago next January" (S, p. 183). Not only does
MM's death coincide with the inception of the poem, but her pro-
gressively unfolded identity, ascending as it does the spiritual hier-
archy, measures the upward progress of the work—a progress
whose very ascent itself demands a series of farewells:

> MM. NO ACCIDENT . . .
>> I AM OF THE FIVE.
>
>> (Those are her words. An icy terror
>>> Flows through our veins—good Lord!
>> Or is it the bereavement we most feel?
>> It's now, Maman, *before* we break the mirror,
>> We lose you?
>>
>>> [S, p. 183]

Knowing that the "logic" of the poem demands that the mirror be
broken at last, the reader begins to feel the emotional momentum
of this great narrative movement from an actual death, to a close
communion with a successively redefined figure of the dead, to a
moment of final farewell and release:

> MM. JM WILL TAKE THE MARBLE
>> STYLUS & GIVING US THE BENEFIT
>> OF A WELLAIMED WORD, SEND OUR IMAGINED SELVES
>> FALLING IN SHARDS THRU THE ETERNAL WATERS
>> (DJ CUPBEARER) & INTO THE GOLDEN BOUGH
>> OF MYTH   ON INTO LIFE   D'ACCORD?
>>
>>> [S, p. 234]

Another crucially timed mortal loss is that of DJ's parents. At
the very center of "Ephraim" we had read "D must cope / With the
old people, who are fading fast. . . . / But that's life too. A death's-
head to be faced" (DC, p. 85). And it is partly in response to this
impending loss that DJ and JM return to the board, thereby begin-
ning Mirabell:

> Those last days before Mary died, we made
> Contact again with Ephraim. As things were,
> Where else to look for sense, comfort and wit?
>
>> [M, p. 6]

The way in which the opening pages of *Mirabell* mingle details of the Jacksons' deaths—the "raw trench" and the "gates of clay"—together with a quickening of new insights from a higher world does much to reinforce the poem's characteristic blend of loss and gain. Significantly, too, this narrative sequence repeats, in little, the pattern noticed with regard to MM: the development from accounts of an actual death, to a period of contact during which the dead are transformed and reborn, to a final act of release ("LET US GO FORTH ANEW / UNWEIGHTED BY [your love]").

In addition to addressing the Jacksons' deaths, the opening of *Mirabell* also repeats the fact of Maria's, pairing it with that of Chester Kallman; while in yet another pairing ("two by two into the ark?") the deaths of George Cotzias (GK) and Robert Morse occur almost at the midpoint of *Scripts,* contributing substantially to the succeeding events. These are only some of the more significant subjects of this multiple elegy—Hans Lodeizen and Maya Deren, for example, being no less important. In each case, the anchoring cables are multiplied and intertwined, while the urgent personal connection to the "lessons" is intensified. Thus, although Hans Lodeizen is the specific subject of the lines "And yet (for all I know) he *is* the key / This opus began and will end in" (*M*, p. 127), there is a sense in which they may apply to several mourned and celebrated figures in the poem, as though these all contribute to a single love object lost and refound, a compounded martyr, god and guide, resembling that "latest / Recurrent figure out of mythology / To lend his young beauty to a living grave / In order that Earth bloom another season" (*DC*, p. 129).

Of course, the dead are more than the mere "occasions" or subjects of inspired triumphs. Each yields a particular leaven, a legacy, such as Hans Lodeizen's unresolved V work, his quotient of poetic talent, which now enriches JM's store (*M*, p. 126). Or Maya's contribution, her work on Haitian divinities, together with her film and her beautiful dream (*DC*, p. 88), so graphically illustrative of such crucial issues in the poem as possession, or the "ritual of transfigured time." Nor do the dead merely bequeath some inheritance to the living. Their affection for their survivors insulates the latter from raw currents of fiery communication as they translate the more abstract linguistic codes of higher spirits into humanly intelligible speech. Some of the dead (MM, WHA, and GK) participate with DJ and JM in the sequence of seminars, conducting research and gathering the very materials of JM's increasing knowledge. Above all, their own evolutionary reincarnations enact the central myth and movement of the poem.

In one of the first dictées, Ephraim had explained how the living each "represent" a "patron" or "secular guardian angel" who, while forbidden to intervene during a life, tries to pluck the soul of its representative out of the dull round of mere (unevolving) reincarnation in order to raise it to the first of nine stages of improvement. Only a small minority of souls, "at most two million relatively fleet / Achievers," are eligible for this elevation, the majority being simply "recycled" after at most a "short pep-talk." Since Ephraim himself is only at Stage 6, little is known regarding the higher stages of the senses they signify, and only in *Scripts* will these superhuman faculties be defined. But Ephraim does suggest that the ninth stage can be reached, and that the earth has already received such "PERFECTED SOULS" as "AMENHOTEP KAFKA DANTES BEATRICE 1 OR 2 PER CENTURY" (*DC*, p. 103). As through the phases of a funerary Mystery ritual, or as through the tiers of Dante's journey, "JM IS GOING UP THE SCALE," and its stages thus constitute a chart of the poem's course.

Within the predominantly memorial world of "Ephraim," the climbing of stages, as the return of senses beyond death, seems to depend on an activity of Proustian recollection, Proust himself "throned on high" above Ephraim, having been able "Through superhuman counterpoint to work / The body's resurrection, sense by sense" (*DC*, p. 120). But as we move on to *Mirabell,* the notion of the refining passion of memory is superseded by a more scientific version of evolution, the genetic "cloning" that occurs within the R (research) Lab. (*Scripts,* in turn, encompasses the dazzling rise to the final stages, while the epilogue, as we shall see, will conclude with JM himself enacting a version of God's tenth sense.)

Now, the R/Lab, in which the chosen souls are cloned and improved by admixtures of certain mineral or vegetal densities, only came into existence in an attempt to protect the current world from the cataclysms that destroyed its former versions and their inhabitants. Reports of these catastrophes not only deepen the historical perspective of the poem but also give it a more broadly elegiac cast. They issue, after all, from Mirabell (also known as 741), the outcast survivor of one such Fall, himself now apparently at pains to expiate his error and to drive a version of his own evil out of mankind. The R/Lab, not unlike the poet, thus performs a reparational and defensive task, cultivating the embers of a fallen world. And our sense of the fragility of this task is intensified by accounts of the residually threatening negative forces in creation, the "dark hands testing the greenhouse pane by pane."

We learn more about the grim threat in *Scripts,* where a precarious balance of opposing forces (a balance mirrored in the book's own "YES & NO" form) is shown to be more than a haphazard misfortune. Rather, it is the very structure of reality, from the atom to the human psyche to the internal tensions of galaxies. As a result, the ultimate danger is that of a wilfully "separatist" self-assertion by the purely negative forces. With man so proud and so technologically capable of satisfying his "will to oblivion," the peril has become immensely real, and the poem gathers a great moral urgency in its almost Miltonic plea for a submissive rather than pridefully exploitative attitude toward the sources of human and natural power. So, too, much of the poem's strength, particularly as a work of consolation, derives from its courageous admission of evil or negation in the world and from its affirmation and indeed sharpened definition of its own values by confronting them dialectically with their adversaries. The powers of obliteration or regression cannot be annulled, can only be persistently withstood.

The R/Lab's first successes were the cloned souls of Akhnaton and Nefertiti, two of the Five ideal souls who are reincarnated in successive generations. While these Five are beyond the nine Stages, each is associated with one human sense (Akhnaton with sight; Nefertiti, taste; Homer, hearing; Montezuma, touch; Plato, smell). By "MAKING SENSE OF THINGS" and reporting directly to God, the Five thus also represent his first five senses. Wonderfully enough, it is with these paragons that such beloved figures as MM, WHA, and GK become associated in the course of *Scripts.* There, too, further correspondences are drawn with the four Archangels, who are themselves associated with a particular element as well as with a sense: Michael, Air, sight; Gabriel, Fire, smell and taste; Raphael, Earth, hearing; Emmanuel/Elias, Water, touch. When MM and WHA are stripped by the seminars to their essential elements, they therefore take on what we now regard as angelic associations:

THESE RETURNS TO THE ELEMENTS ARE NOT
SAD OR SINISTER BUT IN FACT SAINTLY ELEVATIONS.
. . . . .

A RETURN
LIKE OUR FRIENDS' IS A NEAR-MIRACULOUS REPLENISHMENT:
THEY WILL BE JOINING THE ARCHANGELS OF EARTH & WATER.
THEY HAVE LONG BEEN CHOSEN
        Becoming—stripped of personality—
        Part of what those angels know and are?
                        OF THE DOMINIONS CHEM & VEG
THEY WILL BE OF THE RULING ORDERS
        But with no way for us to get in touch.
                        THEY WILL MAKE THEMSELVES
KNOWN TO YOU BOTH   THEY WILL CHARGE U WITH ENERGY & WAIT
TO LEAD U TO THEIR MASTERS
        Localized—here Daphne in young leaf?
        There the chalk face of an old limestone cliff?
                        AH THEY WILL RIPPLE   THEY WILL
JOLT THRU THE WAVES OF TREES & WARPS OF EARTH   THEY WILL
        CARRY
MESSAGES IN THE GRAIN OF ROCK & FLOW IN THE GREEN VEINS
OF LEAVES FOR THOSE 2 GODS' VAST NETWORK KEEPS THE GLOBE
        INTACT
                                        [S, pp. 27–28]

In these lines, with their antiphony between the majestic voice of assurance and amplitude and the vulnerable voice of wonder and need, and with their superb blend of the mythological, the naturalistic, and the personal (MM having been a passionate gardener, WHA "consistently homesick" for a limestone landscape), we come to the very core of the elegiac tradition—the dead, like vegetation deities, descending to animate and to humanize the world of their survivors. Acknowledgeing the tradition, JM goes on immediately to cite "Adonais" as an example of the basic myth: "Like 'Adonais'—all of life imbued / With the dead's refining consciousness." But as we see, Merrill's revision does, for all its spirituality, have its "MUNDANE," even scientific, application. The ascent to the angelic orders is not, as it had so fiercely been for Shelley, incompatible with a descent into the physical world. As with his clear-eyed confrontation of evil, Merrill's fidelity to the given world and to the changing rather than the constant light, is one of the most moving aspects of his poem. After all, the trajectory is always one of reincarnation—not a shedding but a renewing of life. Here the imperishable physical components of MM and WHA live on to affect the possible improvement of life on earth. So, too, they penetrate the various strata of existence to yield the descriptions and insights that make this poem such a remarkable entry into the nature of the physical world. (Accounts of these researches are found, for example, in the "&" section of *Scripts*.) And it is this very entry of the mind into nature, a process never before so minutely and grandly imagined, that is itself identified as the ultimate pursuit of an Edenic world: "every grain / Of dust, each waterdrop, to be suffused / With mind, with *our* minds. This will be Paradise" (*S*, p. 26).

In what follows, I shall turn away from sketching the "career" of an identity so amazingly ramified as that of MM. (Her identification with Plato as one of the Five, for example, means that in addition to her vegetal descent, she will also return in the next incarnation of the philosopher, as an Indian priest and scientist.) Rather, I shall suggest the ways in which so many of the entire poem's motifs converge in the epilogue, with its account of the rebirth of Robert Morse and its luminous preparation for JM's performance of the concluded poem.

Robert Morse is introduced near the close of *Mirabell* as a gifted and versatile friend and as a valued respondent to the work in progress. His death is mentioned with that of George Cotzias almost midway through *Scripts*:

> The second death. We're just back from the island—
> Hall strewn with tar-flecked towels, a straw hat, stones
> And suitcase—when Long Distance telephones:
> Robert Morse died in his sleep last night.
>
> [*S*, p. 93]

The news interrupts and seems to seal off the world of the momentary and the near at hand. But then, opening out into formally perfect yet limpid decasyllabics (the form, incidentally, of God's survival song), the verse modulates to lines of simple ceremony, with their balance of loss and gain and their emblem of figurative art itself pushing against the brine:

> A sense comes late in life of too much death,
> Of standing wordless, with head bowed beneath
>
> The buffeting of losses which we see
> At once, no matter how reluctantly,
>
> As gains. Gains to the work. Ill-gotten gains . . .
> Under the skull-and-crossbones, rigging strains
>
> Our craft to harbor, and salt lashings plow
> The carved smile of a mermaid on the prow.
>
> Well, Robert, we'll make room.
>
> [S, p. 94]

"Room" is of course already waiting in a world that the poem has now made familiar and hospitable. WHA and MM receive RM still blurred by pain and boredom but on the verge of "coming alive" in the briskly social "circles of the brilliant and creative." Among others, the set includes Proust, Wilde, Sarah Bernhardt, and Jane Austen, who

> tilts but keeps her head,
> Addressing him, after a moment's droll
> Quiz of gray eyes beneath the parasol,
> As *Mr. Robert*—a shrewd estimate.
>
> [S, p. 101]

It is a wonderful touch, the kind of witty jeu d'esprit that not only shares in that glittering milieu but also suggests the poet's underlying confidence in his vision. He can afford such playfulness. The device that has lifted RM to heaven works with apparently effortless ease, indeed with surplus wit.

RM enters the R/Lab to be prepared for his next life as a composer. This gives us a chance to see the Lab at work, the clearest example thus far of the actual procedure of evolutionary reincarnation:

THE NEXT RM:
STRAVINSKY POWDER A HALF CUP   A TEASPOON
OF MOZART   DOLLOP OF VERDI   THESE AS U KNOW,
ASPECTS OF HOMER . . .
. . . . .
THUS THE MELODIC SENSE REFINED IN LIVE
ALEMBICS THRU THE CENTURIES WILL GO
LARGELY TO RM.

[S, p. 215]

Within the playful recipe lingo, there is, of course, the reference to the refining alembics of alchemy, and the passage reads like a sketch of tradition itself in operation. Once again, the general theme of purgative stripping is also present: "THE VARNISH / STRIPPED AWAY & THE WILD OATS I SOWED / EATEN BY UNI" (S, p. 217). Only rigorous training allows for the transfer and compounding of "ingredients," and RM has only eleven months in which to reach the frontiers of Western musical composition.

As we may expect from our growing understanding of the V work, this carefully selected composer will have a specific mission in his approaching life. The mission relates to MM's and WHA's task of affecting natural resources in order to reduce the earth's population to a desirable number. RM is to be the musician who, elegiacally perhaps, celebrates those who survive:

'MR ROBERT, MAKE US A MUSIC TO
CLEAN UP & THIN OUT THE WESTERN SCENE'
THESE WORDS NO SOONER UTTERED I BEGIN
TO HEAR SOMETHING   THIN   NONREPETITIVE
IS IT AN ECHO OF PURCELL?   THE FLEET HIGH
FLUTE OF A HIMALAYAN SHEPHERD'S LAMENT?
. . . . .
'AM I TO WRITE THE SUPREME LULLABY?'
'NO, MUSICIAN, THE SWEET REVEILLE
FOR THOSE STILL LEFT TO WAKE.'
                    The cup moves sadly—
It *is* an awesome task to undertake.

[CLS, "Coda"]

Undertaker and composer of a *wachet auf,* player of last post and reveille, RM is associated with the flute. The association is consistent and is worth interpreting further.

From the pipings in Theocritus's First Idyll, to those of Spenser's mournful Colin Clout or of Milton's uncouth swain, the flute has been *the* instrument of elegy. In fact, flutes or pan pipes provided the music at both Egyptian and Greek funeral rites, and the elegy originated as the metrical form of flute songs. The legendary account of the flute's invention is itself a narrative of loss and consolation—Pan's loss of Syrinx and discovery of the mournfully musical reeds. In his poem "Syrinx," Merrill had wittily referred to Pan as the "great god Pain," and we remember WHA's description of God's song (His tenth sense, exercised outward in an eerie broadcast to the universe):

> WELL THE 1ST THING WE HEARD WAS A FAINT PIPING
> NOT UNLIKE A SHEPHERD'S FLUTE   THIS GREW,
> RESOLVED INTO NO MELODY BUT TONE
> LEVELS & INTERVALS OF UTTERED MEANING:
> PLAINTIVE? AFFIRMATIVE?
>
> [S, p. 80]

Pan and the flute are also associated with Marsyas, and in a densely suggestive passage, of which I have already quoted the beginning, WHA offers:

> AS, OH, TO MILTON THE DROWNED LYCIDAS,
> SO SOC TO PLATO. . . .
>   HIS WHOLE LIFE & DOOM
> FURNISHED THE GOLDEN SCRIBE WITH 'LIVING ROOM'
> DJ (under his breath): A thankless task.
> I CAN'T AGREE MY DEAR. THE SOCRATIC MASK
> BECAME THE FACE OF THE GOAT GOD SILENUS
> WINEBAG FLUTEINVENTING COUNTERPART
> TO MICH/APOLLO IN THE DAWN OF ART
> To be flayed by him like Marsyas? OF COURSE
> BUT WHAT WERE SKINS TO SUCH A MYTHIC FORCE!
>
> [S, pp. 190–191]

RM's connection to this flayed or stripped martyr-flutist figure of elegiac mythology is made quite unmistakable:

> Oh Robert . . .
> Will it be taken from you now, that ingrained
> Callous of the Self? ALL   ALL SKINNED OFF.

BEFORE ANOTHER TINY MARSYAS
CAN STAND UP TO APOLLO, FLUTE IN HAND . . .

[*CLS*, "Coda"]

Can we avoid also hearing the prayer of Dante at the outset of *Paradiso*? Emerging, significantly enough, from *his* purgatorial ascent, Dante prays to no other than "O buono Apollo":

Entra nel petto mio, e spira tue
sì come quando Marsia traesti
della vagina delle membra sue.

[Do thou
Enter into my bosom, and there breathe
So, as when Marsyas by thy hand was dragged
Forth from his limbs, unsheathed].

[*Paradiso*, Canto I, ll. 19–21; trans. Cary]

The actual reincarnation or resheathing of RM necessarily involves his gradual reattachment to the five senses, a theme we have seen expanding in significance since "Ephraim." Connected now with the immortal Five, and with the archangelic elements and attributes, and with the first five senses of God, a reentry of the five senses into life entails a renovation of the divine fabric of creation itself, as the epilogue's five "ceremonies" of reincarnation show. It is a breathtaking tour de force, with the Archangels themselves bestowing the senses on the reborn infant.

But this feat is not all! For Merrill has woven yet more strands into this final miracle. Raphael, Archangel of earth and hearing, whispers RM's new name:

Raph. HEAR, HEAR!
YES BABE, TODAY YOUR NAME YOU'LL HEAR
FROM OLD GRANDFATHER CLAY. YES, YES . . .
LONG DOUBTING THOMAS, LEND AN EAR
AND WITH A KISS I WHISPER IN IT: T O M !

If we wonder what's in a name, the clue comes immediately:

DJ. That's his new name?
JM. So it would seem. The cast
Of the next *Rake* assembling? They work fast.

[*CLS*, "Coda"]

The Rake's Progress (whose protagonist is Tom Rakewell) is apparently being reborn. In fact since "Ephraim," it seems to have had a phoenixlike capacity: "here is La Fenice where the *Rake* / Rose from the ashes of the High Baroque" (*DC*, p. 125). And toward the end of *Scripts* we had a forecast of Raphael's future "ALL STAR REVIVAL OF THE RAKE / AS A GARDEN TOOL," in which the prompter will whisper "'ADAM, THIS TIME GET IT RIGHT'" (*S*, p. 226). Auden's and Kallman's libretto for *The Rake's Progress* itself allows for this assimilation of Tom to Adam. As the opera's epilogue confirms, Tom is after all a version of the everyman Adam who always gets it wrong—the rake, reborn now as perhaps an instrument that may restore the forfeited garden. Playing further on the name, we come also to "ATOM," as WHA approves; "& TOM OUR THREATENED ATOM" (*S*, p. 203). Even the atom, whose fate has been of continuing interest throughout the poem, is thus itself being reborn. We may remember Mirabell's speculation: "THE ATOM, IS IT THE VERY GOD WE WORSHIP?" (*M*, p. 130).

Finally, in this so widely associated rebirth, we may hear Tom-Adam-Atom-*Adonis*. We are pointed to this last inclusion by the very section of *The Rake's Progress* chosen by Queen Nature for her masque during the last lessons of *Scripts*:

> COME, COME ON THE MILD NOTE OF LOVE
> AMID THE REVELRY,—Tom's aria,
> Forbidden its librettist to revise,
> Starting exactly here, the first word *Love*—
>
> [*S*, p. 203]

The aria is not quoted, but a look at the libretto shows it to contain nothing other than an appeal by Tom to Mother Nature-Venus, entreating her to intercede on his behalf at the moment of his death. He will of course die under the assumed identity of Venus's martyred lover, evoking these concluding lines of the opera: "Mourn for Adonis, ever young, the dear / of Venus; weep, tread softly round his bier."[4] With the birth of Tom-Adonis in Merrill's epilogue, we are therefore once again at the heart and origin of elegy, witnessing a ceremony that, in its gathered skein of interrelationships, suggests no less than a "REINCARNATION OF THE GODS." And that, as Mirabell had proposed long before, is after all no less than "THE GREAT MIRACLE" (*M*, p. 131).

Most elegies traditionally draw attention to themselves as performances. They do this both to emphasize that a ceremony of some kind is being successfully completed and to focus on the poetic powers (frequently defined or enlarged by the elegiac performance itself) of the survivor. Hence the motifs of tests or contests and rewards, to foreground the singers' skills and their effects within the originally eclogic elegies. And hence the rhetoric of performance in many later elegies: "Begin again . . . Yet once more . . . I come to pluck . . . Weep . . . Weep no more . . . Thus sang . . . Tomorrow to fresh woods . . ." Once again, *The Changing Light* is brilliant and ample in its relation to such conventions.

Throughout the poem, Merrill has found ways to set off the performance of the work. As already mentioned, its action is marked by a carefully designed yet exuberant proliferation of masques, fetes, galas, pageants, and lessons (complete with A's and A + 's). Similarly, the poem's very texture displays the author's virtuosity in a deliberately and intricately varied array of verse forms—couplets, sonnet sequences, and terza rima, to name a few—while, as we have seen, the mirror and board are constantly under focus as the work's very "field" of activity. In addition, the poem is itself a continuing subject of its own narrative and commentary, from the opening lines discussing its "present form" to the final revelation of its ordained provenance. From the bright line of the January light falling on Merrill's page as he begins "Ephraim" to the shower of drops that pucker the onionskin manuscript of the epilogue, the poet thus invites an abiding attention to the grand unfolding as well as to the minute formal, even physical, characteristics of the written poem.

Each major section of *The Changing Light* begins with a remarked gesture of commencement: "Admittedly I err by undertaking / This . . . ; Oh very well, then. Let us broach . . . ; Yes, Cup Glides from Board. Sun dwindles into Sound. / DJ and I look at each other. Well? . . . A new day—world transfigured yet the same— / We're back at our old table." We see the effect not only of repeated self-presentation but of a work continually resumed, as in the "Begin again" refrains of early elegies. So, too, the endings of such sections share a sense of resolution, of the poet's having worked his way into the receiving and hallowing presence of the ageless woman of the world, or of Michael, or of God, or of the assembled hosts. It is on this last resolution that I would like to dwell—the development by which JM prepares to perform his poem to his extraordinary audience.

As early as in "Ephraim," the dead had expressed a fascinated approval of the poem thus far ("To my surprise, all burn / To read more of this poem . . . / POPE SAYS THAT WHILE BITS / STILL WANT POLISHING THE WHOLES A RITZ / BIG AS A DIAMOND" (DC, p. 116). Appropriately enough, it is RM, shortly before his own reincarnation, who becomes an agent of JM's final and most complete emergence as performer. For it is RM's hints about the poem's "revelations" that awaken the desire of the spirit world to hear the completed work actually read out loud. It is with great excitement and very high spirits that the poem moves toward this climatic debut. But there are important interruptions.

Almost immediately after the "launching" of the reborn RM, and amidst a flurry of further news regarding the careers of the reincarnated MM, WHA, and GK, news comes of the unexpected death of Mimí, wife of the novelist Vasili Vassilikos. Continually open to such "buffeting of losses," the poem "makes room" for this new grief:

> We don't quite understand—it's not yet morning—
> Vasili's voice, from Rome, expressionless:
> "Instantaneous . . . no pain, no warning . . ."
> Dead? *Mimí*? And dressed in the white dress.

From such fragmentary and literal snatches of bewilderment, the following ten lines enact the poem's inclusive ceremonies of containment, moving towards the language of artifice and toward the prosodic resolution of an adjusted yet recognizable sonnet form:

> We reach her, but she's dazed by the prompt call
> Or the ungodly hour: BUT WHERE AM I?
> WHO'S THIS   VASILI ARE YOU HIDING   WHY?
>
> So Ephraim guides her from our love, which hurts,
> Back to her patron's dim confessional
> Where (though harp and trumpet fill the air)

> She must sit upright on a little bench
> And not cry if her finery reverts
> To homespun rags, and shake out her long hair,
> And be a candle for the dawn to quench.
>
> [*CLS*, "Coda"]

Mimí is taken up by the poem's established elegiac machinery, as Mirabell explains that she had incarnated a talent or density whose cycles were more rapid than those of human life. The theme and figures, however modernized, are essentially those of the familiar vegetation myths: "A DYING AS THE SEED / CYCLE CLINGS TO A PERENNIAL TALENT FAR BRIEFER / THAN HUMAN LIFE CYCLES" (*CLS*, p. "Coda"). And as the heavenly guests gather to hear JM's reading, Mimí herself is found among them in a place of honor. She is introduced to the assembly and is praised by no less a figure than Mother Nature, who "drawing Mimí to her breast . . . dries her tears" ("And wipe the tears forever from his eyes").

Yet more important, in several respects, is the figure of the mourner, Vasili. Indeed, it is upon him that the supervisory powers of Nature have come to bear. She admits having contrived to include him in the earthly contingent of the audience—an audience, we are now reminded, whose primary need may after all be that of consolation and whose faculties are perhaps best refined by grief itself: "I HAD PLANNED: / TO DRAW TO OUR CRITIQUE A GREEK, A LIVING EAR / SHARPENED BY LOSS" (*CLS*, "Coda"). So it is that Vasili arrives at the house in Athens at the precise moment that JM is about to begin his performance:

> MAJESTY AND FRIENDS—when shatteringly
> The doorbell rings. Our doorbell here in Athens.
> We start up.

Once again, the world of the poem is jarred open to admit bereavement.

> David opens to a form
> Gaunt, bespectacled, begrimed, in black,
> But black worn days, nights, journeyed, sweated in—
> Vasili? Ah sweet Heaven, sit him down,
> Take his knapsack, offer food and brandy—.

> He shakes his head. Mimí. Mimí in Rome
> Buried near Shelley. He can't eat, can't sleep,
> Can't weep.
>
> [*CLS*, "Coda"]

Vasili's grief seems thus to challenge the very work of mourning and consolation and threatens a more than momentary disruption of Merrill's poem ("live despair [takes precedence] / Over a poem or a parlor game"). And yet, of course, so much of this poem is addressed precisely to such as Vasili. "Merely to listen" will help "to keep his head / Above the sucking waves, merely to listen / A little while." The poem is testing and defining its particular strength, even as it seems to let us know, as Stevens's elegy had, that the consoling forms we are about to see are "visible to the eye that needs."

The physical scene for JM's reading is the house in Athens. But the heavenly audience is accommodated in a "celestial ballroom," which in turn resembles the ballroom of "the broken home" of JM's childhood, Sandover. By a magnificent coup de theatre, this is now a rejuvenated version, a reincarnation, of that original place: "How many years before your 'restoration' / Brought to light this foreign, youthful grace" (*CLS*, "Coda"). Restoration, bringing to light, revelation of youthfulness and grace—these are, of course, central projects of the poem at large. Had not Mirabell insisted that the scribe's task is precisely "TO RENOVATE THE HOUSE OF MAN" (*M*, p. 145)? And had not JM himself speculated:

> Who can compete
> With Nature? She's Mind's equal. Not a slave
> But mother, sister, bride. I think we're meant
> To save that marriage, be the kids who stay
> Together for their parents' sake. DJ:
> Who wrote "The Broken Home"? No accident!
>
> [*M*, p. 135]

No less a part of that project is the raising of an earthly object or locale to its celestial version, particularly a version that replaces a scene of loss, displacement, and isolation with one in which the poet is truly found and "made at home" among a dazzling audience of those whom he most loves and admires.

I have already mentioned how most elegists rehearse, for themselves, the immortality established for the figures they mourn. In a sense, JM himself is sharing, at the level of an aesthetic performance, the reception or assumption that the dead have enjoyed within his poem. Like them, like Lycidas, he enters among "the sweet Societies / That sing, and singing in their glory move." And yet, whereas Lycidas, for example, is "entertained" by such societies, it is JM alone who sings. Perhaps to enter most truly among the dead, to take one's place most forcefully within tradition, is to play host to them, to entertain them. As Mirabell said, "YET YOU HOUSE US FOR ALL THAT WE / DO LITTLE BUT TAKE UP YR ROOM" (M, p. 163).

Of course, Merrill does not let us forget that the actual realm that includes both the mundane and celestial ballrooms is the mirror, mercurial region of the poem itself. It is just outside the mirror frame that JM waits, in the wings, while the guests take their seats. And it is into the mirror that he begins to read. This climactic image of JM reading into the mirror-ballroom-universe may well remind us of the image of God B singing alone into galactic space. For each, as for any elegist, there is a peculiar blend of pathos and grandeur in this act of utterance, an act so precariously having to sustain itself, having even to create its addressee. Of all poets, the elegist most needs to imagine that he addresses more than himself. The very presence of the mirror here, serving once again as threshold and field of transformation, rather than as terminus or medium of self-reflection, may therefore serve to emphasize how Merrill's poem is precisely *not* one of sheer self-communion. God's highest sense was, we recall, "EXERCISED OUTWARDS." And it is that most poignant and most performative aspect of language that the poem has so thoroughly advanced.

Indeed, language itself has been a steady object as well as means of this poem's devotion. "THE REVEALED MONOTHEISM OF TODAY IS LANGUAGE" (M, p. 145). And is not Merrill's poem circling to begin its rites again? *The Changing Light*, as the great vehicle of language and the "recurrent muse," thus also finally takes its place among its objects of reincarnation. And as the poet steps forward to utter the last and first word of his great work, the circle, emblem of eternity, closes and reopens.

Finally, lest we think that Merrill has lapsed from his revisionary myth of evolutionary reincarnation to one of mere recurrence, we should recognize how differently we now reread the beginning word and its successors. Like everything else in the poem, the word "admittedly" returns with refined and augmented meaning: what appeared at first reading as a concession of error, is now, in the context of what follows, a vindicated and rechosen way of beginning, signifying also the great theme of admittance. Like the poem, the word has been reincarnated at a higher level of interpretation. The readers, too, begin now at a higher level, as members of an audience of which they had not heard before reading the poem. We, ourselves, have thus become admitted, or perhaps translated, to the celestial ballroom and its guests.

Among the concluding lines of his beautiful poem, "Lost in Translation," Merrill had written:

> But nothing's lost. Or else: all is translation
> And every bit of us is lost in it
> (Or found—. . .

[*DC*, p. 10]

CHAPTER 7

Breaking the Mirror:
Interruption in Merrill's Trilogy

Willard Spiegelman

> I'll break my staff,
> Bury it certain fathoms in the earth,
> And deeper than did ever plummet sound
> I'll drown my book.
>
> —*The Tempest*, V, i, 54–57

> A song means filling a jug, and even more so breaking the jug. Breaking it apart. In the language of the Kabbalah we perhaps might call it: Broken Vessels.
>
> —H. Leivick (quoted as epigraph by
> Harold Bloom in *Kabbalah and Criticism*)

The breaking of the mirror at the end of *Scripts for the Pageant* enacts, as a form of closure, a final rupture with the past, an abjuring of the "rough magic" of the Ouija board and all its hocus-pocus in James Merrill's great trilogy. Here Merrill sets the seal on his own V work, turning away from the agents and angels, his equivalents of Prospero's elves and demipuppets; overthrowing his own charmings, he stands before us at the end with his own considerable strength. When, in the epilogue to the sacred books, he rises before the great society of the noble dead—friends, relatives, persons real or imagined—who have gathered in the schoolroom at Sandover to hear their poet, the cynosure of all eyes, he ends his epic with its own performance: "Admittedly." In one sense broken, the circle is, in another, completed.

Merrill's decision to go it alone is the last and strongest rupture in a work where breakups, interruptions, and disruptions have operated as a major theme and as a manifold device. *Scripts* is distinguished from its two predecessors by its length, its relative stateliness and formality of method, a larger cast of heavenly characters; it is also the book in which the fewest, but the most important, interruptions, occur. The fluidity of Time that Stephen Yenser finds beneath the surface of "The Book of Ephraim"[1] runs, in *Scripts*, its truest course, without damming, diverting, or channeling of other sorts. Conversely, "Ephraim" is both shorter and more deliberately confused: the mortals at the board must adjust themselves to divine harmonies that sound, at first, cacophonous (just as novice readers of the trilogy feel that they have been released into a world quite different from their own). God B's plan for the universe is revealed circuitously and with much misinformation, and as one speaker replaces and corrects his predecessors, the "hand" and "scribe" at the board only gradually accustom themselves to their foreign visitors. Although Ephraim is the most congenial of their callers from beyond, he is also the most frivolous; appropriately, his book, with much stichomythy, and the most frequent interruptions of dialogue, also contains JM's lost, unfinished novel, which interweaves itself into JM's and DJ's lives during a twenty-year period.

Merrill has said: "Manners are for me the touch of nature, an artifice in the very bloodstream."[2] The commonest, and most wrongheaded charge continually made against him is that he is a poet in whom manners have hardened into mannerisms. On the contrary, his work absorbs "interruption," a basic gaffe in manners, into the lifeblood of poetic revelation. From voices cut off by new ones (and all are disembodied) that float in from the other world, to single articulations interrupted in mid-sentence, to broken or "phantom" rhymes, we can understand the major struggle in the trilogy as the attempt to achieve *politesse*, hard won in *Mirabell*, and accepted as given in the pageantry of *Scripts*.

Interruption has recently found its own literary theorists. For

Harold Bloom, reflecting on the cosmology of the Kabbalah and finding in the schemes of Isaac Luria and others a prototype for literary tradition, all acts of creation are catastrophes, broken vessels glued together: "Reality for Luria is always a triple rhythm of contraction, breaking apart, and mending, a rhythm continuously present in time even as it first punctuated eternity."[3] Restitution, in Luria, Freud, or Ferenczi, involves of necessity a previous fracture. More recently, Stanley Fish has reopened the question of interruption, via the several voices, in *Lycidas*, to discover that the multiplicity of voices renders the poem "finally anonymous," as if an *embarras de richesses* is in some way self-canceling.[4]

Clearly, *Lycidas* baffles its readers because its transitions are never clearly defined, its voices never adequately differentiated; it seems, like Merrill's trilogy, quite modern in its brokenness, which challenges us to invent or to discover schemes for mending it as our own act of creative understanding. Other works of literature that we may think of as "seamless" (e.g., the romantic conversation poem or the modern novel floating on a fictional stream of consciousness) pose different but equally deep challenges. Merrill, however, has always been concerned with breakings and interruptions, and it is to these that we should attend in order to restore and appreciate the harmony of the whole.

In three of his shorter poems, we can see Merrill's various interruptions at work, undermining and creating the substances of which they form an important part. In "The Broken Home" (*Nights and Days*) he rehearses an obsessive theme, a family romance torn apart by divorce, and he prepares us for the nursery at Sandover, which becomes the schoolroom in *Scripts*, the scene of instruction for Maria Mitsotáki and W. H. Auden and of the performance of the trilogy in the epilogue to the work. The fall from primal unity, the dissevering of the marriage of "Father Time and Mother Earth," as he refers to his parents, the greater intensity of the past than the present: all these elements prove that although time flows continuously, we have still to acknowledge those fallings from us— "vanishings," as Wordsworth called them—that betoken not just loss but the destructive interruption of original innocence. "The Broken Home" traces what M. H. Abrams, showing how the romantics appropriated biblical tropes, terms "the circuitous journey," whereby a secular modern artist can refuse to relinquish the myth of unity, division, pilgrimage, and restitution at the heart of biblical narrative.

The road away from house and home leads ever back to it, just as the speaker of this poem continues to honor and obey, however inversely, his own parents. The adult's great refusals—to vote, to buy a newspaper, or to tend a garden—imitate the child's petulant rebellion against his parents but testify equally to their hold over him. The elder Merrills have broken a marriage and a home; this divorce forces the adult to collect the shards of love and possession and to improve the past within the present. His old house has been transformed, by the vagaries of real estate dealings, into a boarding school (nice detail: children in a prep school are separated from their homes, however happy these may be). At the same time, the poet envisions a later harmony that does not simply reestablish primal innocence, which may never in fact have existed. Educational seriousness succeeds social elegance, as a new student replaces the lost child:

> Under the ballroom ceiling's allegory
> Someone at last may actually be allowed
> To learn something; or, from my window, cool
> With the unstiflement of the entire story,
> Watch a red setter stretch and sink in cloud.
>
> [ND, p. 30]

The poem began, however, with a parody of mystic revelation: "I have lit what's left of my life. / I have thrown out yesterday's milk / And opened a book of maxims. / The flame quickens. The word stirs." The true milk of instruction flows at the end as the unspecified "someone," not the adult, but resembling him, relives and therefore completes the poet's own childhood. The puns do the job of restoration, since the new student sees both a setting sun (which may remind us of Wordsworth's at the end of the Immortality Ode), and little JM's own Irish setter, Michael, who appeared earlier in the poem. Likewise, "the entire story" combines architectural and narrative references to prove the relation of this child both to the real child the speaker sees along with his parents in an upstairs window of his present residence at the poem's start and to some improved version of himself who has been at last released from his own autobiography through the mercies of art. Someone—we may wonder who—has repeated the poet's life, thereby idealizing and healing it.[5]

In one of the two long poems in *Nights and Days*, Merrill tries for the first time his later favorite form: "The Thousand and Second Night" is a diary, a medley of styles, forms, and effects, honoring both a flow of consciousness and the intrusions upon that consciousness by strong foreign fires. Throughout, the poem deals with figurative or actual breakings: the schizophrenic city, Istanbul, poised between "the passive Orient and our frantic West," the metamorphosed Hagia Sophia, church, mosque, museum, whose dome is now "bald of mosaic" and whose facade covers up its genuine face just as the mudpack of the poet, applied to remedy the peculiar paralysis that affects half of his face, "effaces" his genuine self beneath.

The poem treats symbolically the crisis of middle age and takes serious tropes of passage literally, as when the poet crosses from Asia to Europe or from Turkey to Greece, returning to the civilized West with his "own little drama," the cracking of "that so-called mirror of the soul," kept secret from his friends. But the disturbance has effects not unnoticed: the poet remains cold and withdrawn from the West, traumatized by his several passages.[6]

Flirting with other poetic forms while remaining true to his beloved quatrains, Merrill ransacks not only his prosodic handbook but also, to complement formal variety, his ventriloquist's luggage. Even before those voices from the other world bombard him, the tones in his poetry are many: he plays the tour guide, the pedagogue, the victim, the storyteller Scheherazade, and the Proustian recollector. The poem ends, as it had begun, with a fiction of the divided self: reminding us of Scheherazade, the poet himself becomes the Sultan ("I saw the Sultan in a glass, grown old"), acknowledging both the interdependence of sultan and slave, body and soul, and the inevitable separations ("headlong emigrations out of life" he calls them earlier), which are another way of naming change, growth, loss, and the farewells to the flesh we are always taking.

The piecemeal forms and recollectings of Merrill's increasingly longer poems, his obsession with the primal broken home, and the weavings of memory, invention, and necessity that keep Scheherazade alive one day at a time, make their most intense appearance in "Lost in Translation," of all the shorter poems in *Divine Comedies* the one that most succinctly dramatizes, through a central image, the literal and figurative restoration of the puzzle that is our daily life and ou creative enterprises. Unfolding like a Shakespearean romance, wh what is lost is found (or maybe not: more on this subject later), the poem mingles a reminiscence of a complex jigsaw puzzle that the child (a "pauvre enfant," according to his part-French, part-German governess and mother surrogate) receives, assembles, and then dismantles in 1939, with the adult's unsuccessful attempt to discover a translation by Rilke of Valéry's "Palme" that he swears he once saw but can no longer find.

Significantly, the translation is mentioned first in a parenthetical aside at the end of the poem's second stanza: parentheses, which Coleridge said contained the very drama of thought,[7] interrupt Merrill's poem at crucial points and then underhandedly propel it forward. The repackaged puzzle is missing one piece: this will be discovered years later (again, in a parenthetical aside) through ESP and a medium's help. Merrill accepts all change as an inevitable loss of unity, an interruption of wholeness, for which restoration may be irrelevant or impossible. Life is a puzzle, the pieces of which one is perpetually forming, losing, seeking, reforming ("So many later puzzles / Had missing pieces"). And the mind functions in the same way:

> But nothing's lost. Or else: all is translation
> And every bit of us is lost in it
> (Or found—I wander through the ruin of S
> Now and then, wondering at the peacefulness)
> And in that loss a self-effacing tree,
> Color of context, imperceptibly
> Rustling with its angel, turns the waste
> To shade and fiber, milk and memory.

> [DC, p. 10]

The self-effacing tree, in its disappearing act, like the literal and psychological self-effacement that Merrill undergoes in "The Thousand and Second Night," participates in a cosmic nutritional cycle. It also turns out to have existed all along. The poem's epigraph, straight from Rilke's readily accessible translation of Valéry, quotes the monitory lines about the Palm's roots that extend deep into the stones of the desert, drinking and discovering nourishment in what are not empty, worthless spaces.

All is translated, and all is found: even the damage of interruptions contributes to the discovery or invention of the underlying order. "Form's what affirms," says the self-parodying Merrill in "The Thousand and Second Night," and his forms, riddled and speckled as they are with parentheses and changing rhymes, begin to assume, in the trilogy, even greater variety, as voices from beyond intercept, interfere with, and then merge with the poet's own. Merrill's music, finally, is chordal, and what may seem at first rudely disharmonious eventually establishes new resounding tonics for our delight and health.

The first breakthrough to the other world (after some aborted communication with one Cabel Stone; see *Mirabell*, p. 169) admits a halting, timid voice. Ephraim's appearance foretells Auden's quatrain, included in the "quotations" of the poem's seventeenth section: "The glacier knocks in the cupboard, / The desert sighs in the bed, / And the crack in the tea-cup opens / A lane to the land of the dead." JM's and DJ's "breathing stopped," when during their first sessions at the Ouija board a voice interrupts and sends their cup on a drunken rampage: "HELLP O SAV ME," followed by a double "YES" and then rapid movement, too fast to be understood by hand and poet, still novices at their enterprise:

> those early sessions
> Break off into guesswork, paraphrase.
> Too much went whizzing past. We were too nice
> To pause, divide the alphabetical
> Gibberish into words and sentences.
>
> [*DC*, p. 51]

The automatic flow, enthralling, frustrating, and swerving, needs to be broken up for the vessel of poetry or knowledge to be constructed and then filled.

The flow of time within a life-and-death cycle is the major story of "Ephraim." Like JM, Ephraim comes from a broken home, and like his scribe, Ephraim creates an identity through successive layerings, deaths, and rebirths. In this modern version of Plato's myth of Er or Vergil's picture of reincarnation borrowed from the darkest Orphic mysteries of the ancient world, Merrill has discovered that death, after all, and despite appearances, is *not* the major interruption of our individual lives. What disrupts is not so much the early death of Hans Lodeizen as the planting of new babies (p. 64) by which Ephraim, with the help of his worldly pals, interferes with the cycle. The pigeonholing of souls turns to disaster, as does (p. 77) the nuclear research that led to Hiroshima and the "AIR ABOVE LOS ALAMOS," which is "LIKE A BREATH SUCKED IN HORROR." We learn (p. 99) that no souls came from Hiroshima; this vacancy, which in *Mirabell* becomes the trope of interruption as vacuum, is the equivalent of an astronomical black hole. Death itself, normally conceived, merely continues the flow of life: it is the *news* of death (throughout the sacred books, as much is taken, much abides: Merrill's friends and relatives take their leave only to be restored to him by the board) that interrupts daily life and shocks the living by a removal from their midst.

If breaking, or interrupting, constitutes the original catastrophe in the life-death continuum, and the starting point of artistic consciousness, then patching, repair, or replacement should form the next stage. And we find a metonymy of sorts right in the middle of the poem: in section L, Merrill reexperiences his last death, as Rufus Farmetton, in South Africa, c. 1925. By reliving (or is it redying?), JM relieves that trauma; his repetition creates by dismantling: "So, bit by bit, the puzzle's put together / Or else it's disassembled, bit by bit" (p. 87).[8] Likewise, in the following section, Maya Deren undergoes the temporary release of her soul, replaced for a night by a former inhabitant of her building. Such, assures Ephraim, was the case with Dante, whose real life was temporarily interrupted so that during sleep he, like Maya, was transported to a heavenly weekend. Someone stood in for the poet in Tuscany while he "toured the spheres," a junket from which the *Paradiso* is the traveler's tale.

Literary and psychological disruption increases in the remaining sections of "Ephraim." A small thing may represent a larger one, for example, the use of enjambment to disturb a word. Maya says that her boss, "ST LUCY,"

> IS LETTING
> ME DIRECT SOME AVANTGARDE HALLUCI
> NATIONS ETC FOR HEADS OF STATE
>
> [DC, p. 108]

Here, the rupture pinpoints both the "LUCY/LUCI" rhyme and the "NATIONS/STATE" connection, as well as reminding us how a hallucination suspends ordinary perception. And we have, as well, the unfinished novel that interrupts but embeds itself in the layers of the lived lives the poem describes.

Like death, revelation signals a break in ordinary communication.[9] In section U, Ephraim's and Maya's voices are jettisoned as a new character, previously unheard and unknown, makes a single, solemn, and archaic statement, an edict unglossed and fearsome: "MYND YOUR WEORK   SIX MOONES REMAIN." Mirabell's interruption of the gavotte with Maya and Ephraim affects hand and scribe. DJ's palm is creased, red, and sore, and "the pencil in [JM's] writing hand snapped." Ephraim, Maya, Maria, and even Wallace Stevens are bowled over, and although Ephraim responds to the mortals' call the following week, "things were not the same."

Merrill has appropriately set the stage for one of his formidable, blazing set pieces, the most intense natural description in the poem. In Venice (section V), considering the decline of the city (the old Ruskinian theme) and the palimpsest of Giorgione's *Tempesta* (continued in section X), JM prepares to fly home to New York when "lightning strikes the set." The eighteen difficult lines that depict the storm test Merrill's readers' ability to withstand his assaults. Elliptical, strenuous, almost breathless, the lines are syntactically demanding, with nouns and verbs, subjects and objects, occasionally difficult to separate:

> Gust of sustaining timbers' creosote
> Pungency the abrupt drench releases—
> Cold hissing white—the old man of the Sea
> Who, clung to now, must truthfully reply—

Bellying shirt, sheer windbag wrung to high
Relief, to needle-keen transparency—
Air and water blown glass-hard—their blind
Man's buff with unsurrendering gooseflesh

Streamlined from conception—crack! boom! flash!—
Glaze soaking inward as it came to mind
How anybody's monster breathing flames
Vitrified in metamorphosis

To monstrance clouded then like a blown fuse
If not a reliquary for St James'
Vision of life: how Venice, her least stone
Pure menace at the start, at length became

A window fiery-mild, whose walked-through frame
Everything else, at sunset, hinged upon—

[DC, pp. 120–121]

The major eruption in the poem dramatically readies us for its most extended revelation. Venice, itself a stage, harboring images of storms and tourists clicking cameras to preserve experiences of the set, opens itself up and unlike the "shatter-proof glass" that reflects the viewers' faces in Giorgione's painting, becomes, now becalmed, a frame through which walks "a youth, to mount the bridge's stairs." Section V is the only one not end-stopped; the space between V and W requires "bridging" as we hold our breath and turn the page. Merrill, shifting prosodic gears from his quatrains into appropriately bravura Dantean terza rima, beholds through the frame his nephew Wendell who, he forgets until after the encounter, is Ephraim's representative. In that break between the sections Merrill shows how the flow of time, consciousness, or syntax must exist simultaneously with, or below, the apparent blankness of page that itself must be bridged (it is cunning of him, too, to place the revelation *on* a bridge). Merrill's technique, for which he is as much notorious among hostile critics (mere showing off, they cry) as admired by sympathetic ones, reminds us, in instances like this, that technique serves vision; as Hazlitt asked, thinking of Venetian painting: "Was Titian, when he painted a landscape . . . pluming himself on being thought the finest colourist in the world, or making himself so by looking at nature?"

"The Book of Ephraim" ends, a year run through, in winter, at "zero hour," with time eroding and things literally breaking down. The furnace does not work; the fire is low; plants are dying; the phone is out of order. In a parody of New Year's resolutions, JM insists that "we must improve the line / In every sense, for life." More important, a burglary has occurred. The house has been broken into, but "Nothing we can recollect is missing" (later, "nothing's gone, or nothing we recall"). We should hear in this the end of "Lost in Translation" as well as the double sense of "recollection." But the unseen thief, like Ephraim himself, remains a "presence in our midst, unknown," as the intruder becomes a symbol of all invasions upon, or from within, the mind. The poem ends with Jamesian stasis: "For here we are" recalls not only the last line of *The Ambassadors* but also that of *Mrs. Dalloway*, and we may remember Merrill's opening reference to the nouveau roman as an "orphaned form," whose followers were "suckled by Woolf not Mann"—yet another broken home. In demonstrating the inevitable presence of the unseen, Merrill concludes by validating the continuity that, far from being disturbed by breakings, is paradoxically strengthened and assured by them.

Mirabell is the crucial volume; like the *Purgatorio* it ties the uncertainties of a previous volume to the mature sureness of a succeeding one. Here, the lessons are more difficult, the dangers more threatening, the interruptions more explosive, than in "Ephraim." In spite of intrusions (the frightening vision of the "winged / MEN B4 MANKIND," p. 7), and censorings of information, or the interruption of news not yet permitted, Ephraim is preparing DJ and JM for new knowledge. The traffic, temporarily halted, will resume, he assures them:

> THE LIGHTS ARE RED
> I CANNOT BE EXPLICIT   WHEN THEY CHOOSE
> A SCIENTIFIC OR ARTISTIC BREAKTHRU
> THE VEHICLE EXPERIENCES HIS WORK
> UNIQUELY & THE RESULT IS   But here Ephraim
> Breaks off. Is broken off. David's left hand
> Has grazed the Board. He cannot lift it.
>
> [*M*, p. 14]

The enlarged cosmic history, Merrill's nominal theme, once he has acceded to the demand for "poems of science," centers on a series of catastrophes, eruptions, and breakings. The Fall, or several of them, the causes of Black Holes, the wreck of God B's greenhouse five hundred million years ago, and atomic fission in 1934 (Laura Fermi's memoir of the first atomic pile, in 1942, is quoted as epigraph to the book), provide the basis for the poem's pseudoscientific maunderings. Readers vary wildly in the seriousness of their responses to Merrill's history, which certainly tests more forcefully than any other poet's major creation since *A Vision* the questions of poetic persuasiveness and literal assent. The themes may be taken as "mere" machinery, like Pope's sylphs and gnomes, or as serious considerations of biological and astronomical problems (and it is curious that many readers, who previously held to the cliché that Merrill was a nacreous poet, all glittering form and no substance, should now object to the "fanciful" because unusual plumbing of serious questions in the trilogy: why are those who are disturbed by puns, spoonerisms, and camp humor also bothered by atoms in poetry?).

Interruption is at the heart of the matter. Inviolability, atomic, personal, or poetic, and threats to integrity are best highlighted by a passage in which JM and DJ consider, as DJ is preparing to enter the hospital for an operation (the actual surgery is never mentioned—it seems, however, that he suffers from an inguinal hernia, that is, a rupture, which requires mending) the deep capacities for Manichean good and evil, within man and the atom:

> Eden tells a parable of fission,
> Lost world and broken home, the bitten apple
> Stripped of its seven veils, nakedness left
> With no choice but to sin and multiply.
> From then on, genealogical chain reactions
> Ape the real thing.
>
> [*M*, p. 98]

"ALL THINGS," says Maria Mitsotáki to her "ENFANTS . . . ARE DONE HERE IF U HAVE TECHNIQUE" (p. 10), and what surprises most pleasantly about *Mirabell* is Merrill's harnessing of technical skill to the demands of theme. Voices interrupt and blend with one another more thoroughly, but with appropriate concern for station (the bat spirits speak in fourteeners, the other dead in decasyllabics, the living in a variety of human speech). The attention to detail continually astonishes, supporting JM's lesson from beyond that there are no accidents. What does one say, for example, about the following moments? Toward the beginning, Maria is cut off as she begins to comfort DJ:

> LIFE TERRIFIES ALL ALL BUT THE UTTER FOOLS
> But you're . . . not living, and still terrified.
> OF THEM AS U ARE   I HAVE MORE TO LOSE
> Literally? I BELIEVE SO   THEY CAN USE
> FI *Censorship*
>
> [M, p. 34]

Has the revelation been made? To the extent that we fill in the "RE," it has, but the reader, like the scribe, must compensate for the initial loss; breakthroughs alleviate breakups. Later, Maria creates a void that she proceeds to fill, after a significant pause:

> I ALWAYS WANTED A MONKEY So did I—
> Perhaps next he'll turn into one? JM
> ARENT U ASHAMED OF YR MONKEY My animal nature?
> Not a bit. O LET ME MAKE THE JOKE:
> —SHINES?
>
> [M, p. 77]

Even more problematic, an exemplary trope of absence, is the striking "phantom rhyme" in Chester Kallman's lament when he learns he is to be reborn as a Black African:

> AH LIFE   I FEEL THE LASH
> OF THE NEW MASTER   NOTHING NOW BUT CRASH
> COURSES What does Wystan say? TO PLATO?
> HAVING DROPPED ME LIKE A HOT   O SHIT
> WHAT GOOD IS RHYME NOW
>
> [M, p. 90][10]

Other ruptures require more time to be healed. DJ and JM are tantalized with a piece of news that they misconstrue (p. 114) and that is broken off. Later, in *Scripts*, strengthened for the deepest revelations, they learn at last that, mirabile dictu, Maria was the latest incarnation of Plato, one of the sacred Five. In *Mirabell*, however, they learn only enough to intuit her elemental qualities, but not enough to be vouchsafed her true identity.

The censorship imposed by the spirits when one of their number goes too far, like the erratic veering of the cup on the board at especially risky moments, allows JM and his readers to fill in what was missing, like adding those letters that were censored, or to infer information given piecemeal. A metaphysics of manners may be developed through these irrational and excited blurtings-out and half-revelations; once again, Merrill's elegance serves his major concerns. Just as one does not reveal everything in polite society, nor risk total intimacy or exposure with strangers, so one must behave with shy circumspection when dealing with creatures from another world. And so do they. *Mirabell's* major moment occurs when the spirit 741 is metamorphosed (the central letter of the alphabet allows JM to confect a veritable M&M factory) into a peacock and enters the human world of manners and *politesse*. And this entry, or transformation, is heralded by interruptions.

Previously, I spoke of interruptions as a form of revelation. In addition, interruption precedes revelation; lack of mannerliness sets the way for induction to human cordiality. An instance of the break that ensures knowledge occurs when JM is burst in upon by his goddaughter (who is also, as she is addressed in "Urania," from *Divine Comedies*, one of his muses), who inspires him with her colloquial, inquisitive, broken English, by posing a question whose answer he just now knows:

> How on Earth to recompose the bits? [of his scattered knowledge]
> Till stair by stair, gradual as heartbeats,
> Two cautious feet approach, a small grave face
> Peers round the gilded, space-dividing frame:
> Urania. Still in the first pride of speech,
> She faces me, then pipes, "Noné (godfather),
> "What's matter?" I face her, and almost know.
>
> [*M*, p. 17]

Surely moments of this kind recall the deification of Apollo in Keats's *Hyperion*, when suddenly, looking into the eyes of Mnemosyne, goddess of memory, Apollo is redeemed by "knowledge enormous," as futurity and pastness merge in a single visionary moment.[11]

At the start of Book 2, the voice/number known still as 741, "our school's / New kindergarten teacher," suggests the neatest symbols for division: punctuation comes to the board, and in addition to the letters, numbers, "Yes," "&," and "No," heretofore their sole resources, hand and scribe now have hyphen, period, comma, and so forth, those interruptors of free and automatic letter-mongering that can distinguish between, by dividing, speakers' voices. Mostly, however, these "tinkering symbols [are] known / Not in themselves, but through effects on tone." Grateful and delighted, JM cannot quite bring himself to address completely his spiritual teacher: "Is it still Bezel—I can't say that name / But you know who I mean: are you the same?" The voice 741 (later Mirabell) and his kind are merely messengers, whose thoughts, like their names, are mathematical formulas that require exposition, usually through metaphor, to be accepted by human minds. At the same time, he is the pupil of his human contacts, who can instruct him in the bonds of human society, namely manners.

The promotion of Mirabell through humane courtesy continues in Book 3, and revelation once again succeeds a breaking. First 741 confesses that "THIS WORLD OF COURTESY" has slowed down the learning process in which all participate. Then,

> Breaking off, the cup strolls round the Board
> As who should take a deep breath before speaking:
>   NOR WD I HAVE COME TO LOVE U
>
>   [M, p. 61]

Illuminated and animated by the human scribes, 741 has "ENTERD A GREAT WORLD   I AM FILLD / WITH   IS IT MANNERS?" Immediately following, 741 begins a defense of homosexuality as a recent product (4,000 years ago) of God Biology to encourage arts and mind. JM demurs, reminding him that "certain very great / Poets and musicians have been straight." The answer is cut off: "NO DOUBT   BUT 4000 YEARS AGO GOD B REALIZ / Censorship." And once more, the break heralds a miraculous transformation: JM urges 741, the erstwhile bat, to speak for himself, not for God, and his kindness encourages the number to assume a new form. Maria announces simply, "MES ENFANTS HE HAS TURNED INTO A PEACOCK."

Mirabell closes with ten final lessons, a countdown review of God Biology's work and the construction of the universe, at the end of which the archangel Michael enters the poem and readies us for the third volume. But immediately before this last series, which begins with lesson 10, concerning the soul, Mirabell receives his name. This entire section (Book 7) works structurally on the principle of breaking, humanizing, and revealing that the smaller moments cited above prepare us for.

The main subjects of the lectures of Book 7 are the appearance and work of Akhnaton and Nefertiti, two of the sacred Five, and, in a larger way, the balance between usefulness and uselessness in nature. JM defends Mother Nature (to whom he had given the last question in "Ephraim") before 741, who relegates what he calls "physical densities" to a relatively trivial position when weighed against "soul densities." Something happens, however, to 741's pronouncement about this maternal figure:

> BUT SHE DOES NOT ALWAYS COMPLY AS U YRSELVES WILL SEE
> WHEN SHE COMES TO U
>   Here the cup sweeps—is swept?—clear off the Board
>   Into the wings, a single violent swerve.
>
> [*M*, p. 137]

Maria now reveals that poor 741 was caught in mid-sentence and was "HAULED OFFSTAGE BY A HOOK LIKE A BAD TAP / DANCER ON AMATEUR NIGHT." Everyone seems to JM "so anti-Nature," and indeed MM and WHA want to leave for a smoke. Gradually abandoned, by his spiritual friends and then by DJ, who goes off to Boston for a medical checkup, JM is left alone with his thoughts, and in a set piece of seven eight-line stanzas, he conjures up Mirabell's name significantly in the middle of a contemplation about his own mother, the Nature figure throughout all his work. What renders the naming so lovely is that it comes almost as an aside, or perhaps as an illumination in the midst of his Yeatsian consideration of the polarity of mind and nature:

Once out of nature, a mercurial
Inch, look back! Sea, jungle, alpine snow,
Buff desert far below
Alternate by "turns" as in a music hall.
So distanced, it could be the way
Of our own world, as the fops in Congreve knew
With their strut and plumage—ah! mightn't Mirabell do
For our peacock's name?—

[*M*, p. 138]

His heart contracting in terror, fearful of what may have happened to his own mother whom he is telephoning long-distance, Merrill gets through at last as the line clears, the phone is answered, and Mother Nature resumes earthly communication.

The newly named Mirabell is restored to his human benefactors and in a mannerly exchange redons his peacock finery (p. 140). A single "please" makes possible the restitution of appearance to voice (although "seen" only by WHA and MM), and a second "please," like the audience's applauding for Tinkerbell in *Peter Pan*, brings back Ephraim, as a special treat to the audiences on both sides of the mirror. The stage is set, and the manners have affirmed polite discourse: Mirabell now begins the last lessons. Addressing his peacock by name for the first time, JM asks, after a thoughtful pause, whether he approves of his fancy name, to which Mirabell replies:

INDEED
IT QUITE SUITS THE PERSON U HAVE MADE OF ME   HAS SOMETHING
OF THE MIRACLE? THE MIRAGE? & SURELY OF THE PLUM!
NOW B4 US LIE OUR TEN RECUPERATIVE LESSONS

[*M*, p. 142]

The mastery of *Politesse* purges the spirits of their formulas by giving them names. It reassures the living by producing a lively, loving commerce with the other world in which the achieved manners are a hard-won victory and an assurance of future communication. The appearance of the archangel Michael at the end of *Mirabell* prepares JM and DJ, as well as Auden, Maria, and the reader, for the sterner stuff of *Scripts* with its headier revelations. Politeness has healed Mirabell of numbers, has humanized through naming. Language is the province of the humans, and it has its intellectual analogue in Keatsian negative capability, another term for the polite willingness to remain content with partial information without any irritating, vulgar groping after personal truth or gain. Although JM acknowledges a wish for "the feather of proof," he has been too polite to ask, and the reward for this self-effacing kindness will be the grander assurances of the heavenly pageant. His legacy, according to Mirabell, for having endured gaps and breakups, will be restitution and wholeness:

> WE & YOU MOVE IN OUR FIELD TOGETHER
> (THERE! STITCHES OUT WHERE THE SCAR'S LIPS MEET INVISIBLY) AH
> WITH WHAT REGRET THAT WE CAN NEVER SAY: CAREFUL DEAR FRIENDS
> DO NOT TAKE THAT FALSE STEP! OR IN ANY WAY PROTECT U
> WHO ARE OUR LOVED ONES   WD THAT WE CD LEAD U TO THAT LOST
> VERMEER THAT MANUSCRIPT OF MOZART OR LEAVE U SIMPLY
> A LITTLE GLOWING MEDAL STRUCK IN HEAVEN SAYING: TRUE

> Dear Mirabell, words fail us. But for you,
> How small our lives would be, how tedious.

> [M, p. 164]

Having been naturalized, the manners will never be relinquished; Michael's chilling last words invite JM and DJ to a meeting of equals:

> I HAVE ESTABLISHED YOUR ACQUAINTANCE & ACCEPT YOU. COME
> NEXT TIME IN YOUR OWN MANNER.   SERVANTS WE ARE NOT.

> [M, p. 182]

From this point on, interruptions will be less frequent.

Scripts seems the fussiest of the trilogy. The level of social politeness is highest; deference is accorded inevitably to Michael, and then to Gabriel, as natural superiors, even though God B's plan is for "A GOOD COMPANY AND A FRIENDLY PLACE" (S, p. 11) where intelligence and talent are everyone's possession. At the same time, the language of the angels is orotund, distant, and icy, with more ritual in the exchanges (the move in the trilogy has been from romance to ritual, JM says on p. 37). So we have regressed, in one way, to a formal scene of instruction (the schoolroom at Sandover was formerly the nursery), although the boys of the earliest visits from Ephraim are now steadied and calmed adults, ready for mature instruction. After all, twenty years have passed since "the Rover Boys at thirty" had their first communiqués. But despite the evenness of tone, the angelic speakers in *Scripts* continue to allude to the most violent of cosmic breaks as part of the underlying scheme of the universe. At the same time, this is the volume of healing and cementing, which neatly and elegantly sews up the seams between life and death, form and matter, God B and Nature, between, in fact, all dualities.

As a visible reminder of the separation without which parallels could not exist, Merrill introduces the ersatz schoolroom from which he and DJ are excluded and uses two typefaces to distinguish between what happens at Sandover and what at the mortals' sites. Often in mid-sentence, roman will give way to italics, signaling how the two scenes intersect and yet remain distinct. The use of the schoolroom encourages as well the stately pomp of *Scripts*'s drama, since Merrill presents Michael as a lighting director, Nature/Psyche as set designer, God as a producer; and in the epilogue the whole cast will reassemble to listen to JM return them to the opening of "Ephraim" as he performs the story of everyone's life.

Having learned that "INTELLIGENCE . . . IS THE SOURCE OF LIGHT" (*S*, p. 14), Merrill includes larger tracts of scientific and philosophical information throughout this *Paradiso*. The lectures are unalloyed and unleavened, but humor is not entirely absent. Now, however, the poem builds toward a major breakdown and breakthrough rather than proceeding around smaller interruptions. One example of Merrill's earlier method, which would be more at home in the other volumes, occurs at the beginning when the four elemental angels are presented. Elias, the water spirit, has made known his imminent arrival, heralded here by the book's lengthiest parenthetical aside, a metaphor of alienation and comfort that steadies *and* overwhelms. Michael is speaking:

> CHILDREN, MY BROTHER ELIAS REQUESTS YOU IN TWO DAYS. HE IS
> AS WATER SWEET & FLUID.
> I HAVE CLEANED THIS SPACE: HAVE NO FEARS, INTELLIGENT ONES,
> HAIL!

Thus as in some old-world Grand Hotel
(Early morning ado; kingfisher streak
Of lift-boy; *Figaro* and eggcup; hall
Porter's flicked ash, a chambermaid's faint shriek;
The beldam, ringlets trembling upon skull,
Chastening marble with her brush and pail
—Inconveniences the clientèle
Must philosophically endure until

A new day's clean white linen runners lie
In place over the antediluvian crimson
Of corridor and stair, down which now takes
—Bonjour, Milord! Il fait un beau soleil!—
His ease a blondness bareheaded and winsome)
THE WHITE HAS BEEN LAID DOWN FOR THESE NEW TALKS

[*S*, p. 19]

From its epigraph, taken from *Jean Santeuil*, *Scripts* proves how the final breaking of the glass will cement knowledge and human love and will assure mature independence. In division is unity. In the middle of the book (the third lesson of "&" when "They've picked this Sunday for our telephone's / Seasonal breakdown. Neither Lab nor Rat / Soul will rescue us with idle chat," p. 113), we learn of the Manichean bifurcation of the universe, the species, and the atom, between good and evil. Psyche or Nature, appearing as a Proustian *jeune fille*, informs us that God wanted to make man surprisingly different from his other species and so decided to divide him (shades of Plato and Yeats filter clearly through Merrill's ontology):

LET US DIVIDE THE FORCE OF HIS NATURE, JUST AS WE WILL MAKE
    TWO SIDES TO ALL NATURE,
FOR IN DUALITY IS DIMENSION, TENSION, ALL THE TRUE GRANDEUR
    WANTING IN A PERFECT THING.

[*S*, p. 126]

As the book proceeds, we hear stronger requests for the breaking of the mirror. The first suggestion (p. 81) is that JM and DJ will risk bad luck at last by "break[ing] the glass / & SEND[ing] US PACKING"; this statement begins a complicated figure of WHA, MM, DJ, and JM in an arabesque of parents and children. Killing the paren-

tal spirits by dropping them ensures, at the end, their rebirth or
recloning; or, vice versa, leaving the boys to their own devices
bestows upon them the maturity which, as far back as "Ephraim,"
they feared they lacked. "With one wise crack," JM will liberate his
masters and himself. If the issue of *Mirabell* is the achievement of
manners, that of *Scripts* is release and abandonment. Dialectic gives
way to dramatic action.

Shattering the glass will grant rebirth to the spirits ("LIKE BABY'S
KICKING FOOT THAT SAYS MARCH ON") and creative growth to JM,
whose major urge has been "to put / These headlong revelations
finally / Between the drowsy covers of a book" (p. 136). It is appro-
priate, then, that the final twenty pages form a stretto to the whole,
repeating themes and worries that filled Merrill's work even before
the trilogy was begun. After Gabriel's tenth lesson (and his set,
balancing Michael's ten, provides the negative "resistance" to the
positive assertions of that spirit of light), JM daydreams in a set
piece that mingles recollections of his own childhood, as he has
presented it from the mid-1960s onward, with parallels to the cos-
mic history he has just absorbed. Significantly, MM finishes a broken
statement:

> Friction made the first thin consommé
> Of all we know. Soon it was time for lunch.
> Between an often absent or abstracted
> (In mid-depression) father and still young
> Mother's wronged air of commonsense the child sat.
> The third and last. If he would never quite
> Outgrow the hobby horse and dragon kite
> Left by the first two, one lukewarm noodle
> Prefigured no less a spiral nebula
> Of further outs. . . .
>   . . . . .
>   Tight-wound exposures lay
> Awaiting trial, whose development
> Might set a mirror flowing in reverse
> Forty years, fifty, past the flailing seed
> To incoherence, blackout—the small witness
> Having after all held nothing back?
> HUSH ENFANT   FOR NO MAN'S MIND CAN REACH
> BEYOND THAT HIM & HER   THEIR SEPARATION

REMAINS UNTHINKABLE. WE ARE CONFINED
BY THE PINK CARNATION, THE FERN FIDDLEHEAD
& THESE BREATHMISTED PANES OF HUMAN SPEECH

That was the summer my par—YR PARALLELS
DIVERGE PRECISELY HERE

[*S*, pp. 213–214]

This section suggests that poetic "style," like the deliberate creation of a personality, is the attempt to cook and serve up bits and pieces of one's early life or, to change the metaphor, to mend an earlier rupture. Both our discontents with civilization and our primitive or juvenile traumas cause poetry.

This simple psychological version of poetic inspiration comple-ments the grander one at the heart of the trilogy: that vast bureau-cracy of patrons, laboratories, clonings, and chemical divisions of "soul densities." The dead are always reintegrated, biologically or chemically, and all life is imbued with their "refining conscious-ness" (p. 28). Merrill begins to sound rather like the Shelley of *Adonais* at moments such as this; or, perhaps, he is reaffirming Eliot's dictum, in "Tradition and the Individual Talent," that the dead *are* what we know." Death itself, Merrill learns in the middle lessons, is the interruption that improves and continues knowl-edge and the race; it is "THAT RESISTANT FORCE DEFINING THE FOR-WARD MOTION OF LIFE" (p. 128). Michael gives a literary version of the same dialectical progress: "ALL GOOD DISCOURSE MUST, LIKE FOR-WARD MOTION, / KNOW RESISTANCE" (Maria is quoting him, p. 132).

Revelation may be the gift of the spirits, but the major prize in this volume, the point to which the whole trilogy has pushed, is adulthood. "MAN MUST PROVIDE," says Maria at Ephesus (p. 214) as mother and father figures prepare to abandon the enfants. Much was made (p. 118) of July 4 as the date of the fourth middle lesson, and Michael at that point presented the tableau vivant of the Muses *en attitude*, like a seamless garland, each picking up the strand of her sisters' speech where it had been broken off. Perhaps their unity is meant to inspire the boys to show their own spirited ma-turity by breaking away. On DJ's fifty-fifth birthday, the blessed release is ordained.

Before the final moment, Nature vouchsafes to JM the answers to some questions he has been meaning to ask, namely, what form "resistance" will take after the gradual perfection of mankind has occurred. From the beginning, all the voices have assured us that resistance is the friction, counterforce, or antithetical principle in dialectical movement. As in other myths of millennial happiness, this element is exactly what will disappear (Merrill differs from Shelley on this point; the apocalyptic end of *Prometheus Unbound* suggests that man, however uncircumscribed and unbound, will still take his chances with death and mutability). Man will become duller, less willful: "IS THAT SHARP EDGE NOT WELL LOST / WHICH HAS SO VARIOUSLY CUT AND COST? / WE WILL WALK AMONG HIS KIND MADE NEW" (p. 230). In Blakean harmonies, all the zoas, mortal and immortal, will mix in bright dance. But by improving the species, Nature and God seem to have eliminated the cutting edge of wit itself. The new world, its population thinned and honed, will admit only of synthesis, not of interruption. The final restitution will arrive, with its own price: no divisions, no breaks.

For all the warnings and preparations, the end comes as something of a surprise. The parent surrogates, about to be reborn or divided among the elements, bless their living friends who are, in a sense, preparing to sacrifice them. While Nature gives encouragement, Maria offers the final instructions:

> JM WILL TAKE THE MARBLE
> STYLUS & GIVING US THE BENEFIT
> OF A WELLAIMED WORD, SEND OUR IMAGINED SELVES
> FALLING IN SHARDS THRU THE ETERNAL WATERS
> (DJ CUPBEARER) & INTO THE GOLDEN BOUGH
> OF MYTH   ON INTO LIFE   D'ACCORD? HUGS   KISSES
> WE'LL WRITE WHEN WE FIND WORK
>
> [*S*, p. 234]

The final twenty lines require quotation in full to show how Merrill's style serves his vision, how the syntactical variety of his quatrains works to support yet subtly to undermine his last revelation, and how breakings and interruptions are far from finished:

> Our eyes meet. DJ nods. We've risen. Shutters
> Click at dreamlike speed. Sky. Awning. Bowl.

The stylus lifted. Giving up its whole
Lifetime of images, the mirror utters

A little treble shriek and rides the flood
Or tinkling mini-waterfall through wet
Blossoms to lie—and look, the sun has set—
In splinters apt, from now on, to draw blood,

Each with its scimitar or bird-beak shape
Able, days hence, aglitter in the boughs
Or face-down, black on earth beneath, to rouse
From its deep swoon the undestroyed heartscape

—Then silence. Then champagne.
                                        And should elsewhere
Broad wings revolve a horselike form into
One Creature upward-shining brief as dew,
Swifter than bubbles in wine, through evening air

Up, far up, O whirling point of Light—:

HERS HEAR ME I AND MINE SURVIVE SIGNAL
ME DO YOU WELL I ALONE IN MY NIGHT
HOLD IT BACK HEAR ME BROTHERS I AND MINE

[S, p. 235]

Four simple sentences precede four single fragments before the complex, interwoven, eleven-line sentence that contains the major action. It subsides, without a genuine stop, into the aftermath of more sentence fragments connoting a gap ("silence") and a celebration ("champagne"). But we should notice that the shattered mirror, in its shapely fragments, recalls the jigsaw puzzle of "Lost in Translation" and possesses the razor sharpness to cut both flesh and "undestroyed heartscape." Even in resolution danger abides. Indeed, provocative resemblances between contraries accumulate: breaking and revealing, closure and fragmentation, climax and indecision, begin to look the same. The poem ends significantly with a dangling subordinate clause. Can Merrill, now lacking some of his wonted apparatus, not yet see clearly this misty apotheosis? Is this horselike form their old friend Unice? Or is it instead all the zoas resolved into "one creature"? Potential answers vanish like bubbles as our questions multiply but are interrupted by a final, equally unfinished, message.

But does it come from the board? Or does this voice in caps at last exist independently? Is it read or heard? Is it God's? Michael's? Life's? The same voice that spoke on page 78 in similar piecemeal remarks? Not only the origin but also the ambiguity of the utterance mystifies. The regressive loss of punctuation requires us to make syntax and sense. Do we hear a farewell: "I and mine survive signal; me do you well" (appropriate since the signals should have stopped by this time)? Or a poignant request for more contact: "I and mine survive; signal me; do you well" (Nature is still in love with the productions of Time)? Perhaps the chilliest possibility is that the message is overheard, directed not at the mortals but solely at the heavenly spirits by one of their numbers ("Hear me, brothers"). Or, more hopefully, perhaps the voice has now included the mortals among his own confreres. Looking into the heart of darkness or of light, what exactly does James Merrill see or hear? A revelation has been begun but is broken off: the rest is silence.

CHAPTER 8

"At the Salon Level":
Merrill's Apocalyptic Epic[1]

Richard Sáez

In guiding students through Dante's *Divina Commedia,* before approaching the *Paradiso,* I ask them to try to imagine what paradise would be like. My purpose is to instruct them in how very difficult this is to do and, thereby, to help them appreciate the full measure of Dante's unique achievement. Responses to my request are usually pretty bleak, but one year a young man answered by describing paradise as "an eternal orgasm listening to *bel canto.*" Here was someone who had taken careful measure of his likes—and dislikes— and had come up with an idea not entirely unworthy of the Florentine master in things paradisiacal. Indeed, the difference between Dante's and this student's view has much to do with the differences between discursive epic and epiphanic lyric poetry.[2] In his conception of an eternal, orgiastic melody the pluses are pretty obvious. But clearly implied are the things the young man disliked! Notice how sex is isolated from all the hard—and occasionally messy—work that leads up to orgasm; how even further removed sex is from any burdensome concept of posterity. And no laboriously modulating recitative or developmental orchestral passages. No; what is wanted is the pure melody of song, the essence of lyricism. Of course, what he doesn't mention, and what is never mentioned in connection with lyric poetry, is the necessary suspension of disbelief. Certain modes of art (lyric poetry among them)— like certain modes of sex (promiscuity among them)—require a massive suspension of disbelief. Indeed, it's part of what they're all about. An orgasm, by its very nature, cannot last forever, and bel canto defies both space and time for a transient victory. A dancer momentarily suspended in air and a soprano's high notes are the slaves of gravity nonetheless. And the full blast of a world's accumulated romantic passion cannot budge its mansion one inch from the places of excrement.

In the articulation of his three-volume visionary epic—"The Book of Ephraim," *Mirabell: Books of Number*, and *Scripts for the Pageant*—James Merrill has achieved some dazzling contemporary analogies with Dante's *Commedia*.[3] But I intend to concentrate here on an essential difference. Instead of Dante's revelation of a planned, ordered, and rational universe with the Christian *mysterium* at its center, Merrill's revelation could well be characterized metaphorically as a series of orgasms listening to bel canto. In this sense he has remained true to his essentially lyric gift.

I am reluctant to describe Merrill's apocalypse in this rather camp tone.[4] Not that the trilogy lacks camp humor. On the contrary, in many respects it is a masterpiece of sustained camp. Unfortunately, I think the camp element may distract some readers from the seriousness of the work, especially because Merrill's medium is a game, the Ouija board. Indeed, one reviewer has already misread an essential element of the work.[5] In the course of the trilogy Merrill contacts and communes with several mediums—each with his own explanation of final causes: Ephraim first, then Mirabell and, finally, Michael and Gabriel, not to mention God Biology himself, among many others. The reviewer thought this sequence corresponds to the frequent changes of lovers in a certain homosexual lifestyle. An interesting idea, but odd, and essentially wrong, as applied to a work that celebrates the twenty-fifth anniversary of the central pair of lovers: JM and DJ. Indeed, an unmentioned but essential premise of Merrill's trilogy is that its revelation—because of the nature of the Ouija board—can come only to a pair who have shared a lifetime.[6] Undoubtedly, because of his brilliant lyricism, Merrill would have a great deal to say about promiscuity, the moments Auden called "the entirely beautiful."[7] But in the epic sweep of his trilogy he is reacting not to promiscuity but,

on a profound level, to the evolution of man's religious conscious-
ness: from primitive shamanism through Judeo-Christian monothe-
ism to the mysterious aspects of contemporary science. It is true,
he reacts to the disappearance of a spiritual mode as one might to
the loss of a lover. But this is a manifestation of his poem's lyric
modality and not of the poet's private life.

In fact, both the camp humor of Merrill's work and its focus
literally on a board game are related to its most serious concern,
and it might be well to discuss that aspect before proceeding. In his
magisterial *Homo Ludens*[8] John Huizinga taught us that all games
contain a deadly humor in that they are related to the central
philosophic and theological concern of man, that is, to theodicy,
the play of good and evil in the universe.[9]

It is difficult to discuss theodicy in a twentieth-century context
without sounding either sophomoric or pontifical or both, but there
is no understanding our epic literature—including Merrill—with-
out it, and most contemporary readers have become rather hazy
about the arguments of Judeo-Christian theodicy. Let's take a bird's-
eye view: If the universe is created by one beneficent, omnipotent
deity, what are evil, pain, and suffering doing in it? Clearly this
God's ways, as Milton put it, must be justified to man. This pro-
cess of justification is the science of theodicy, and Merrill's epic—
no less than Dante's and Milton's and Blake's—is very involved in
it. All games are related to theodicy, for the latter responds to evil
by conceiving life as a game that is either won in salvation or lost
in damnation. All evil, pain, and suffering encountered in life are
essentially testing, tensional elements against which man exercises
his free will. In this view, as represented by Dante via Saint Augus-
tine and Saint Thomas, evil can be an absence, a distortion or a
corruption of the good, but it has no metaphysical existence in and
of itself.

Essentially, there have been two branches of theodicy: the Au-
gustinian and the Irenaean (Irenaeas, Bishop of Lyons, 130–202 A.D.).
In assessing responsibility for the existence of evil, Saint Augustine
emphasizes will: human failure, original sin, man's fall, and his
continued imperfection. In Irenaean theodicy the emphasis is on
God's own purposes toward universal beneficent ends and his cre-

ation of human existence as a vale of soul making. There are subtle anticipations in Irenaeas of contemporary schools of theology which seem to see God himself as in a process of evolution.

Unless we abandon logic, there is only one possible alternative to theodicy's denial of metaphysical existence to evil, and that is Manichaeism in any of its forms: the precept that evil itself is an independent force at large in the universe. (Again, according to the logic of the discursive modes of theology and epic, Judeo-Christian monism and Manichaean dualism cannot simultaneously be true because two and one, as Merrill well knows, add up to three—result in a triadism. They do not miraculously reduce to one. Such a suspension of disbelief is apparently allowable in Eastern forms of mysticism and in lyric poetry [chiastic rhyme is its prosodic form],[10] but it has not yet been made to work in Western philosophy and narratives.) The most extreme forms of Manichaeism, as in the works of the Marquis de Sade, Céline, and Jean Genet, decide that evil is the stronger force in the universe and, therefore, worship it rather than a beneficent but weaker deity. This latter heresy seems to be gaining currency in the contemporary age, where satanic and sado-masochistic cults seem to flourish, and Merrill's epic is well aware of these "Mineshafts"[11] of contemporary Manichaeism. As we shall see, Merrill's aesthetic modes of song and his association of them with the "Ewig-Weibliche" (S, p. 23) ultimately save him (and us) from men's most pernicious and ever-threatening heresy. Not at all surprising when one considers that it was J. S. Bach's theologically inspired harmonic treatment of "demonic" dissonances which determined the development of Western music.[12]

Merrill's relationship to theodicy is not easy to grasp in a casual reading of his trilogy. Although I think there are major polarities in the work, he at times seems to touch all bases, and I would like to illustrate several of them. The many modes of pop-spiritualism in recent times, such as UFOs, ESP, reincarnation, mediums, astrology, palmistry, numerology, sci-fi, and so on, are simply inversions of Sade's Manichaeism: that is, they displace all responsibility to supranatural powers beyond the will of man. Probably the most sagacious and kindly view of these phenomena interprets them as attempts to make the self interesting to itself. In Merrill this mode of narcissism becomes an aspect of his mirror imagery to which I return. Though the many forms of contemporary pop-spiritualism litter *Comedies*, they are really aspects of its camp humor, which is about more serious things. Throughout, Merrill's carefully honed literary sensibility alludes to the beneficence of suffering—so integral an aspect of Western man. In "Ephraim" theodicy is given doctrinal expression:

> Wrong things in the right light are fair, assuming
> We seize them in some holy flash past words,
> Beyond their consequences and their causes.
>
> [*DC*, p. 107]

This mode of theodicy grows in depth and complexity—and beauty of lyric expression—throughout the three volumes. One would have to say that Merrill has made a significant contribution to this vein of lyric theodicy in twentieth-century literature. But in his epic, lyric expression is balanced by an Augustinian sense (which Merrill seems to derive mostly from Dante) of a specifically theological plan involving man's participation:

> [']SISTER, TAKE COMMAND OF HIS . . . RESISTANCE? HIS 'UNGODLY'
> SIDE. MAKE HIM KNOW DARK AS WELL AS LIGHT, GIVE HIM
> PUZZLEMENT, MAKE HIM QUESTION,
> FOR WOULD WE NOT LIKE COMPANY?' I AGREED.
>
> [*S*, p. 126]

I think it would have to be said, however, that Merrill's theodicy is more essentially Irenaean, and probably Manichaean, because of the crucial role he gives to what he calls "cloning," "V work," that is, divine agents who create man rather than man growing through the agency of his own free will. In discussing *Comedies* as an epic, one should observe that it differs radically from the Western epic tradition in that it is not about the regeneration or moral development of its hero. Indeed, it is questionable whether any form of Manichaeism would allow for our sense of the development of character, a notion that seems to be a literary by-product of biblical and Augustinian metaphysics. As we shall see, the absence of characterization points to the essentially lyric ethos of Merrill's work.

To return to the question of theodicy, however, there is a dichotomy in *Comedies* in that despite the many references to the monistic tradition of a beneficent evil, Merrill seems finally to accept a Manichaean dualism. The tripartite structure of *Scripts*—" Yes," "&," "No"—seems to signal an acceptance of Manichaeism, as does making Michael, the Angel of Light, the voice of "Yes" and Gabriel, the Angel of Death, the voice of "No." Still, however, there is a return toward the end of Gabriel's pageant to an affirmation:

> DJ: They're all on the side of life, then? YES
> Gabriel had us frightened. HE IS GOD'S,
> AT MOST INHERITING HIS MOTHER'S ONE
> BLACK OR 'RESISTANT' GENE AS LIAISON
> WITH THE CHAOTIC FORCES But in fact
> Nature said Yes to man—the question's settled.
>
> [*S*, p. 210]

Indeed, all along Michael and Gabriel, God Biology and his twin Nature, good and evil, work hand in hand in what seems to be a clear case of Judeo-Christian theodicy. But in yet another turn Merrill also provides a cosmology that separates the forces of good and evil:

> WE MUST PRESUME THAT THE ORIGINAL
> PACT WAS BETWEEN GOD BIO & THE BLACK
> The Black beyond black, past that eerie Wall—
> PAST MATTER   BLACK OF THOUGHT UNTHINKABLE.
>
> [*S*, p. 158]

When I first learned about Merrill's poem, I wondered what his lyric genius might do with the farthest out elements of contemporary physics which describe black holes as universes collapsing into white holes—other universes: a cosmic theodicy! Rather unexpectedly, in *Comedies* black holes are seen as repositories of this negative force. The poetic-theodisic possibilities of nuclear physics' conception of antimatter are also voiced dualistically rather than as a paradoxical monism. Nonetheless, the lyric voice continues to crop up from time to time, for example, in imagining the original conquest of chaos as a form of fratricide:

WAS IT FRATRICIDE
THAT PUTTING DOWN OF CHAOS? Yes, is Chaos
Gabriel? If so, he's anti-Life
Or Lord of Antimatter—

[S, p. 41]

But Manichaeism seems to win irrevocably when God B himself looks wistfully into the black spaces of other universes over which he has no control.

The most lyric—as opposed to doctrinal, philosophic, theological—treatment of theodicy is embodied in a tradition that goes back to Saint Augustine, flourishes in the seventeenth century—especially Shakespeare—and is echoed in modern times by T. S. Eliot among others.[13] It is a tradition that distances good and evil into modes of memory. In contrast to Freud's conception of an unconscious blocking mechanism, remembering and forgetting are seen as functions of the free will. To remember something is to say yes to it. To forget is to say no. Merrill approaches this mode of thought several times:

'SON MICHAEL, SHEDDER OF LIGHT, REFLECTOR, NOW HELP MAN
    FORGET'
AND SO MY THIRD NATURE: SLEEP, THE REPOSE FROM DAYLIGHT TO
    DAYLIGHT.

[S, p. 64]

But once again, the absence of free will invites something closer to Manichaeism. God himself asks to forget—a literal black hole(!)—one of the unsuccessful stages of creation: 'HELP ME FORGET. TAKE ON YOUR SECOND CHORE. BURY THEM' (S, p. 188). It is, of course, this unassimilable negative force that accounts for the doleful tone of Comedies. It is Merrill's poetic genius that turns even Manichaeism into a display of sustained camp pageantry.

Although Merrill's theodicy remains problematic and contradictory, divided as it is between Manichaeism and what my essay will analyze as a sublimated acceptance of the Judeo-Christian view, I hope this brief discussion at least reveals his trilogy's deepest concerns to be those of the major epics within the Western tradition. How could it be otherwise? Merrill writes in Milton's language and Dante's form, with Blake, Pope, and Yeats as additional models.

Perhaps it is best to consider theodicy in *Comedies* not as a thematic argument that must come to some resolution but rather as a musical motif that modulates tonalities and melodic configurations but ultimately resolves only in the integrity of the poet's voice. In any case, it would be an unfortunate misreading of the work to see it, on the one hand, as merely a symbolic action for private lives or to imagine, on the other hand, that in a few mystical allusions Merrill successfully resolves man's most irresolvable philosophic question. I wish to discuss further the trilogy's epic nature by concentrating on a comparison of the personae of his lyric poems and those of his epic. I will then proceed to a discussion of the nature of the trilogy's apocalyptic revelation, which is, on the contrary, expressed in a more lyric vein.

2

My concern with Merrill's epic personae and the metaphysics of his revelatory moments leads me inevitably to draw some analogies with Dante's *Commedia*. But though purely lyric elements, such as Merrill's *son et lumière* response to Dante's Aquinian metaphysics of light, are remarkably analogous, I think it is the differences within the overall structural similarities of the two epics which predominate. I have already noted the obvious absence in Merrill's eclectic poem—which draws on influences both East and West—of the ordered and rational Aristotelian-Aquinian ethics and metaphysics of Dante. Even the broader tripartite structure harbors an essential difference. Dante's three canticles—*Inferno, Purgatorio,* and *Paradiso*—are, in addition to being fixed places within a structured universe, modes of being: the damned and lost, the striving and hopeful, and the beatific redeemed. Merrill's three books are not as easily divisible, but it is helpful to distinguish major concerns within each. The "Book of Ephraim" is the most personal, concerned with the past, present, and afterlives of the poet's family and friends. It has a very personal religious stance that essentially confirms private and personal attitudes. *Mirabell* takes a historical perspective: the trajectory of God B's creative experiment and of the poet's career. *Scripts for the Pageant* is structural in approach: the natural and metaphysical structure of the universe and the poet's oeuvre. In general, the infinite finiteness of the alphabet ("Ephraim") results in better sound and sense than the finite infinity of numbers (*Mirabell*) or the *hemiola* of pivoted opposites (*Scripts*)—the secret of which Brahms seems to have taken to his grave. There are, of course, exceptions to this evaluation. "Samos" and the collectable interstices describing the changing lights at Sandover (both in *Scripts*) are lyric masterpieces in the language.

Dante's location of his characters within a specific geography, which is also a mode of being, is precisely what allows him the extraordinary depth of characterization achieved in figures like Farinata or Picarda or Pia. Their reality and individuality are so intense as to be transcended into a metaphysical mode of existence.[14] Merrill's much more fluid world, in which the personal, the historical, and the universal never quite blend, leads to a persona that is more like caricature. His own metaphor for this kind of characterization is the "silhouette": one of the modes in which the absent presence of the haunting figure Hans Lodeizen appears (*DC*, p. 105) and in which the figures of the pageant reveal themselves (*S*, p. 39). This use of caricature is, of course, wonderfully complementary to the camp modality Merrill maintains throughout, and it is important to remember—such is the weight that Dante, Shakespeare, and the realistic characterizations of modern literature have imparted to us—that it is not a value judgment to describe something as caricature. It is merely a generic and, I hope, accurate statement. Perhaps Merrill's approach is most readily appreciated if we look at DJ (David Jackson), a character essential to the trilogy who is caricatured throughout as the slightly abused, alter-ego partner ("CUPBEARER" [*S*, p. 234]), existing more as an aspect of the poet's life than in his own right. Caricature is similarly apparent in Chester Kallman—Auden's companion. Behind both of these personae stands the weighty archetype of the skeptical, pragmatic, and realistic Sancho Panza, but, significantly, they never come to reside in that identity in the way that, for example, Merrill's lyric childhood home "18 West 11th Street" becomes the House of Atreus.[15]

I think we learn most about the nature of the personae and phenomena that appear in Merrill's trilogy by comparing them with the personae and phenomena of his lyric poems. In an earlier essay, I described Merrill's method of taking several analogous elements—a series of lovers, homes, landscapes—and coalescing them through a meditative process into the icon of the particular lyric:

> Each poem begins after a physical or emotional crisis has enervated the poet, effecting something like Proust's intensified sensibility after an asthmatic attack. A delicate but incisive sensuous perception leads from the present to related scenes in the past. . . . Movement is more in the rhythm of ritual dance—measured, repeated steps with darkly significant variations—than narrative action . . . eroticism is closer to the core than to the surface. When the focus has narrowed sufficiently to burn through the poet's self-absorption, remaining under the thin gauze of ashes is the poem: a cooling artifice which coalesces and refigures the past.[16]

In these poems both nature and the arts are symbolic of the spirit, carefully chosen words are pregnant with presences; meditated on long enough through symbols and words, nature reveals transcendent messages and a series of lovers or landscapes coalesces into a platonic essence.

"Lost in Translation" is a masterpiece in this genre, and it is particularly interesting for us in that, like *Comedies*, it focuses on a board game and contains a poetics as well as mediums. In it a poem by Valéry, its translation by Rilke, a scene from the poet's childhood when he put together handmade puzzles in the company of a governess, the life of that governess, scenes from the poet's adult life (including one in which a medium identifies the handmade piece of a puzzle), and the exotic Arabian scene of the puzzle itself (involving an Oedipal triangle similar to that of the poet's childhood family life)—all these scenes, and more, are coalesced through the magical alchemy of Merrill's poetic craft into the stanzaic pattern of the poem, itself compared to a crafted puzzle:

> Out of the blue, as promised, of a New York
> Puzzle-rental shop the puzzle comes—
> A superior one, containing a thousand hand-sawn,
> Sandal-scented pieces. Many take
> Shapes known already—the craftsman's repertoire
> Nice in its limitation—from other puzzles:

Witch on broomstick, ostrich, hourglass,
Even (surely not just in retrospect)
An inchling, innocently branching palm.
These can be put aside, made stories of
While Mademoiselle spreads out the rest face-up,
Herself excited as a child; or questioned
Like incoherent faces in a crowd,
Each with its scrap of highly colored
Evidence the Law must piece together.
Sky-blue ostrich? Likely story.
Mauve of the witch's cloak white, severed fingers
Pluck? Detain her. The plot thickens
As all at once two pieces interlock.

[DC, p. 5]

Here life is sacrificed to its transcendence into art. It is no wonder that nothing is lost, or all is lost, or all is found in the suspension of disbelief allowed to lyric poetry:

But nothing's lost. Or else: all is translation
And every bit of us is lost in it
(Or found—I wander through the ruin of S
Now and then, wondering at the peacefulness)
And in that loss a self-effacing tree,
Color of context, imperceptibly
Rustling with its angel, turns the waste
To shade and fiber, milk and memory.

[DC, p. 10]

(A lost piece—remaining in the boy's "pocket"!—is incidentally compared to a soprano's lost high notes: "Maggie Teyte's high notes / Gone at the war's end." I'll return to those notes later.) In such lyric triumphs a science of theodicy is hardly necessary, unless disbelief were to reawaken.

There is something very Proustian in Merrill's sense of life sacrificed to art, as well as in the haunting guilt that sacrifice awakens in him.[17] In an important respect the epic trilogy is an attempt to assuage that guilt. An aspect of its dynamics is located in Merrill's unfurling the icons of his lyrical poems, which are alluded to throughout, into their constituent elements, that is, in a favorite Merrillian image, running his poetic camera backwards:

> Tight-wound exposures lay
> Awaiting trial, whose development
> Might set a mirror flowing in reverse
> Forty years, fifty, past the flailing seed
> To incoherence, blackout—the small witness
> Having after all held nothing back?
>
> [*S*, p. 213]

(The same image had already occurred in "18 West 11th Street," a poem that anticipated Merrill's liberation from his lyric identity.) *Scripts* has an epigraph from Proust's *Jean Santeuil* which alludes, indirectly, to the Proustian apocalypse achieved when the enslaved habits of passion are freed by rupturing their icons to release the colors, sounds, smells, touches, and tastes of which they were composed. And the sacrilegious act is rewarded!

> Il ne pouvait pas la quitter et lui avoua tout bas qu'il avait cassé le verre de Venise. Il croyait qu'elle allait le gronder, lui rappeler le pire. Mais restant aussi douce, elle l'embrassa et lui dit a l'oreille: "Ce sera comme au temple le symbole de l'indestructible union."

In the early *Jean Santeuil,* the breaking of the vase refers to the Jewish wedding ceremony, but toward the end of *À la recherche* Proust had expanded the same image into the radical metaphor for two volumes: *La prisonnière* and *La fugitive.* Through his obsessive, romantic passion the narrator has made his captive love herself a prison, which he describes repeatedly as a vase, containing all the joys and sensuous qualities of life. Only with her death is the vase broken and the constituent elements of his life slowly restored:

> Albertine m'avait semblé un obstacle interposé entre moi et toutes choses, parce qu'elle était pour moi leur contenant et que c'est d'elle, comme d'un vase, que je pouvais les recevoir. Maintenant que ce vase était détruit.[18]

But I'm running a little ahead of my argument. The refraction of wholes into constituent elements is endemic to allegory and essential in almost all epic poetry. Thus, a perfect individual is represented by the several knights of various virtues, or a single nation is refracted into the various levels of its body politic. Images of unwinding, dismantling, or unfurling present themselves numerous times in Merrill's trilogy. And they occur in the most surprising guises. Whereas Merrill's various homes have always been frozen into powerful mythical icons in his poems, in *Comedies* these homes, and their various bric-a-brac, literally unfurl into life. The designs of a rug and wallpaper, and "a painted tin / Dimestore peacock" become the animated angelic and demonic voices of his visionary experience—another camp dimension from the fairy-tale world of *L'enfant et les sortileges*. The Victorian mirror of the Stonington house, in which the otherworldly characters of his epic appear, could function as a symbol for his lyric poems reanimated into multiple individual forms. But the mirror is more specifically one of the revelatory symbols to which I will return.

The refraction of poetic realities into individuated elements has many other manifestations throughout the trilogy. It is present in the cast of colors which is part of the vision in *Mirabell* Book 6 (anticipated in section K of "Ephraim"), and in the individuated elements of *Scripts*—Light, Water, Earth, and Air—and the angels who represent them—Michael, Emmanuel, Raphael, and Gabriel. One sees it again in the treatment of the memory of a paradisiacal past, compressed into the word "toy" and its cognitive rhymes in "18 West 11th Street," but unfurled into a succession of Atlantises in *Mirabell* and *Scripts*. At times it seems as if Merrill is processing the icons of his life into a digitalized code.

This urge toward individuation is even present in the refraction of spiritual force (compressed into a concept like translation or an object like a precious stone in the lyric poetry) into the figures of *V*, who in turn are refracted into various constituent elements. Merrill's tour de force in this radical urge toward refraction is his exquisite treatment of light, which is worthy of his masters in Dante and Shelley. Even his previous tendency, not only in his lyric poems but in his novels and dramas as well, toward a "composite" mythical hero[19] moves toward refraction in *Comedies* as the characters' various identities peel off from a central seed or atom—Adam.

Merrill is also fascinated in his trilogy by the painted-over scene that the "X Rays" of art historians have unfurled beneath the surface of Giorgione's *Tempesta*. This leitmotif keeps surfacing: in, for example, sections V and X of "Ephraim" and both the "Yes" and "No" sections of *Scripts*. Merrill reveals layers of meaning which no X ray could possibly unravel. The paintings (St. Theodore leaning on a staff and a nude lady "with a child / who needs explaining" painted over a "Nude arisen . . . From flowing water") echo the Oedipal concerns of Merrill's lyric poetry, the more so since he uses the occasion to abjure—at least for the moment—his own lyric method:

> One more prompt negative. I thanked my stars
> When I lost the Leica at Longchamps. Never again
> To overlook a subject for its image,
> To labor images till they yield a subject—
> Dram of essence from the flowering field.
> No further need henceforth of this
> Receipt (gloom coupleted with artifice)
> For holding still, for being held still. No—
> Besides, I fly tomorrow to New York—
> Never again. Pictures in little pieces
> Torn from me where lightning strikes the set—
>
> [*DC*, p. 120]

Nonetheless, his *Tempesta* meditation goes on to discuss an Oedipal substructure:

> All of which lights up, as scholarship
> Now and then does, a matter hitherto
> Overpainted—the absence from these pages
> Of my own mother. Because of course she's here
> Throughout, the breath drawn after every line,
> Essential to its making as to mine.
>
> [*DC*, pp. 127–128]

This presence-absence of Merrill's mother is a leitmotif in itself. The trilogy contains several such references to subtexts, most notably in the memory of an early passion remembered after decades of lovers and a twenty-five year "marriage":

> Hans. Dead now a quarter century.
> A note gone tinny on my keyboard, false . . .
> And yet (for all I know) he *is* the key
> This opus began and will end in. Someone else

> Pausing here might note each modulation
> Away from, back to his blue tonic gaze.
>
> [M, p. 127]

This is a poignant archetype of lost innocence, Merrill's biographi-
cal fall. But the theodicean dance of good and evil is more specif-
ically—and abstractly—alluded to in the extended Giorgione medita-
tion. It occurs in the more specifically theological *Scripts* as Merrill
puns on "negative":

> Think, before you give
> Way to panic, of what other meanings
> The word "negative" takes on in *Ephraim*:
> X-ray images, or Maya's film
> In which the widow turns into the bride.
> Tricks of the darkroom. All those cameras clicking
> In Venice, on the bridge. For now a new bridge—
> Can it be crossed both ways?—from Yes to No
> Is entering the picture. DJ: So
> Is Venice, if our plans firm up. JM:
> By which time, from the darkness you foresee,
> Who knows what may develop milkily,
> What loving presence? (Odd, not long ago
> Our daydreams were in color, that tonight
> Print out in Manichaean black and white.)
>
> [S, p. 80]

For an epic poem, Merrill's trilogy is notably lacking in multi-
tudes. Rather, it tends to the nucleus of an exclusive salon: a "petit
noyou" assembled at "stage center": "Wystan, Maria, you and I,
we four / Nucleate a kind of psychic atom," (M, p. 97). However,
as if haunted by his own childlessness—the absent infinity of pos-
terity—the poet has attempted to compensate by peopling his uni-
verse with the unfurling of his icons. Within the greater expanse
of an epic structure, Merrill is using this extended unfurling and
refraction to provide the biographical background for his lyric po-
ems. Just the title of one of his lyrics, "The Friend of the Fourth
Decade," implies other friends, not to mention the expanse of forty
years, compressed into the icon of one poem. And to a lesser
extent contemporary modes of sexual liberation direct the expan-
sive energies of the trilogy into something far more worked than

confessional poetry but nonetheless related to it. The essential thrust of these books is stronger and more profound, however. It goes back to Merrill's Proustian sense of the ruthless exercise of poetic will in sacrificing life to art. I do not wish to belabor this point, but for Merrill the crucial sacrifice of life to art is expressed by the artist's childlessness, if his aesthetic vocation is considered responsible, as it is in *Comedies*:

> KEEP IN MIND THE CHILDLESSNESS WE SHARE THIS TURNS US
> OUTWARD TO THE LESSONS & THE MYSTERIES IT IS A
> FINE POINT: THE TYPE U SET JM, INVERTED & BACKWARD,
> IS YET READ RIGHTSIDE UP ON THE BIOLOGICAL PAGE.
>
> [*M*, p. 122]

In her review of *Mirabell*, Helen Vendler referred to the poem's central, almost obsessive concern with "childlessness" without discoursing on it.[20] I will return to this theme in describing Merrill's dialogue with the soprano voice as a sublimation of his sexuality, but for the moment it can be said that there is a relationship between the trilogy's concern with childlessness and its apparent surrender to Manichaeism. The surrender of free will in a universe created by the cloning of supernatural agents or the control of a mechanistic Monitor (not a flesh and blood Minotaur) at the earth's core is also a surrender of any personal responsibility for the sacrifice of life—childlessness and all—to an aesthetic vocation. I have written at some length in my previous essay about the moral and political commitments of that supposedly amoral, apolitical aesthete, James Merrill—commitments that involved not only sexual matters but also Merrill's place in the hegemony of a capitalist society. Throughout the trilogy, Merrill's references to "High Class Queers," the reincarnation of his financier father as greengrocer, and so on, are delicious bits of camp humor! But the washing of the hands represented by a cloned, mechanistically controlled universe far transcends the metaphysics of camp. It is, in fact, a vigorous assertion of the free will in the disguise of passivity.

For the moment, I want to return to a comparison of the refracted personae in Merrill and the characters of Dante's *Divina Commedia*. While Dante's characters and landscape are also elements of a whole, Dante's superstructure allows him to remind the reader constantly of the relationship of part to whole. Nowhere is the metaphysical unity of Dante's symbols more evident than in his most specific treatment of song. In Canto II of *Purgatorio*, in the ante-purgatory, Dante recognizes his old friend Casella among the souls about to be purged. A famous musician, Casella had sung many of Dante's own songs. Dante tries to embrace him three times. Each time, in a forceful reminder of the difference between the spiritual condition of the afterlife and the human condition before death, Dante's arms pass through the shadow of Casella's spirit and return to his own breast. Somewhat frustrated, Dante makes a further appeal to vanity and asks Casella to sing one of his own (Dante's) songs. Soon all present are lost in a trance at the beauty of Casella's singing, and they must be forcefully called back to the onerous chore of purgation. Bliss comes later. In this vignette, Dante delineates three levels of self-transcendence: the physical in the vain attempt to embrace Casella (which only comes back to the self), the aesthetic in the transient escape through Casella's singing (which is a prototype of the third and final form but can interfere with it), and the spiritual in the reminder of the purgatorial and paradisiacal road ahead (which is the only real form of transcendence to which the other two aspire). Dante allows a lyric suspension of disbelief, but only momentarily, and he makes it a perfect symbol of the spiritual transcendence that, when it comes, will be accompanied by the harmony of the spheres.

How does Merrill integrate lyric into epic? Contained within *Comedies* is a substantial collection of lyric poems as distinguished as any of Merrill's recent volumes. Whether these poems are fully integrated into the epic (in Dante's manner) is another matter, however. One of these poems, written in seven, eight-line rhymed stanzas, appears in Book 7 of *Mirabell*. It describes an evening phone call the poet makes to his mother. The initial intention to write to her is interrupted by the poet's celestial meditations on the supranatural, which he opposes to the world of nature below:

> Up there's the stratosphere
> Of (how to put it) Mind, that battiness
> Chose over some maternal Nature's less
> Perfectly imagined realm down here

> Of random tide and gale, of sweet and bitter
> She calls home. . . .
>
> [*M*, p. 138]

There are even telling questions of choice and free will:

> Sent reeling by her kiss,
> Did we *choose* artifice,
> The crust, the mirror meal?
>
> [*M*, p. 138]

The poem also associates the aesthetic choice with camp ("the fops in Congreve") and homosexuality, and it contains one of the most striking evocations of the soprano voice:

> She answers with a tug of the old magnet,
> Making me look up from where I sit.
> Cocked to those infinite
> Spangled thinnesses whose weave gosling and cygnet
> Have learned already in the shell,
> The mind's ear registers her vocalise.
> Flagstad herself had no such notes as these
> Of lashing hail and rapturous farewell.
>
> [*M*, p. 139]

The poet returns from his reverie, telephones his mother, is temporarily alarmed by her failure to answer, and then rejoices in the final "presence":

> —But no, she answers. And a spate
> Of what she still calls news (weddings and weather)
> Sweeps me away, bemused, glad to be with her,
> Communing where we don't communicate.
>
> [*M*, p. 139]

All the themes I am articulating are here: the choice of artifice over nature, the blackness of camp humor devoid of posterity, theodicy, choice, mirrors, the soprano voice. This passage could be taken as one of the lyrics that Merrill is unfurling in the course of his trilogy, and it is like Dante's Casella "Canto" in its power of concentration of the epic into the lyric. Where it differs from Dante is in the integration of the lyric into the whole. Casella's singing func-

tioned as a symbol for celestial harmony. Instead of Dante's si-
multaneous blending and delineation of lyric transcendence with
the Christian apocalypse, Merrill presents a dichotomy that can be
represented by his own juxtaposition of "communing" and "com-
municate." In a book that communicates abundant information about
numerology, astrology, myth, and science fiction in endless stac-
cato lines, Merrill (and the reader) retreats to the more intimate,
intuitive, and ritualistic mode of lyric discourse which has ever
been his maternal, his Oedipal language. One can have a dialogue
in *verse* with the *past* because it has already played itself out in time
and space, and verse is literally (and etymologically) the discourse
of recurrence. But one cannot hold such a dialogue with posterity,
for it belongs to the future and needs another mode of discourse—
one that includes biological and moral regeneration: a discursive
mode in which the Oedipal passions of mother and son cannot be
mirrored or cloned but must be painstakingly modulated into a
distant but inherent tonality, as the son evolves into the father of a
daughter. This is the world of Shakespeare, for example, where the
homoerotic and triadic sonnets evolve into the father-daughter
centered romances.

In a work that refers to childlessness so frequently, the poet's
relationship to his own mother is of necessity especially poignant.
But nothing is more poignantly symbolic of the homosexual's child-
lessness than his almost hysterical passion for the *soprano voice*.
This phenomenon, frequent enough in popular culture, is not par-
ticularly prominent in literature. There are the many hyperbolic
references to the soprano Marietta Alboni in Walt Whitman, but a
more contemporary analogy could be found in several works by
such film directors as Pasolini, Bertolucci, Zeffirelli, and Visconti.[21]

Future critics are sure to comment on Merrill's use of the so-
prano voice. Once again, I hope their inevitably camp analyses
will be worthy of the complexity of his work. My discussion fo-
cuses on the transience of a voice that holds a note for an instant.
For Merrill that transient high note has the resonance of one of his
lyric icons: it seems to symbolize the mystery of female sexuality
and childbearing.

It would be difficult to work out a satisfactory phenomenology

of the relationship of some male homosexuals to the super-culti-
vated, hothouse voices of great operatic sopranos. But some of the
ingredients are obvious: as opposed to the inextricable blood ties of
procreation, the art of the operatic soprano is a highly stylized,
distanced—but also heightened—form of reality. For Merrill in par-
ticular, any such phenomenology would have to consider the op-
eratic plots of poems focused on the Oedipal triad of his childhood,
and take special note of "Matinees," which is set in an opera house
and talks about love:

> You and I, caro, seldom
> Risk the real thing any more.
> It's all too silly or too solemn.
> Enough to know the score
>
> From records or transcription
> For our four hands.

[*FS*, p. 50]

Unfurling the disk surface, "the real thing" could refer not only to
performance but also to another love affair in the fifth decade.
In the light of Merrill's entire oeuvre—especially within the walls
of Sandover, resounding as they do with so many great soprano
voices—the real thing would have to refer as well to female sexual-
ity and childbearing.[22]

This reading, I am well aware, goes against the affirmations of
"v work" in *Comedies*, especially in *Mirabell*. These statements are,
however, intermittent and hardly in the poet's own voice, whereas
the longing I am referring to is a more constant element in the
fabric of the epic. Besides, in his now lengthy oeuvre, Merrill has
never been a poet who characteristically affirms directly. His more
important messages—such as the politically revolutionary stance of
"18 West 11th Street" or the poetics of "Lost in Translation"—
reveal themselves only through an arduous combination of intu-
itive and analytical reading. *Comedies* seems to me no different.

<h1 style="text-align:center">3</h1>

Another aspect of the unfurling and refraction of aesthetic icons is
an obviously complementary and recurrent image—the turning of

records and cassettes. Whereas the tendency toward refraction suggests an epic modality, the transient moments preserved in recorded song are essentially lyric in nature—but not simply so. Without having done a count, I would say that song—usually recorded on discs or cassettes—is the predominant symbol in Merrill's trilogy. And the favorite mode is theatrical song in grand opera. There are an astounding number of specific references to composers, operas, scenes, characters, arias, and performers. But as we shall become increasingly aware, Merrill's addiction to bel canto is not innocent of Bach's theodiceanly inspired principles of harmony and counterpoint. Merrill also occasionally invokes music with the image of a chord: the triadic foundation of all Western music, strong enough to encompass not only passing dissonance and Oedipal triadism but evil itself.

The "Yes" and No" sections of *Scripts* culminate in pageants with songs at their center, and God B himself performs a ditty that is interpreted by Auden. Michael's fete at the culmination of "Yes" combines the celebration of JM and DJ's twenty-fifth anniversary with their final lessons: "(The ring, the silver rose, the Jubilee, / Everything fits unbelievably)" (*S*, p. 74). Indeed, the artful coincidence of highly stylized artifact dominates the fete. The background music is "ROSENKAVALIER / SIDE ONE," evoking the presence of Strauss himself to hear Flagstad sing a fifth "Last Song." And in what must be the ultimate symbol for intense but distanced and stylized song there is the presence of Schwarzkopf, "who had dubbed a high / C in that late *Tristan* Flagstad made."

God B's song is an uncomfortable reminder of the fatalism so close to the trilogy's core:

AH   SO HEARTBREAKING   SO THAT WAS IT
He's singing to the Pantheon. OR ALONE
KEEPING UP HIS NERVE ON A LIFERAFT
Far cry from the joyous Architect
Michael told us of at the beginning—;
But He gets answered. DOES HE? Yes. The angels
Spoke of signals. DO THEY KNOW? I see.
They've never heard the Song. ONLY WE 4
& THAT'S AS HE WOULD SAY THE HALF OF IT

What was the song's effect on you? MM
KNEW HERSELF TO BE AMONG THE STARS
THE WORLD LOST, OUT OF EARSHOT. I WAS KEEN
UPON THE SOUND ITSELF   THOSE TONES WERE EITHER
THOSE OF AN ETERNAL V WORK OR A MACHINE
SET TO LAST   UNTIL THE BATTERIES
RUN DOWN   OR . . . ?

[S, pp. 80–81]

The section ends with a lyric, inspired by God B's song. It presents a "HOMESICK, HEARTSICK" tenor and is mindful of a "WRONGED & WILFUL QUEEN." The Oedipal triangle, posterity, and childlessness are very much at the heart of the matter:

A SHIPBOARD SCENE,
TRISTAN ACT I OR LES TROYENS ACT V:
HIGH IN THE RIGGING, FROM
BEHIND THE GOLD PROSCENIUM,
ABOVE THE ACTION'S THRIVING
CITY WITH ITS WRONGED AND WILFUL QUEEN,

ONE SAILOR'S CLEAR
YOUNG TENOR FILLS THE HOUSE, HOMESICK,HEARTSICK.

[S, p. 83]

But song is not the only way in which Merrill's apocalypse reveals itself in transient moments. There are many related elements, and I would like to delineate a few of them before returning to song in its theatrical mode. The work bristles in the poet's own voice with poetic notions, aperçus, and feelings that are themselves transient modes of thought—too lightly presented to be properly considered as ideas. Every reader will have favorite examples. A few come to my mind: (1) in the afterlife people achieve the age at which they first became aware of their own mortality, (2) God's putting down of chaos as a form of fratricide, (3) and time as the "soil of feeling."

The endless clutter of "bric-a-brac"—the carpets, the wallpaper, the statues, and the objets d'art that fill the poet's two homes (Stonington and Athens)—could not be more different from the deeply symbolic fireplace of "Mornings in a New House," or the Oedipal family of "The Broken Home" and several other lyrics, or the mythic ruin of "11 West 18th Street."[23] These *disjecta membra* of the trilogy are to the monadic symbols of the lyric poetry as caricature is to deeply structured characterization, or, perhaps, as the flatterers and acolytes of a salon are to the blood ties of posterity. And the spiritual force of the world's great religions, which I doubt even a thinking atheist would deny, is reduced to the political, social, and accidental nature of transient historical institutions by the way in which Moses, Jesus, Buddha, and Mohammed are presented. Their appearance in *Scripts* (pp. 160–168) is profoundly disturbing. Because the historical emanations of these spiritual leaders appear "hollow" and "exhausted" to the salon of Merrill's epic, their spiritual energy (which for Dante, incidentally, by its very nature can only multiply) is flushed into a "Mineshaft" of contemporary history. And again unlike Dante, Merrill does not link the trilogy's light show to a transcendent hierarchy of angelic powers; rather it too seems intimately responsive to the sense of a passing moment:

> Music. A single pure white beam one knows
> Floods the mirror room, which undergoes
> Instant changes. Dewy garlands deck
> The staircase. Statue, pictures, candlestick,
> Each is prismatically multiplied.
> The Ouija Board drifts upward on a tide
> Of crystal light—ethereal parquet
> Where guests will presently join WHA
> And MM. (DJ and JM appear
> Twice, outside and in, both 'there' and 'here'.)
>
> [S, p. 72]

Finally, much is revealed about the transient and Manichaean nature of Merrill's vision in the appearance of the mirror in *Comedies*. The troubadour poets, whose lyrical ethos of romantic ecstasy so much of Dante's *Commedia* is in antithetical response to, had made the Narcissus myth into a favorite trope. Whereas Narcissus mistook illusory reflection for reality, Dante the pilgrim mistakes reality for an illusory reflection. In Canto II of the *Paradiso*, when Dante encounters his first paradisiacal beings, he is confused by their etherealized condition and imagines them to be reflections on

the face of the moon. He turns around to see the true beings, only
to be chided by Beatrice, who forces him to realize his error. What
we have here is Dante's final rejection of romance's narcissistic
projection of the self in favor of the externally manifest universe—
historical and spatial—of God. Merrill, loyal to his own lyric im-
agery in which the Oedipal triangle is so prominent, turns the
mirror, finally, into a triadic symbol: two spaces (his home and the
school room at Sandover) and the meeting ground of the mirror.

As with the son et lumière, Merrill makes the mirror responsive
to several of the major themes of his poem. It first appears with
playful sexual overtones:

> [(]Noons, D and I might row to a sandbar
> Far enough from town for swimming naked
> Then pacing the glass treadmill hardly wet
> That healed itself perpetually of us—
> Unobserved, unheard we thought, until
> The night he praised our bodies and our wit,
> Our blushes in a twinkling overcome.)
>
> [DC, p. 50]

In *Mirabell*, it has become one of the vehicles of the epic's Man-
ichaeism:

> With new eyes we confront the mirror,
> Look *beyond* ourselves. Does he appear?
> Never plainer, never more hidden, his glassy
> Foyer, his permeable impasse.
> Reason might argue that to enforce our absence
> Upon it wipes the gleaming slab
> Of him as well. Instead, this quasi-
> Liverish cloud betrays
> A presence hitherto unseen; this acne,
> Not yet disfiguring, points to . . . a black
> Alter ego? an alchemical Jekyll
> Mapping the orbit of the long, long trek
> Back? To what? . . .
>
> [M, p. 155]

The room within the mirror that JM and DJ cannot enter is pre-
sented in many ways as a complement to, as well as an inversion
of, their own room. They do on occasion seem to pass mystically

into the world of the mirror: with a phonograph obligato in the background, no doubt. And we never lose sight of Merrill's frequent play on the etymological pun on room ("stanza") and the prosodic stanza. (By the third volume of the trilogy the reader should be well aware that he is dealing essentially with a poetics.) The mirror is also the proper abode of the Lady of Sandover, the only female among the many mediums—Ephraim, Mirabell, Michael, Gabriel—in the trilogy. In subtle ways the elaborately triadistic, mirrored *mise-en-scène* in *Scripts* reminds the reader of sexual antithetical and complementary opposites—phallus and testes inversely reflected in vagina and ovaries:

> But now my question:
> Is there no Ewig-Weibliche in sight?
> AN EWIG SHALL WE SAY HERMAPHRODITE?
> YOU HAD THOUGHT ERZULIE WAS FEMALE? HE/
> SHE IS/WAS RAIN SOIL SEED SUN STARLIGHT
> PHALLUS & VAGINA   OMNISEX.
>
> [S, p. 23]

How revealing that in his cosmology Merrill presents God B with a female twin: Nature ("Known also as Psyche and Chaos"). It's as if in an elaborate Platonic myth he has presented God B as a sexually mirrored reflection. One might argue from this that just as Merrill has compensated for the absence of posterity by refracting endlessly the personae of his poetic lives, so has he projected a heterosexual structure onto his universe—a structure that accounts for the Manichaean duality God B encounters when he gazes into the mysterious universes beyond his own. The trilogy is aware of the mirror as a potential symbol for posterity:

> Like mirrors seen in mirrors down the whole
> Length of the gallery. Not just Body:Soul
> Or Angel:Bat, in frame on gilded frame
> Varying terms reiterate the same
> Proportion.
>
> [M, p. 144]

But the mirror in *Scripts* does not reach into that infinity. It is soon to be broken:

                                                        THAT DAY
        ENFANTS TAKE OUT A SMALL EXPENDABLE MIRROR
        ONTO THE FRONT STEP   KISS & WITH ONE WISE
        CRACK SET US FREE.

                                                        [S, p. 82]

This is the epic's final, doleful transience—albeit a rather theatrical one.

Like games, theatricality is profoundly related to the problem of theodicy in man's consciousness. If life is a temporary game to be won or lost for the highest of stakes, it can also be seen as a dream or transient drama that resolves the conflict of good and evil in its characters and then as in Shakespeare's *The Tempest*:

> The great globe itself,
> Yea, all which it inherit, shall dissolve
> And, like this insubstantial pageant faded,
> Leave not a rack behind.

The masques in *Scripts* are Merrill's most elaborate indulgence in this form, extraordinary in the way the revelation of the masques is the pageant itself. And extraordinary in the sense they give of life as an occasion for which one dresses up. As with Merrill's symbolic use of song, the tone is very subtle. It touches both melancholy and camp and seems to emphasize the transient, the artificial, the distanced—qualities that heighten the intensity of the experience. The Lady of Sandover is given the most elaborate mise en scène:

> *Enter—in a smart white summer dress,*
> *Ca. 1900, discreetly bustled,*
> *Trimmed if at all with a fluttering black bow;*
> *Black ribbon round her throat; a cameo;*
> *Gloved but hatless, almost hurrying*
> *—At last! the chatelaine of Sandover—*
> *A woman instantly adorable.*
> *Wystan, peeking, does a double take:*
> *Somewhere on Earth he fancies he has seen*
> *A face so witty, loving, and serene*
> *—But where? Some starry likeness drawn by Blake*
> *Perhaps for 'Comus'? or the one from Dante*
> *Of Heavenly Wisdom? This, then, is the third*

And fairest face of Nature (whom he'll come
To call, behind Her back of course, Queen Mum).
Glance lively with amusement, speaks. Each word,
Though sociable and mild, sounds used to being heard.

[S, p. 125]

The most revealing of these theatrical entrances (Sarah Bernhardt's)
is in *Mirabell*, Book 6:

She stood (wrote Jules Renard of the divine
Sarah) in one place, letting the stair unwind
Her profiles, eerily descending wand
Of the still center, or its weathervane.
Gone, she endured. Globes lit the banister's
Counterspiraling ascents of bronze
As in remembrance Lalique's cabochons
Waxed and waned upon that brow of hers

Like this pale purple atom (phosphorus)
Periodic among satellites,
Messengers, sugar chains and residues
—*Her* memories of past performance? Cues?—
Whereby the curtain on a triple thud
Has risen. It's the theatre in our blood.

[M, p. 109]

In a lyric vein here, Merrill has created a theatrical equivalent for the
epiphanic suspensions of song and dance: "Gone, she endured."
But the lyric continues to find a literal equivalent for the "theatre in
our blood" in a museum model for the DNA molecule: a brilliant
metaphor for Sarah Bernhardt's descending wand:

22.vii. Boston Museum of Science
Studying a model (2.5
Cm. per angstrom) of the DNA
Molecule—a single turn blown up
Tall as a child. My ignorance reduced
To jotting down—red, blue, black, yellow, white—
Colors of the bit-player beads, the carbons
And nitrogens all interlinked, on pins
But letter-perfect, purines, pyrimidines,
Minute intelligences that indwell
The chromosome and educate the cell . . .

> Even grossly simplified, as here,
> It's too much. Who by reference to this
> 3-D Metro map's infernal skeins
> And lattices could hope to find his way?
> Yet, strange to say, that's just what everyone
> On Earth is promptly known for having done.
>
> [*M*, p. 109]

As if this lyric virtuosity were not enough, a third metaphorical level is applied in the succeeding stanza as DJ is "wheeled up from surgery":

> "There was this kind of
> Slow green climbing, and all round me lights
> Higher and higher . . . "
>
> [*M*, p. 110]

In fact, there is such abundant lyricism here that the reader could easily miss the museum's model DNA molecule as dead center for Merrill's imagery of the unfurling of icons and procreation both. A radical metaphor for the entire trilogy even in regard to the model's plasticity: a Shakespearean, tightly knit web of complex organic imagery![24] This section is halfway between the reduction to an icon and the limitless refraction of those icons of Merrill's lyric and epic voices. Of course, a close reading of the poem reveals just about every fraction within that wide spectrum.

The background music for Gabriel's masque—as much an ecstasy of transience as Michael's—is Stravinsky's *The Rake's Progress* ("SIDE TWO, BAND ONE"), which reminds us of the failure of Anne Truelove to reform the hero. This sense of failure—the absence of moral regeneration, a light, greyish cloud of suicidal thoughts—reveals itself through the camp humor only after many readings of the epic. But it is a tone that seems to become increasingly important, and I want to discuss it briefly.

As Dante well knew—and represented graphically in his *Commedia*—violence against the self can take a physical form (suicide) or a moral one (a Faustian pact with evil). For the poet of "CHILD-LESSNESS" with his eyes turned "OUTWARD TO THE LESSONS & THE MYSTERIES" the question is a little academic. What is the significance of personal suicide in the shadow of an abnegation of posterity? And "THE LESSONS & THE MYSTERIES" are certainly beyond ordinary good and evil. Nevertheless, suicide is specifically discussed in connection with one of the poet's "quintessential" spirits, Maria Mitsotáki, and it continues to haunt him in his final pages:

> 6:00. Stone and words. The balustrade
> Pressing back the harder I press down.
> Three-story drop. A cat stares up in dread.
> Faces streaking through me of the dead,
> Traffic whizzing—how the old motor races!
> How simply, too, the urge is gratified:
> Just shut the eyes . . .
>
> [S, p. 232]

This lyric meditation goes on to flower in a transposition of the past and the future through, this time, the rearview mirror and headlights of cars:

> But here inside my head
> No question of total blackout. Lights all along
> Following closely, filling the rear-view mirror,
> Forcing upon whichever of us drove
> Illumination's blindfold—those lights now gather
> Speed to pass. Our own weak dashboard aura,
> Our own poor beams that see no further than needed
> Will have to guide us through the homeward ride.
> Still not alone. Despite the Doppler drop in pitch,
> That disappearing car will make things round the bend
> Shine eerily, a tree, an underpass of bone;
> Or else a dip between hills miles from now
> Will glow in recollection—
> As DJ
> Takes his place, beyond words, at my side.
>
> [S, pp. 232–233]

Memory—"recollection"—is the proper final note here: the time modality of lyrical poetry into which Merrill has lapsed. In fact, Gabriel's masque concluded with the poet's most poignant memory of the triadic tragedy of his childhood:

> Between an often absent or abstracted
> (In mid-depression) father and still young

Mother's wronged air of commonsense the child sat.
The third and last. If he would never quite
Outgrow the hobby horse and dragon kite
Left by the first two, one lukewarm noodle
Prefigured no less a spiral nebula
Of further outs. Piano practice, books . . .
A woman speaking French had joined their sunstruck
Looking-glass table.

[S, p. 213]

The Faust myth, among several allusions, has a section to itself—
Mirabell, Book 2—in which Merrill blends if not coalesces the Faust
and Pope Innocent vi myths in order to allow himself the pun
"Faust was Innocent." But both suicide and Faust are forcibly and
not so innocently present in the diluted lyricism—Merrill's willing
surrender of his poetic will—which is such a constant feature of
Comedies.

And maddening—it's all by someone else!
In your voice, Wystan, or in Mirabell's.
I want it mine, but cannot spare those twenty
Years in a cool dark place that *Ephraim* took
In order to be palatable wine.
This book by contrast, immature, supine,
Still kicks against its archetypal cradle.

[M, p. 167]

A darker side of this surrender of poetic will and its modality of
memory is the recurring importance of forgetting, which I have
already discussed in connection with theodicy. It is one thing for a
minor character like DJ's father to celebrate forgetting in light tones:
"BUT LIFES JOB IS TO FORGET / FOR THOSE OF US NOT SPECIAL" (M, p.
14). But like God B's rueful glances at the black spaces of universes
beyond his control, Michael's articulation of his function is rather
more haunting:

'SON MICHAEL SHEDDER OF LIGHT, REFLECTOR, NOW HELP MAN
    FORGET'
AND SO MY THIRD NATURE: SLEEP, THE REPOSE FROM DAYLIGHT TO
    DAYLIGHT.

[S, p. 64]

No less haunting are the final notes at Sandover of "the school-room empty" and "condemned building":

> —Leaving the schoolroom empty. Never to be
> Realized again with such fidelity?
> The big old globe, each mooned-over pastel
> Nation in place and river legible;
> Grain of each desk-top; the minute sky-grid
> Sliding across an inkwell's cut-glass lid;
> Chintz roses bleached and split; chalk mote arrested
> In mid-descent by sun; the horseshoe rusted
> To scabby lace, nailed between sepia 'School
> Of Athens' and Ignoto's 'The Pure Fool';
> Moot intercourse of light and shade above
> Our heads, familiar shapes we've learned to love
> Emerging this last time from the cracked ceiling
> As if they too shared the unspoken feeling
> That once we've gone, nobody else will thumb
> The pages of our old Curriculum.
> The manor is condemned. One doesn't dare
> Say so flatly, but it's in the air.
> The fine italic hands that have to date
> Etched the unseen we blankly contemplate
> Must now withdraw . . .

[S, p. 200]

Condemned buildings have long been an image Merrill uses for transience, but rarely as beautifully as here. If we wanted to locate an archetype for these condemned buildings Valhalla would do, and in the epic we find it reflected in the soprano voice:

> However a wrong turn
> Discovers where the Master of the Ring
> Once dwelt, the same who made Brünnhilde spurn
>
> Heaven's own plea, ecstatically cling
> To death-divining love, while the sky-folk
> —Scene I, so help me, first heard Flagstad sing—
>
> Touched by her tones' pure torch, go up in smoke.

[DC, p. 125]

Memoria and amnesia, epic refraction and lyric epiphanies, "Yes" and "No," free will and cloning, melodic line and harmonic structure: there are many dichotomies in the trilogy, and as with most dichotomies in literature they are manifestations of a troubled spirit. Although the work's major premise is Merrill's surrender of his poetic will in favor of the voices who propound the doctrine of a mechanistic, controlled, and cloned universe, there is a pull in the opposite direction toward the exercise of free will. Merrill provides another tantalizing analogy with Dante in *Mirabell*, Book 6, when he is remembering the death agonies of his friend Maria Mitsotáki:

> Oh Maman—
> POSO AKOMA (her last words, "How much more?")
> I CROAKED NOT TO POOR LOUROS BUT THE RAYS:
> HOW MUCH MORE WD THEY TAKE FROM ME B4 . . .
> (This is the point, I later tell DJ,
> When Dante would have fainted dead away.
> But cloned with minerals, heartsick, eyes red,
> I see no way out but to forge ahead.)
>
> [*M*, p. 114]

Dante's acceptance of Augustinian theodicy's doctrine of free will and all its awesome responsibilities for individual salvation paradoxically allows him the escape of those three fainting spells in the *Commedia*. In a rational universe, controlled by one beneficent deity, temporary individual absence is an affordable luxury. The world goes on "travailing towards perfection."[25] But when presence is robbed of posterity, when there is no doctrine of a monistic beneficence, there are no luxuries. There is "no way out but to forge ahead." This is a weary, a moving, indeed, a heroic tone more a part of the essence of *Comedies* than of its surface. While God B calls for oblivion, JM remembers his plea, and while his poem rejects Judeo-Christian theodicy, it seems to ache longingly after it as the poem aches after the mysteries of that female voice. A recurring image is that of dual vision reduced to a single glass:

> TRUE, FROM ONE END OF THE SPYGLASS
> And from the other?
>
> [*S*, p. 209]

If the two are thus accommodated to the one, Merrill's obsession with refraction, numerology, and correspondences seems equally an accommodation of the many to the one. As varied as the poem's doubles, fives, twelves, and 12:88 ratios may be, they all refer to "Number" in the singular. I can think of nothing in literature since or before Calderón's *Autos Sacramentales* as elaborate as *Comedies'* correspondences of spiritual, human, animal, vegetable, and mineral worlds. "Samos," the jewel-like centerpiece of *Scripts*, is one of the few lyric expressions worthy of comparison with Calderón's absolute mastery of lyric-dramatic correspondence. Indeed, the kinship of Merrill's epic to Calderón's religious masques is remarkable. For Calderón, the *Autos* were very consciously a vehicle for the theodicean doctrine of monistic beneficence. And Merrill—possibly through Shelley—remembers more of them than he is able to admit. What he has chosen to forget is that an endemic aspect of Calderón's *Autos*—as of all literature concerned with the problems of theodicy—is the Augustinian exercise of free will toward the *regeneration* of the hero.

From the myopic present, it is difficult to tell whether the troubled spirit of Merrill's *Comedies* is an aspect of that "disunity" in great works about which John Bayley has written so cogently,[26] or whether it is the result of an unfelicitous joining of lyric and epic modalities. In discussing recent failures of American foreign policy, a *New York Times* editorial observed that while it was permissible for individuals to have attitudes a government must exercise policy. A similar distinction between the private and the public holds for lyric and epic poetry. What seems to me clear about Merrill's apocalyptic epic is that the essentially lyrical epiphanies in which the two and the many are accommodated to the one are not sufficient answers for a work of epic scope to what has always been and remains man's most serious theological and philosophical concern: the problem of evil.

Poetry and doctrine? Well, in apocalyptic epic poetry, yes! One has only to compare the way doctrine allows each ledge—each step—of Dante's *Purgatorio* to be an inverse mirror reflection of the ridges of his *Inferno* and how these ledges and ridges are—again, step by step—remembered and forgotten in a triumphant exercise of free will in his *Paradiso,* to compare this with the uneven contours of Merrill's trilogy.

All the familiar subjects of Merrill's lyric poetry are present in the trilogy: biography, nature, the particularities of time and place (especially his several homes), the adventures of travel, the stages of love and death, the ecstasies and agonies of encounter and departure, and the memory of literature and the other arts. What is new is the doctrine of a Manichaean, monitored universe, as well as the camp tonality in which it is rendered. It might be very rewarding to read the poem as Merrill's camp response to the idea of translating the archetype of man's epic quest toward a beneficent and omnipotent God into "a poem of science."

4

In approaching a conclusion to this essay on Merrill's extraordinary work, I was haunted by various thoughts that wouldn't quite come into focus. Didn't the spyglass image remind me of some pre-Dantesque, medieval definition of God which involved two circles reduced to a unity? Does Merrill's surrender of his own lyric voice in favor of his mediums prevent his poem from being one of the modern masterpieces of epic literature? And does the history of literature instruct us about the possibilities and dangers of revoicing? Must the poet's sacrifice of life to art be so painfully tragic? If so, does the world's accumulated wisdom offer any balm for this particular wound? And in connection with Merrill's final longing for a world in which a mirror can be simply a piece of furniture, I wondered whether it were possible to present the weighty concerns of theology, religion, and philosophy—so important to the trilogy—in a mode closer to Merrill's genius for the lyric expression of human relationships?

In my frustration at not being able to resolve these questions, I decided to adopt Merrill's Ouija board method.[27] Here is what a voice, identifying itself as "BOTH THE CENTER AND THE CIRCUMFERENCE OF THE COSMOS," communicated:

ON ITS MOST SERIOUS LEVEL, MERRILL'S CAMP EPIC IS HIS POETICS. TOWARD THAT END, HE SHOULD REVOICE ALL SECTIONS INTO HIS OWN LYRIC MODES. BUT ONLY AFTER EXPOSING TO THE CHANGING LIGHTS AT SANDOVER:

1 CALDERÓN'S AUTOS SACRAMENTALES WHERE ALL CORRESPON-
DENCES AND RELIGIOUS DOCTRINES ARE POETICALLY DOMESTICATED
TO THE GAME OF THEATRICAL PAGEANT.

2 TASSO'S ORIGINAL AND THEN REVISED GERUSALEMME LIBERATA SO
AS TO KNOW HOW TO PLAY BACKWARDS TASSO'S PROCESS OF RUIN-
ING A GREAT EPIC POEM THROUGH THEOLOGICAL REVISION.

3 SAINT AUGUSTINE ON THEODICY WHERE THE RELATIONSHIP BETWEEN
GOOD AND EVIL IS THE WILL INVOLVED IN WHAT ONE CHOOSES TO
REMEMBER AND TO FORGET.

4 KING LEAR WHERE THE MULTIPLICITY OF THE WORLD'S RELIGIOUS
DOCTRINES ARE DOMESTICATED IN A FAMILY DRAMA ABOUT THE
CONSECRATION OF SHARED SUFFERING, FOCUSING THE VAST COS-
MOS ON AN INDIVIDUAL BREATH OF LIFE BETWEEN FATHER AND
DAUGHTER.

CHAPTER 9

The Names of God:
Scripts for the Pageant

Stephen Yenser

Some twenty-five years ago, without an inkling of the prodigious consequences, James Merrill and his friend David Jackson contacted the other world by means of the Ouija board. For a couple of decades thereafter, they communicated primarily with a witty, kind, and surprisingly sensuous spirit, the eponymous hero of "The Book of Ephraim," the first volume in Merrill's recently completed trilogy. After telling them what he knew of the empyrean, putting them in touch with various dead loved ones, and becoming a dear friend himself, Ephraim eventually gave way to certain chiropteran superiors, who identified themselves as "THE SONS OF CAIN" and claimed to speak "FROM WITHIN THE ATOM." These bizarre figures turned the next round of Ouija sessions, which we heard about in *Mirabell: Books of Number*, into seminars intended to prepare JM to write "POEMS OF SCIENCE" that would advance their own project: the creation of Paradise on Earth. In this "v WORK," which they undertook as penance for destroying a prehistorical Arcadian civilization, they cooperate with "THE 5," an elite group of immortals whose avatars help to shape the course of history, and report to their overseers, the angels (also known as "THE 12" and "THE 12 PER CENT"), who are in turn responsible to God Biology, the presiding power in our sector of the universe and a member of the intergalactic "PANTHEON."

Just as in the second volume the shades of their friends Maria

Mitsotáki and W. H. Auden joined the two mortals in the class-
room while Ephraim was replaced by Mirabell and his colleagues,
so in *Scripts for the Pageant* new students arrive and even more
imposing instructors take over at Sandover—the name, we discover,
of this little academy founded by God B and his complex twin,
Nature/Psyche/Chaos. From time to time the new teachers, the
angels themselves, correct and supplement Mirabell's notions of
things. His obsessively applied 12:88 ratio is a "FAULTY READ-OUT,"
for example, and the Muses, when they appear, remind one less of
his "GOLDEN / CONTAINERS" than of petulant dancing girls haled for
the visitors' sake into the sheik's tent. As for UFOs, which Mirabell
worried might be scouts for alien powers, they are the angels'
"TEASPOONS TESTING THE SOUPY ATMOSPHERE." Unlike their counter-
parts the bats, the angels seem infallible in what they know, but
they do not know all. "MUCH HERE IS PURE & SIMPLE MYSTERY," one
of the new, highly placed sources tells us—and at the same time
tells us, although we do not realize it until we get to the recently
published "Coda," how some of that "MYSTERY" resolves itself.

Meanwhile, the angels: they turn out to be four brothers, one
for each of the elements, but then each of them has three natures,
so poor, chagrined Mirabell was not entirely wrong about "THE
12." No one who has followed Merrill's catoptrics this far will be
surprised to find that these four, introduced one by one in succes-
sive orientation sessions, divide into pairs. Thus we have Michael,
"the Angel of Light," and Gabriel, "the Angel of Fire and Death,"
coupled by a tension born of their equally powerful and seemingly
antipodal natures. "AIRY MICHAEL," God B's favorite, is the most
extroverted and charitable of the four, and it appears at first that he
runs the show. Patient, warm, gentle, blessed with a sense of
humor, he radiates sublime intelligence unalloyed with mere per-
sonality. A stunned WHA describes his entrance:

> WE LOOKED UP:
> A GREAT ORIGINAL IDEA   A TALL
> MELTING SHINING MOBILE PARIAN SHEER
> CUMULUS MODELED BY SUN TO HUMAN LIKENESS.
> IN SUCH A PRESENCE WHO COULD EXERCISE
> THE RIGHTS OF CURIOSITY: HAIR? EYES?

> O IT WAS A FACE MY DEARS OF CALM
> INQUIRING FEATURE   FACE OF THE IDEAL
> PARENT CONFESSOR LOVER READER FRIEND
> & MORE, A MONUMENT TO CIVILIZED
> IMAGINATION . . .
>
> [S, p. 4]

The poet among the angels, Michael shows a suitable fondness for rhyming the word "DAY" (and "JOUR"). His moods run mainly from joviality through playful indulgence. (He teases WHA about the latter's comment on angelic enjambment: "TOO MODERN? EVEN BAD? . . . RUNOVER, HMM. THAT'S A WHOLE NEW DIMENSION.") But he can also speak with grave eloquence, as when he addresses Gabriel as "RED SOLEMN THOUGHT, O DECIMATOR, / CHAOS FROZEN INTO ORDER, WINTER."

The volatile Gabriel strikes one as more human, which is both fitting and paradoxical, since he is "YOUR BLOOD, YOUR LIFE, AND YES, ALAS, (pause, then a volley of cold fire) YOUR DEATH." Evidently kind enough by nature—legend has it that Gabriel diverted the stream to free St. Theodore's mother, we learned in section X of "Ephraim"—he must see to both the individuals and the species who have outlived their usefulness, and his dreadful responsibility has bred in him a cynicism that he masks with captivating shyness. He is God B's "SENIOR SON"—Justice, or perhaps Necessity, to the sunny Grace of Michael, who characteristically softens his features: "THE SHY BROTHER IS, LIKE HIS FATHER GOD, BENEVOLENT. / BOTH SHIELD THE FLAME OF HUMAN LIFE & WHEN WASTED TALENT / MAKES THE FLAME GUTTER, GOD TURNS AWAY HIS FACE. THE SHY ONE / PUFFS JUST ONCE"[1] (S, p. 32). If Michael is "A GREAT ORIGINAL IDEA," Gabriel's special province is thought, and thought, MM observes, destroys ideas. But whether Michael or Gabriel ranks higher remains an unresolved issue—and, finally, a false one.

Emmanuel (or Elias) and Raphael (or Elijah), the angels of the other two elements, water and earth respectively, are even more closely related, as the similarity between their alternative names suggests. Fortunately for the poem, neither has the distinctiveness or the force of Michael or Gabriel, though each speaks and provides occasions for some of this volume's finest "word-painting." Here is MM on Emmanuel's first appearance:

FIRST MICHAEL IN HIS GLORY
THEN HE TURNED & A SHAFT! A RAINBOW SPOKE
& AS WE KNELT IN WONDER MELTED INTO
WHITE CLOUD WHICH NEXT GREW SOLID How baroque!
A GIANT ALL HOAR & SPIKY ICE   A HISS
OF HAIL & OUR BLUE ROBES CLUNG WETLY TO US!
ELIAS ROSE IN A TALL DAZZLING VAPOR
& MICHAEL'S LAUGHTER MADE ALL HEAVEN QUAKE

[*S*, p. 20]

The grandeur and brilliance of such passages distinguish the pre-
dominantly visionary mode of *Scripts* from what JM, with a glance
at the history of Greek drama, calls "the black / Fustian void of
Mirabell, against which / At most one actor strutting in costume /
Tantalized us with effects to come, / And the technician of the
dark switchboard / Tone by tone tried out his rainbow chord."
More practiced by now, that "technician" comes up with some of
the most breathtaking inventions in recent poetry. JM can set them
down the more easily, if I can put it that way, because he discards
early in *Scripts* the method used in *Mirabell* and exemplified in the
reports quoted above: "why need we—just because / It 'happened'
that way—wait till end of scene / For Wystan and Maria's mise-en-
scène?" Instead, he will "now and then incorporate / What David
and I don't see (and they do) / Into the script," while "Italics can
denote / Their contribution."

What "they" see, in this schoolroom equipped with spectacular
teaching aids that project "against nothingness" vividly evanescent
environments, often makes one speculate on the future of cine-
matic special effects. Take this key setting for one early lesson:

The schoolroom stretches to a line. It breaks
Cleverly into two floating poles
Of color that in dark 'air' glow and pulse,
Undulate and intertwine like snakes.
Whatever road we travel now, this twinned
Emblem lights, and is both distant guide
And craft we're sealed hermetically inside,
Winged as by fever through the shrieking wind.

[*S*, p. 54]

"ALL THINGS ARE DONE HERE IF U HAVE TECHNIQUE," MM joked in
Mirabell. In this instance, technique permits the uncanny vehicle

that transports our students to be the very art that creates it. Those two aspects of the *"craft"* can no more be separated than can this passage's import and form. The rhyme scheme, a *"twinned / Emblem"* itself, with its own fusion and fission, its coupled and split rhymes, intertwines with the unity in duality that is its subject. These quatrains gain a special resonance from WHA's later irreverent reflection on the angels' private name for God, "ABBA," which reminds him of "ONE OF JM'S FAVORITE RHYME SCHEMES"—but more of the metaphysics of Merrill's poetry, or the poetics of his philosophy, soon enough.[2]

Scripts contrasts with *Mirabell* also in its cleaner, more classical structure. At one point, Plenorios, the architect of the now delapidated Temple of Artemis at Ephesus, outlines his aesthetic for DJ and JM. WHA, forced to paraphrase ideas that yield only "Broad 'visionary' movements of the cup," tells them that Artemis appeared to Plenorios in a dream, offered him her breasts, one of which represented "PROPORTION" and another "SPLENDOR," and said that she wanted to be sheltered "IN GRAND / & SIMPLE BEAUTY." Just as Merrill's own work in large part honors Mother Nature, another goddess whose "proper sphere is the earth, and specifically the uncultivated parts, forests and hills" and who is also the twin of a sun god, so his design emulates the Greek architect's.[3] It makes sense, then, both that JM gives his "Full concurrence" to the proposition that *"The House / Is Mother"* and that Gabriel designates the alphabet the "MATERIALS" for a "NEW FAITH" whose "ARCHI-TECTURE IS THE FLAT WHITE PRINTED PAGE." Its own *"edle Einfalt und stille Grösse"* notwithstanding, however, Merrill's structure calls little enough attention to itself, hidden as it is by continual references to day-to-day life.

As in "Ephraim," the foreground events in *Scripts* take place in about a year. Prominent among them is the composition of *Mirabell,* which goes on at the same time that JM accumulates material for *Scripts.* Early on, during the fall of what must be 1976, while JM is in Stonington, we find him at work on the second volume, quarrying "from the transcript murky blocks / Of revelation, now turning a phrase / To catch the red sunset, now up at dawn / Edging into place a paradox" (*S,* pp. 15–16). By February, after he has returned from a month in Athens, "*Mirabell*—by now more Tower of Babel / Than Pyramid—groans upward, step by step," and it occurs to him "to make each book's first word its number / In a different language."[4] In May he flies back to Athens, where he remains (except for one trip to Samos and Ephesus in the summer and another to Venice in September) until this volume ends, sometime in October. Early in the summer, when we have got almost halfway through *Scripts*, he approaches the end of *Mirabell*. This last reference to that volume, occasioned by the death of an old friend, Robert Morse, characteristically entangles past with future and fact with fiction:

> Well, Robert, we'll make room. Your elegy
> Can go in *Mirabell*, Book 8, to be
> Written during the hot weeks ahead;
> It's only fiction, that you're not yet dead.
>
> [*S*, p. 94]

And of course it was back in 8.8 (where the echo of Mirabell's charmed number perhaps "foretold" the end of his life) that Morse made his first and last appearance as a living person in the trilogy. A delightful and inspired device, this inclusion of the previous volume's composition among the events in this one decoys the skeptical intelligence (just as JM's dissatisfactions in *Mirabell* anticipated it) and lends an air of immediacy to *Scripts*.

But there is nothing slapdash about the book's governing design. Once more taking his cue from the Ouija board, Merrill divides this volume into three parts, entitled (and beginning) "Yes," "&," and "No." The nearly equal first and third sections enclose a slightly shorter middle section (whose two set pieces, "Samos" and "The House in Athens," neatly frame its conversations with the other world). Merrill enforces this symmetry by giving "Yes" and "No" ten lessons each, while "&" has only five. To describe this structure in one way that has ramifications for the content of this volume, whose central question is once more whether humanity can save itself from destruction, "Yes" and "No" mirror one another. In other words, the middle section is a "bridge" that JM suspects "Can . . . be crossed both ways" or the center of a scales in which "Yes" and "No" are the pans in equipoise. In view of the significance it invests in the image, we might even say that the poem resembles an hourglass, which gets turned over once the sand has run through the neck to one of the interchangeable bulbs. Sandover. In this context, the very name of the academy suggests inversion and reversibility. But here again metaphysics begins to creep, like the deserts JM reads about (where else but in *Time*?), into adjacent fields.

Each of the three sections turns on its set of lessons, and the sets of lessons come at nicely judged different points. In "Yes," discussions in the wake of Michael's entrance and then the introductions of the angels precede "The First Lessons," which are followed only by the brief postmortem the students customarily conduct among themselves after a seminar ends. "The Middle Lessons" in "&," in contrast, prefaced by "Samos" and assorted extracurricular activities and succeeded by more socializing and "The House in Athens," come precisely in the middle. "No" completes the pattern by turning around the arrangement in "Yes." Introduced only by a verse paragraph of stage directions, "The Last Lessons" come early and then give way to a series of postgraduate activities (including the time-honored trip "abroad" and a grand "Finale").

This gracefully balanced structure must be considered along with the internal organizations of the sets of lessons. Each trimester builds to what seems a high point in the penultimate lesson and then continues to a second sharply different but more truly climactic point in the last. (The essential differences among the sets of lessons, from a structural point of view, derive from the "ELE-VATOR" principle: at the end of each set DJ and JM have risen to a higher level of understanding.) In "Yes," for example, a festive party attended by the most distinguished shades culminates in the ninth lesson in a miniature silver jubilee, during which the other-worldly guests get to see themselves wondrously multiplied in different colors by means of "'sense / Prisms' conferred on them by Michael" and to hear a fifth "Last Song" by Strauss sung by Flagstad. Lesson 10 throws this gala into relief and surpasses it in drama. There the mediums abruptly discover WHA and MM adrift in a "*bitter-black and vast*" sea of absence, "RISING RISING INTO

. . . A VOID & HOWL" we soon understand to be God B's own dark
night of the soul, while at the board DJ and JM pick up a transmis-
sion from a "galactic radio"—an eerie ten-line message in decasyl-
labics, addressed to his brothers in the Pantheon by God B him-
self, who proclaims repeatedly and at first enigmatically that "I
AND MINE HOLD IT BACK AND WE SURVIVE." Their experience of
"THE BLACKNESS" so shocks WHA and MM that they must be re-
vived by Mirabell, who "STOOD BRAVELY BY WITH SMELLING SALTS &
ST / BERNARD FLASK."

Similarly, in "&" the astonishing appearance in Lesson 4 of the
Muses (who perform a sort of anti-masque that parodies the cele-
brations in "Yes," 9 and "No," 9) pales beside the entrance in
Lesson 5 of Nature/Psyche/Chaos in the second, most demure of
her aspects:

> Enter—in a smart white summer dress,
> Ca. 1900, discreetly bustled,
> Trimmed if at all with a flowering black bow;
> Black ribbon round her throat; a cameo;
> Gloved but hatless, almost hurrying
> —At last! the chatelaine of Sandover—
> A woman instantly adorable.
>
> [S, p. 125]

There follows one of the most important revelations in *Scripts*, as
Psyche discloses God B's thoughts on "DUALITY" at the time of the
creation. Finally, Lesson 9 in "No" presents a glorious fete *cum*
masque for which Nature has the grounds at Sandover utterly
transformed:

> MICHAEL, FROM YOUR BOREALIS
> MAKE FOR US A SHINING PALACE!
> ON THIS CLAY GROUND, EMMANUEL,
> A SHIMMERING LAKE, A WISHING WELL!
> NOW GREEN TREES HUNG WITH UNCUT GEM,
> YOU RAPHAEL, SEE TO THEM!
> AND FOR FANCY'S SAKE A CHANDELIER,
> GABRIEL, HANG UP HERE & HERE!
>
> [S, pp. 201–202]

Soon MM enters on an ecstatic unicorn, Yeats delivers an enco-
mium, and Nature grants selected wishes out of hand. (She com-

mands that DJ and JM never be separated, gives Ephraim back his vision, and quenches the "nuclear fire-ache" in Mirabell's eyes and installs him henceforth in her own garden.) Nothing could rival such revelry—except a visit by God B. And in Lesson 10 God B speaks directly to the mortals for the only time.

These three twin pinnacles, located at approximately equal intervals and toward the volume's center, each affording a grander view than the last, provide for much of the "PROPORTION" and "SPLENDOR" in the last part of the trilogy. The different locations of the lessons within the sections serve other structural ends as well. Just as the delay of the introductory lessons until late in "Yes" keeps that first climax from coming too soon after Michael's initial, awe-inspiring appearance, so the placing of the concluding lessons early in "No" separates their epiphanies from the affecting denouement of the plot which the poem has been developing.

The plot that I have in mind involves the fortunes of those spirits whom DJ and JM knew as people. In addition to Maria Mitsotáki and Auden, these spirits now include Robert Morse and George Cotzias. Although Maria Callas, Vladimir Nabokov, Robert Lowell, and other notables also drop in shortly after their deaths, these two are the only other shades admitted to the little class. Cotzias (or Kotzias, in stricter transliteration) is the Greek-American research biologist Merrill met through his sister. Toward the end of *Mirabell*, JM feared that Cotzias, who had become "Gravely ill" in the course of developing a hormone to prevent aging, might be among those "CERTAIN HIGHLY CLONED / SCIENTIST SOULS forced back from the frontier" by the overseeing powers, loath to let humanity advance too quickly. Exactly so. When JM last sees him in the hospital early in *Scripts,* Cotzias assures him that he will "Turn up" in Athens—but it is only thanks to the board that he does so. Meanwhile, owing to a high level black bag job, his theorem for immortality, which he gave to JM, gets stolen and "FILED SAFELY" in the other world until its time has come. Like MM, who we were told in *Mirabell* would return to Earth in some vegetable form, and like WHA, who we learn early in this poem will come back in mineral form, GK spends his vacation preparing for reentry, when his energies will somehow be distributed among "18 LABS THRU-

OUT THE WORLD." Until then, he eagerly pursues his work ("WE'RE SETTING UP A LAB!"), joins the seminar, and, lest the world go up in flames, helps the others try to justify the dubious ways of man to the angels.

So does Robert Morse. Back in *Mirabell*, in the "elegy" touched on above, he foresaw the course that DJ and JM would follow. He took his leave of them on the Feast of the Assumption with a blend of sly blasphemy, coy self-deprecation, and shrewd advice all his own:

> "Today
>
> We celebrate Maria's Himmelfahrt
> And yours. You're climbing, do you know how high?
> While tiny me, unable to take part,
>
> Waves you onward. *Don't look down.* Good-bye."
>
> [*M*, p. 162]

What RM, as he was shortly to become, did not foresee was that he would play a part in the ascent.

Not that he has really been "unable to take part" before. On the contrary, as the elegy constrained to appear in disguise discreetly attested, he has an intricate relationship to Merrill's poetry, a relationship that illustrates the way in which the work and the life have both fed the flame that Merrill once called "the consuming myth." An accomplished amateur pianist with a gift for outrageous wordplay as well as a penchant for the pseudo baby talk that E. F. Benson parodies in his Lucia novels, RM can be traced back to Andrew in "The Summer People" (*The Fire Screen*)—or rather Andrew can be traced back to Morse, one of the people to whom *Water Street* was dedicated. In *Mirabell*, 8.8, JM called him "Closest of our summer friends in Stonington" and gave him anew a witticism that Andrew had coined in the ballad: "'Ah lads,'" he says of the stack of transcripts that brought forth that poem, "'it's taxed my venerable beads'" ("'Me giddy fwom / Uppercut of too much uppercase'"). JM confirms this connection later in *Scripts* when he records a meeting in the other world between RM and Andrew Marvell ("I called *you* Andrew in 'The Summer People'") and perhaps implies that it was his friend's wit that had suggested the fictional name in the first place. Morse also contributed to "Ephraim," as Merrill hinted in 8.8 when he referred us to a poem by his friend that Auden collected in *A Certain World* under "Spoonerisms." That poem, "Winter Eve," concludes with lines whose elegiac overtones (though not their bawdy) harmonize with Merrill's purposes in 8.8:

> I'll hash my wands or shake a tower
> (a rug of slum? a whiskey sour?)
> water my pants in all their plots,
> slob a male hairy before I seep—
> and dropping each Id on heavy lie,
> with none to sing me lullaby,
> slop off to dreep, slop off to dreep.[5]

"Ephraim"'s "figure in the mirror" (section T), naturally given to reversing things, not only uses this Morse code (coarse mode, he must have said someplace) but also borrows this excerpt's first phrase. For such reasons, one imagines, Merrill cast their brief last encounter in a dramatic terza rima lightly reminiscent of one of Dante's meetings with some dead "master."

When RM reappears in *Scripts* on the other side of the mirror, he has lost none of his piquant wit, as his sulky response to a run-in with an overbearing Pythagoras proves: "HAVE WE A SLASH MARK? LET HIM TAKE THAT / ." He has, however, gained a certain single-mindedness, a capacity for what Ephraim (in his eloquent speech in section Q) called "DEVOTION." Hence, perhaps, his close association with another new character, Uni, a sweet, hornless unicorn (a descendant of the centaurs destroyed by Mirabell's race), who virtually embodies constancy. Hence, too, after an orientation period during which he is excluded from discussions of top-secret matters, RM's emergence as a great composer to be (who will come back to Earth after the other three). Thus when he joins the seminar, the class gains a musical genius, as well as a gifted scientist in the person of GK. The ghastly convenience of it all provokes Merrill to poignant musings on

> The buffeting of losses which we see
> At once, no matter how reluctantly,

As gains. Gains to the work. Ill-gotten gains . . .
Under the skull-and-crossbones, rigging strains

Our craft to harbor, and salt lashings plow
The carved smile of a mermaid on the prow.

[S, p. 94]

But those losses become gains must turn back into losses, more
final losses—for once their friends have returned to this world,
DJ and JM can no longer contact them. They cannot, that is, un-
less we take seriously the rendezvous they schedule with Maria
for 1991—a rendezvous possible only because she is to be reborn,
not "AS A TREE" after all, but as a Punjabi male who will invent,
twenty-seven years later, "A POLLUTION-EATING ANTIGAS." Indeed
it is one of the trilogy's most startling revelations that Maria is "OF
THE FIVE," who, we now discover, are no less than "GODS" them-
selves. Specifically, she is Plato, Nature's "DARLING," and "NEAREST
THE ANGELS."

Someone has laid the groundwork carefully but unobtrusively.
As early as *Mirabell*, 1.3, where she suddenly snatched control of
the teacup from the still intimidating bats (probably, in retrospect,
because they momentarily arrogated the angels' powers to them-
selves), MM had about her a curious air of authority. When Mira-
bell held forth in 5.8 on the continuous mining of "PLATO'S POW-
ERS" and the "GOLDEN / CONTAINERS" that he presumed the Muses
to be, she kept so quiet—"eyes / Lowered while the menfolk theo-
rize"—that DJ and JM thought she had left. Now one can see that
she was biding her time, for as she asks in "No," "HOW . . . WD YOU
HAVE TAKEN IN THE TRUTH?" Throughout *Scripts* DJ and JM are
subtly prepared for the disclosure. In "&" JM regrets that his "chron-
ic shyness / Vis-à-vis 'ideas'" has kept him from seeking out Plato,
and something inspires DJ to guess that "*Wystan is Plato. Has been
all along.*" While they debate whether to tell their friend that they
have guessed his secret, WHA tries to steer them in the right
direction by letting slip that he is on to something himself: MM
"HAS THE (M) SPECIFIC GRAVITY / OF A CULT FIGURE   PUREST GUESS-
WORK   BUT / NO I'LL PUZZLE IT OUT." (Since DJ and JM miss the
point, they cannot detect the gentle irony in his later regret, pro-

voked by reflections on Plato's "PEARLS" of wisdom: "& ME / WITH NO THREAD TO MAKE MM A CHOKER.") Such hints, even though overlooked, justify MM's contribution to the varied refrain in "No"'s beautiful ballade, JM's "SONG OF . . . MISGIVINGS" in response to the upsetting discovery that the mortal being they loved was only a disguise: "Was anyone prepared for it? U WERE." We all were. As WHA asks much earlier, "IS GOD GEORGE ELIOT?"

Dismaying as it is to DJ and JM, MM's unmasking cannot diminish their ultimate loss, especially since (except for one moment during Nature's masque in which she appears proleptically as a "chubby brown young man we've never known, / Dressed in white *Nehru* jacket and puttees") she stays in character for the rest of this volume. Their grief becomes both harder and easier for them to bear when they realize that they themselves—by smashing a mirror, the symbol of communication between the two worlds—will have to break the connection and dispatch MM and their other two friends to earth. This discovery so unnerves them that WHA offers a means of cushioning the blow: "TAKE A BOWL / OF WATER WE CAN SLIP INTO & OUT / WITH A GREAT SPLASH INTO A PLANTED POT." But JM immediately spots the aesthetic problem: "No. Back to flames, back to the green / Rhine go the rings in Wagner and Tolkien. / The poem's logic, though I hate to say, / Calls for the shattering of a glass" (p. 82).

So in the end they adopt DJ's compromise, break a small looking glass into a bowl of water (the "Marble wedge" they use to break it appropriately "stops a door downstairs"), then pour the water into a potted, blooming cassia (the tree of life in one Chinese paradise), which MM discovered in the wild and which was (also) "transported by her." Merrill has put earlier, in "Glimpses of the Future," the few events that follow this incident, and consequently he avoids an anticlimax. These lines come from a set of quatrains, once more rhymed ABBA, near this volume's conclusion:

> Giving up its whole
> Lifetime of images, the mirror utters
>
> A little treble shriek and rides the flood
> Or tinkling mini-waterfall through wet

Blossoms to lie—and look, the sun has set—
In splinters apt, from now on, to draw blood,

Each with its scimitar or bird-beak shape
Able, days hence, aglitter in the boughs
Or face-down, black on soil beneath, to rouse
From its deep swoon the undestroyed heartscape

—Then silence. Then champagne.

[*S*, p. 235]

Thus the relationship with MM, WHA, and GK ends. After a few more lines, Merrill and Jackson, forced to survive their friends once more, sign off with a three-line reprise of God B's own proud, lonely, survivor's message, first heard in Lesson 10 of "Yes," to his brothers in space:

HERS HEAR ME I AND MINE SURVIVE SIGNAL
ME DO YOU WELL I ALONE IN MY NIGHT
HOLD IT BACK HEAR ME BROTHERS I AND MINE

[*S*, p. 235]

At which point metaphysics and physics alike will out.

2

God Biology's relationships to his brothers in the Pantheon and to the "IT" he opposes or withstands are central mysteries in *Scripts*. We learn from MM and the angels that "THE GALACTIC COUNCILS" gave God B, the "'YOUNGEST BROTHER,'" a charter to create life on Earth. According to the angels, the other gods stipulated only that he regard his creation as "'ONE WITH ALL. NOTHING IN IT WILL BE ENEMY TO OUR REALMS.'" As soon as he descended from the Pantheon, however, another, potentially destructive force, "THE BLACK" or "THE MONITOR," also entered the world. Whether God B brought this "FOREIGN GERM" with him or it arrived under its own power, whether his brothers had deceitfully sprinkled it along with the sand on to "THE SEALS OF THE COMPACT" he carried with him or were ignorant of it, whether God B knew that he had received a "TWO-EDGED GIFT" as WHA speculates or did not: these issues baffle even the angels. We get no closer to an answer than in Lesson 10 of "No," where God B summarizes the school year for DJ and JM thus: "MY SON MICHAEL LIT UP YOUR MINDS   MY SON / GABRIEL TURNED THEM TO THE DARK FORCE WE / CONTAIN."

This dark force sometimes seems to be an invading power, as when Gabriel recalls God B's warning that they are "HARD PREST" by "GODS AS POWERFUL" as he from "OTHER GALAXIES." Again, JM equates it with a continuous bombardment of antiparticles that would extinguish life on Earth except that "Our Lord of Light / Darts promptly forward to annihilate" them. The dark force is "kin," he suspects, to "that insane / Presence beyond our furthest green-house pane" which we heard about in *Mirabell*. More often, especially when viewed as the Monitor, this "GREAT OPPOSING FORCE TO MATTER" seems to reside in the heart of the Earth. As Gabriel warns, "BENEATH US . . . IS THE CAPPD VOLCANO." On their field trips to the underworld, the shades in the class approach the raging center of things (at one point identified with the planet's molten core, at another with a subterranean nuclear explosion) and return with harrowing reports. To complicate antimatters even further, while they sometimes associate the dark force with "EMPTINESS," they sometimes believe that "NOTHING" itself paradoxically shields us from "THE OTHER." We cannot even be certain that the dark force is flatly evil. True, Michael says early on that God B "KNEW THE FORCES ARRAYED AGAINST HIM: THE NEGATIVES, THE VOIDS" and "NAMED THEM EVIL." But the term "EVIL" stands out here because it occurs so rarely in this volume, and much later Michael argues that the Monitor is "NOT OUR ENEMY," that it is "NOT AS EASY AS THAT." It is instead "THE REFLEXION, THE UNDOER TO DOING." At another juncture, the Black seems tantamount to "the screen / Of self which forms between God and His creatures," and elsewhere it takes the form of Time.

Obscure or mercurial though this force is, the necessary response to it is nonetheless clear: it must be "contained," as God B puts it in a term reminiscent of the cold war, or "resisted," to use the word that JM and the others resort to time and again. God B's message to his brothers—that eldritch "Song of the blue whale / Alone in space"—assures them simply that "I AND MINE HOLD IT BACK" and that therefore "WE SURVIVE." "MATTER'S VERY NATURE &

ORIGIN ARE THIS RESISTANCE," GK postulates, and JM guesses that "The Greenhouse from the start had been / An act of resistance." Resistance even seems to be the essence of progress, whether in time, space, or thought. "Friction made the first thin consommé / Of all we know" (i.e., the original chemical soup), and MM reveals that the apparent hostility between Michael and Gabriel in the opening lessons was a necessary deception, "MICHAEL'S INSPIRA-TION: / 'ALL GOOD DISCOURSE MUST, LIKE FORWARD MOTION, / KNOW RESISTANCE.'" But then the principle of the value of resistance generates *its* contrary. The impulse to oppose, which JM once glosses as "Nature's gift to man," cuts two ways—as Nature confirms when she answers his question about the role resistance will play in the "Alpha" period, or Paradise: "THE RESISTANCE? NONE." The post-human creature "WILL, YES, SWIM & GLIDE, / A SIMPLER, LESS WILL-FUL BEING. DULLER TOO? / IF SO, IS THAT SHARP EDGE NOT WELL LOST / WHICH HAS SO VARIOUSLY CUT & COST?"

Interpreted that way, this impulse seems virtually a manifesta-tion of the dark force, as it does when WHA identifies one of the oo, Mirabell's master and the blackest of the bats, with "RESIS-TANCE." But that paradox is no problem for this poem—or rather it is the whole problem in small, for the Black contaminates every-thing. GK links it with "THAT IDEA OF DESTRUCTION WHICH RESIDES / BOTH IN MAN & IN THE ACTINIDES." If at the level of human life it shows itself most flagrantly in "THE DULLWITTED, THE MOB, THE IDIOT IN POWER, THE PURELY BLANK OF MIND," at the level of the angels it takes the form of Gabriel, who claims to "SIT ON A BLACK THRONE AT MY FATHER'S RIGHT." JM wonders whether Gabriel is not "Lord of Antimatter," and GK suspects that he might be "THE MONITOR ITSELF," since "IN G'S VOICE I HEARD / THE HUM   THE SUCK THE CONTRADICTING WORD." When Emmanuel boasts that he and his twin buried the two earlier species that succumbed to the dark-ness (a race of creatures on the Chinese plain antedated *Mirabell*'s centaurs) and still strive to "HOLD IT BACK," Gabriel rejoins with a cool, nonplussing "IT?"

Mirabell looks forward to escaping the "BLACK" he comes from when given the run of Nature's garden, but she too has touched pitch. One of her aspects is Chaos, a term that Michael uses for

Gabriel, and GK thinks that she might be Gabriel's mother. In view of WHA's hypothetical distinction "Between NATURAL (PSYCHIC) & UNNATURAL CHAOS," one might presume Nature and Gabriel innocent—but the distinction is so tenuous as to be legalistic. Besides, his later verdict on this relationship is that while Gabriel is "GOD's," he has inherited "HIS MOTHER'S ONE / BLACK OR 'RESISTANT' GENE AS LIAISON / WITH THE CHAOTIC FORCES." Gabriel, who nevertheless aligns himself with the powers that "HOLD IT BACK" in the eighth lesson of "No," refers to the "TWO SIDES OF MATTER" and makes it clear that one is the dark side; and "MATTER," according to Mirabell's unchallenged proposition, is "MATER" or Nature.

Like Gabriel, then, whose ambivalence projects itself as *Fire fighting itself—fire its own screen*," she works in opposing ways. As Melville's Old Miser puts it in *The Confidence Man*: "'Look you, nature! I don't deny that your clover is sweet and your dandelions don't roar; but whose hailstones smashed my windows?'" It is she who insists on the "THINNING" process, the reduction by any convenient means, however repugnant to us, of lives on the increasingly overpopulated Earth. Compare with the charming figure in "&" this harridan, who appears just before MM, WHA, and GK are to return to this world:

> CITIES, FORESTS, THESE WE KNOW ABOUT, MUCH THINNING TO
>   COME IN THE FORMER, BUT JUNGLES!
> WHO CAN COUNT THE LIVES THERE? CAN I? NO, IN A WORD.
>   O THERE'S MUCH TO BE DONE!
> POET THINK ON THAT WHEN YOU GO LIKE A FOX TO EARTH, HAH!
>   & REPORT TO ME, ME!
> NOW COME ALONG MY DEAR, SO SORRY ABOUT INDIA BUT WE CAN'T
>   ALL HAVE DISHWASHERS & ELECTRICAL GADGETS I'M SURE!
> BEAT YOUR SERVANTS, THEY'LL WORSHIP YOU!
> YOU OTHERS, LOOK ALIVE! MUCH TO DO! THE SUMMER TO GET
>   UNDER WRAPS!
>   [S, pp. 224–225]

Granted, this is less the point of view of the Monitor than of the frenetic, tyrannical mistress of the plantation—and her "THINNING" might be justified in terms of some quasi-Augustinian doctrine—but her affinity with destruction inevitably associates Nature with the dark force.

In short, *Scripts* presents us with a dualistic universe, through-out which light and darkness oppose one another. GK tells us that the atom comprises a "BLACK VOLATILE HALF" and a "WHITE HALF, DEPENDABLE," and JM earns his instructors' praise when he asks this question: "When we suppose that history's great worm / Turns and turns as it does because of twin / Forces balanced and alert within / Any least atom, are we getting warm?" (*S*, p. 196). What he calls an "innermost dichotomy" lay at the very heart of God B's blueprint, as Nature discloses when she recalls one early tête-à-tête:

'SISTER, BEFORE I CALL FORTH INHABITANTS OF THIS PLACE,
    LET US PLAN.
WHAT POINT IS THERE IN AN IMMORTAL BEING (THOUGH LESS,
    MUCH LIKE OURSELVES) IF HE CONTAINS NOTHING NEW, NO
    SURPRISE TO CALL HIS OWN?
LET US DIVIDE THE FORCE OF HIS NATURE, JUST AS WE WILL MAKE
    TWO SIDES TO ALL NATURE,
FOR IN DUALITY IS DIMENSION, TENSION, ALL THE TRUE GRANDEUR
    WANTING IN A PERFECT THING.
SISTER, TAKE COMMAND OF HIS . . . RESISTANCE? HIS 'UNGODLY'
    SIDE. MAKE HIM KNOW DARK AS WELL AS LIGHT, GIVE HIM
    PUZZLEMENT, MAKE HIM QUESTION.
FOR WOULD WE NOT LIKE COMPANY?' I AGREED.

                                                [*S*, p. 126]

This passage itself creates a certain "TENSION," since if any god must be judged by his creations, God B must also fall short of "A PERFECT THING." GK raises this last possibility when he toys with the idea that the creation was an act of "DISOBEDIENCE   GOD AS PROMETHEUS"—and so does WHA, when he argues that the "DE-SCENT" from the Pantheon was actually a "F A L L" from "THE GA-LACTIC PRECIPICE."

Whether or not God B has fallen, the poem leads us to believe that he includes his own opposite, that even he knows duality. His allusion to "THE DARK FORCE WE / CONTAIN" is after all as Delphic as anything here, since it might mean not only that he and the angels limit or confine it but also that it exists within them. Early in "No," GK asks provocatively whether it was really God B that DJ and JM heard in Lesson 10 of "Yes." Mightn't it have been "the Black God? God A / For Adversary?" Or the voice of a blindingly "WHITE

REASON" that has driven the truly creative powers into exile in the universe's black holes? Ostensibly, GK still distinguishes one god from the other, but his theorizing, with its transposition of black and white imagery, has the effect of yoking them together, and we must wonder whether God B and God A are not different names for the same power. Every elementary particle, modern physics teaches, has a corresponding antiparticle: electron and positron, neutron and antineutron, and so on. In the case of the photon, however, the particle is its own antiparticle; and while God B sheds the "*Light*" at the beginning of "No," the Monitor itself later appears to WHA as "A PURE / WHITE LIGHT, THE NEGATIVE OR 'EYE' OF BLACK." In other words, B might also stand for Black—and God B refers to Gabriel as his own "'DARKER SIDE.'"

Consider too that name the angels use among themselves for God B: "ABBA." Now "Abba" is New Testament Aramaic for "Father" (i.e., God), but it suggestively combines the two significant initials. A palindromic word, it mirrors itself. Because this is the sort of linguistic event that enchants both Islamic mystics and the poet of "Syrinx" and "Dreams about Clothes" (*Braving the Elements*), it is no surprise to find Merrill intrigued by the notes on symbolic calligraphy which WHA has picked up from a "SLOEEYED SUFI (13 CENT)." Meditating just before the fourth lesson in "No" on an ornate version of the Arabic phrase "*Bismillah* ('in the name of Allah')," JM points out that the non-Arabic or "backward reader" of the script will find "*Ism* (world of names, empty phenomena) / Within the broadly tendered palm of *ba*," its first letter. *Its* "Initial meaning," he continues, is "God B knows what." Why, precisely— not only because God B is that palm, but also because *ba* combines B (Biology or Black) with A (Adversary or Allah).[6]

No matter which of the elements in Merrill's universe we analyze, we end up fumbling at yin and yang, whose inextricable workings Chinese philosophy supposes to produce all things. If "Abba" can be simplified to *ba*, so *ba* can be reduced to that letter's diacritical mark, to which JM's lyrical explication of *Bismillah* pays special attention. A mere subscript dot, it is God's protective hand in the form of a "fist" closed on all existence. According to the Sufi tradition surely behind JM's lines, this dot "symbolizes Divine Essence itself, the mystery, the abysmal darkness. It is single in itself but embraces all phenomena. With the Sufi, it corresponds to the Heart's centre; it is that to which desire is directed," "the Divine Source," and "the Prototype of the world." In JM's double pun, this "inky star," a tiny synecdoche, is "the Whole Point." In a recent essay on Dante, Merrill draws our attention to two crucial "points" in the *Divine Comedy*: one a virtual "black hole" at the nadir of hell in the *Inferno*, the other the "infinitesimal, intensely brilliant point" that is God in the *Paradiso*. His own "Point" must be "Whole" partly because it combines these other two. Like the atom—"in our day, the point on which all nature and its destruction depend," in Merrill's words—it unites the positive and the negative.[7]

At exactly this point, then, duality can hardly be distinguished from unicity. If all things share duality, mightn't they all be the same thing—or the same indivisible but double force differently manifested? At the same time that dark and light mingle within God B, he pervades existence. It is he "Whose body is Earth. Whose eye—the glowing sun— / Upon the sparrow also is the sparrow," in JM's tentative formulation in "Yes." The angels also seem to be his emanations, as their private name for him perhaps confirms. If we take A and B as symbols, "ABBA" stands for the four brothers, the twin major angels separated, as though by buffers, by the twin minor angels. (Sufism has a rough analogy, for according to one authority, "the four angels Gabriel, Michael, Seraphial, and Azrail correspond to four aspects of the name *Allah*. The four letters ALLH correspond to the mystic's Heart, Intellect, Spirit and Soul."[8]) "DAZZLING TO SET FORTH INITIALLY / THE WHOLE DESIGN," WHA quips—although he has in mind four other letters that represent the angels: MEEK, where K is G because they are "TWINS / PHONETICALLY." He needn't have gone so far afield. Or he might have gone further, since if the meek are to inherit the Earth they must inherit it from their father, Abba.

"Maddening the way / Everything merges and reflects," JM reflects—and his rather delighted complaint anticipates that of the reader searching for even the ghostliest demarcations. God B turns out to be Innocence itself, while his "star-twin" Nature embodies

Idea, but they blur in unexpected ways into Michael (who shares God B's light yet speaks for Idea) and Gabriel (who merges with Chaos but takes the part of Innocence). Then, too, Gabriel's fire gives Michael's light. Other sets of twins include GK and RM ("TWINS SCIENCE & MUSIC"), WHA and JM ("TWIN SCRIBES"), MM and DJ ("MADAME SECRET WEEDER & TWIN SECRET HAND"), not to mention such odd couples as Nefertiti and Plato, and Eurydike and Calypso (the Muses, in this startling version, of tragic and comic drama respectively, who combine to create "LAUGHING GRIEF," which would be one way to describe the tone of this volume's conclusion). Just as JM suspected that the instructors in *Mirabell* were Ephraim in disguise, so now he imagines that Ephraim might have been "our quick-change Michael." "St. Agatha," the mysterious figure whom Maria has assisted all along in cultivating nightmares to be implanted in the minds of politicians, seems in the end to be another name for Nature—but then "Maria" is another name for Plato, and he (or she) turns out to be "ALL NINE" of the Muses, whose mother is Nature (not Mnemosyne, who is instead one of the Muses herself). WHA and MM, *Mirabell*'s "Father of forms and matter-of-fact mother," reflect God B and Nature (MM's initials even condense the matter/mater pun), and they also tend to merge. At least twice, camping it up, WHA refers to himself as "YR MOTHER," and since it is Maria, the mother figure, who emerges as Plato (hitherto associated, like WHA, with mind), one has to wonder whether there was not something to DJ's inkling about WHA after all. It begins to look as though the angels and the shades leave such incipient identifications undeveloped simply out of respect for the dependence of human understanding upon *some* distinctions.

Such insistent fusions and doublings, that is, imply a single, comprehensive union, which gets one of its most explicit and yet compressed treatments in Lesson 9 of "Yes," where Strauss improvises a clever *"four note theme, BDEA,"* for Michael's fete. Perhaps inspired by Bach's famous BACH motif (in which, according to German terminology, H is B natural while B is B flat), Strauss's little theme works out as IDEA (since in our notation B and I would be identical). It follows that *"I come to Be, is the Idea."* And indeed, as "Ephraim" first suggested, it is the idea of the trilogy that humanity and divinity come to themselves through one another, that the race is God B in the process of evolving. That is one aspect of the idea anyway—the Jungian aspect. The other aspect recalls Spinoza or Whitehead, for Strauss's theme further intimates, as the two earlier volumes did on occasion, that if humanity is one name for God, Nature is another.[9] Nature embodies Idea, we remember. Moreover, Strauss's B (or I) makes sense only when joined with the easily translatable DEA. Using the other letter motif, WHA similarly encodes the identity of God B and Nature when he refers to the latter, whom he often calls "QUEEN MUM" or "QM," as "QUEEN M(AB)." It is as though M(AB), BDEA, ABBA, and *ba* were different ways of writing one name.

Not that *Scripts* testifies to the unity of things any less equivocally than to their duality. Like "Ephraim" and *Mirabell*, it everywhere bears witness to Evelyn Underhill's observation:

> The Unconditioned One . . . cannot of itself satisfy the deepest instincts of humanity: for man is aware that diversity in unity is a necessary condition if perfection of character is to be expressed. Though the idea of unity alone may serve to define the end—and though the mystics may return to it again and again as a relief from that "heresy of multiplicity" by which they are oppressed—it cannot by itself be adequate to the description of the All.[10]

JM seems to make the same point in his sonnet on *Bismillah*, when he notes that his "characters, this motley alphabet, / Engagingly evade the cul-de-sac / Of the Whole Point," even as he finds himself "drawn by it." If the ineluctability of diversity helps to account for JM's view of God B, Nature, and the others as entities, its counterpart—the attraction of the One—helps to explain why God B must nonetheless be God A and thus why Nature, who has at least as much say in this matter as he, must balance "Yes" and "No."

Ever since "Ephraim," the crucial question has been whether humanity will survive, in God B's words, to "CREATE . . . A PARADISE," whether we can achieve, in Michael's phrase sung by Flagstad, "THIS HEAVEN IT IS GIVEN YOU TO WIN." The ampersand at the center of the only possible response is the Gordian knot, or Whitman's "old knot of contrariety"—or the untied naught, the "CIPHER" we might still make of ourselves. It is also that bridge that can be crossed both ways, as JM muses just before setting foot upon it, and the subsequent revelations bear him out. Just after the last lesson in "&," as the class moves inexorably toward "No," Nature, in response to the students' anxious pleas, seems to tip "THE SCALE" to "Yes"—to decide to give humanity another chance. To move into "No" is to negate its negation. Or so it seems at first. Anyone who recalls JM's earlier reminder of the positive "meanings / The word 'negative' takes on in *Ephraim*" will be prepared, however, for the mirroring affirmation with negative overtones in "No." It comes at the end of Nature's masque, as the sun sets:

> NOW MARCHING TUNES!
> MICHAEL YOUR RAINBOW LINE, IT IS OUR WISH
> YOU REEL US IN LIKE FLOPPING FISH,
> BUT LET ME CRY A LAST RESOUNDING YES
> TO MAN, MAN IN HIS BLESSEDNESS!

[*S*, p. 207]

WHA teases out the ambiguity, as sly as that in God B's containment speech, a couple of pages later:

> Nature said Yes to man—the question's settled.
> SHE SAYS DEAR BOY E X A C T L Y WHAT SHE MEANS
> LOOK IT UP   "A last resounding Yes."
> LAST? The fête was ending. JM: Or
> Because man won't be hearing Yes much more?
> AH SHE SETS MEANING SPINNING LIKE A COIN.
> HEADS UP? You're asking us? TIP SCALE TO YES
> & ALL'S THE GLINT OF QUEEN M(AB)'S ALLEGRESSE.
> LEAN TOWARD NO, & NO AMOUNT OF SKILL
> WILL KEEP HER IMPS LOCKED UP IN GABRIEL'S SCHOOL.
> *We* do the judging? Everyone? INDEED.

[*S*, p. 210]

God proposes, at best, and man disposes. WHA has said of the angels that "I BELIEVE WE SHALL DISCOVER / THEIR POWERS ARE IN US QUITE AS MUCH AS OVER," and MM's "Sermon at Ephesus" has much the same message: "'PREPARE TO WEAN / YRSELVES OF THE

FATAL DELUSION OF ALLPROVIDING HEAVEN. MAN MUST PROVIDE." At
another point, defending humanity's dangerous "CURIOSITY," she
infers that it must have been inculcated because "WE, MANKIND,
MUST DO / IMMORTAL WORK" and argues that one day when "EARTH
BECOMES / PARADISE" we will emerge as "THE ELDERS IN A RACE OF
GODS." The theme goes back to "Ephraim," along with the image
that occurs to JM when he guesses at humanity's purpose: "To
feed the earthward flow / Of Paradise? That final waterfall . . . "
Late in "No" RM advances his "THEORY . . . THAT PARADISE / ON
EARTH WILL FLOOD EACH EMPTY PIGEONHOLE / OF THE BUREAUCRACY
WITH RADIANCE," and MM and the other two return to their V
work on Earth by means of that "mini-waterfall" at the end. Yet for
all the sanguine predictions, precisely because the future is in hu-
man hands, the scripts must remain plural and the drama's out-
come uncertain. Doubtless because she knows all too well that the
future hangs in the balance, Nature—Queen Mum indeed!—refuses
to read two of her lines in the masque: "'NOW LET US BANISH
GLOOMY DREAMS / FOR HEAVEN ON EARTH MOST LIKELY SEEMS.'"

Frustrated by such paradoxes and intricacies, and in spite of the
richness of such formulas as those noted above, JM finds himself
after Lesson 3 of "No" despairing of "Language's misleading ap-
paratus" and sympathizing with Pound, "Who 'said it' with his
Chinese characters— / Not that the one I need here could be found."
But two such figures do turn up. Gabriel dictates one of these in
Lesson 8 of "No" and draws it in chalk on his blackboard while JM
puts it down in pen, element by element, on his white page. The
finished product looks like this:

The upper X, we learn, represents at once the "IT" of God B's
message, humankind reaching for enlightenment (the figure stands
on the Earth), and an hourglass or Time. The angels do not say,
although they might have, that the X is itself a reflected V, as
though it signified the combined V work of heaven and Earth, with
the point of each V indicating the direction or focus of the labor.

The horizontal line between the "ARMS REACHING UPWARD" repre-
sents the sand in the hourglass, which symbolizes "ANY SURFACE
FUEL" that humankind converts to energy ("NATURAL POWER," as
GK has called it earlier). In the "DOWNWARD ENIGMA" or reflected
X, the "SAND RUNNING UP" represents "DEEP FUELS TAPPD," an "UP-
WARD VOLATILE FORCE" ("UNNATURAL" power, especially petroleum
and atomic power) that threatens to destroy the world and that we
and the angels try to hold back even as the ground bulges with the
pressure from beneath.

The "SAND RUNNING UP," we gather from Lesson 3 of "No," also
indicates "TIME SET RUNNING BACK," or evolution inverted. If souls
like Jesus and Buddha urge us on toward an Earthly Paradise,
those like Caligula and Hitler, hearing "ANOTHER SIREN SINGING,"
lure us toward self-annihilation. By taking to an extreme the task of
"THINNING" which is part and parcel of the creation of Paradise,
the latter have gone over to the Monitor or God A, whose name we
could put beneath the ideogram (the triangle with legs at the bot-
tom *is* an A), just as we could put God B's name above it. And
there we are: one with a symbol doubled against itself, using all
the fuels at our disposal to create Paradise and simultaneously
developing the means to bury ourselves, with time running out
and explosives piling up.

God B supplies the other of these figures in this volume's last
lesson. Taking over the cup himself, he traces out a "Quincunx,"
the salient points of which are Yes, No, A, and Z. The very crux of
the matter, this figure elegantly abstracts Gabriel's reflected hour-
glass, as God B implies in his gloss:

MY UPRIGHT MAN
FULL OF TIME HE STRUGGLES TO HOLD IT BACK
AND CREATE FOR ME A PARADISE I
IN MY OWN UPSTRETCHED ARMS WILL SHOW CRYING
SEE BROTHERS WE HAVE HELD IT BACK SEE SEE
I AND MINE BROTHERS IN OUR DAY SURVIVE

[*S*, p. 212]

"FULL OF TIME": with time to spare, that is? Or handicapped by it?
As JM sees immediately, the closed St. Andrew's cross that God B
draws might represent either "the mark / That cancels, or the letter
writer's kiss," a "Twinbladed axe" or a "Fulcrum and consort to

our willowy &." "Thy word is all, if we could spell," as Herbert has it. Perhaps because we cannot spell, "God B His Mark" also forms "The X / Of the illiterate." Being humanity, that is, God B can hardly read his own nature before completing its creation. Paradoxically, however, his mark must also be one way of writing the All. If the X stands for the unknown, as in algebra, it also stands for the conjunction of divinity and humanity, as in Christianity, and for the intersection of the other world and this one. The various meanings of it all have been there from the outset, then, latent in the board's layout. As a Sufi says of an analogous synecdoche, "The meaning of the four sacred books / is contained in a single *alif*" once its ramifications have been understood.[11] It almost seems inevitable that the nearest tropic relative of God B's diagram would be chiasmus, the figure of "crossing," which rhetoricians sometimes represent by the letters ABBA.

So the hourglass is our glass, which perforce reflects opposite images at once. The hourglass's sand itself serves this volume much as the "current"—continually fluctuating between plus and minus, creative and destructive power—served "Ephraim," as the relationship between Raphael and Emmanuel could suggest. To the extent that the "THINNING" process facilitates the creation of Paradise, the sand falling into the "RISING DUNE" contributes to the "FLOOD" of "RADIANCE" that RM and Ephraim envision. Gabriel, on the other hand, uses that dune as a metaphor for a reservoir so dangerous that he likens it to "ATOMIC WASTE"—a "RESERVOIR OF SPENT TIME." (This phrase gives RM's cute Bensonian version of "au revoir," "AU RESERVOIR," a grimly ironic edge—especially when Nature, in a peevish mood, adopts it herself.) Water and sand, positive and negative foreshadowings characteristically combine in JM's touching figurative anticipation of his friends' return to Earth:

> (. . . The ninth moon setting—at whose full
> Enormous turtles, barnacled like moons,
> Eggs buried in the lap of silver dunes,
> Regain the ebbing world they mustn't fail.)
>
> [S, p. 219]

While his treatment of Earth in terms of the sea and his fine choice of "lap" blur the distinction between the realms of sand and water, the boundary between Yes and No becomes just as indeterminable. The "eggs" in the "silver dunes" point in one direction, "the ebbing world" and perhaps "buried" in the other.

As in "Ephraim"'s section V, "the ebbing world" takes shape as the "drowning, dummy paradise" of Venice, which Merrill—now rhyming with the flair of Byron, now brushing in a scene in shimmering, translucent colors—describes once more in his inimitable terza rima. And here again, as in section M of "Ephraim," an account of a film by Maya Deren summarizes some chief concerns. Merrill's art and Deren's converge during the trip to Venice when DJ discovers that some students are showing her film as "Part of some sort of anti- / Biennale." The same documentary that MD happens to have compared early in *Scripts* to JM's project, it records a voodoo ceremony that she participated in while in Haiti, which would have been about the time that DJ and JM first contacted the spirit world ("How many years ago now, twenty? Thirty?"). As the "Credits flicker" and the camera takes in "A bare beach" and "Glinting wavelets," Merrill's opening in *Scripts* flashes to mind: a list of "Speakers" and the "Sun [that] dwindles into Sound." Deren shot her film in "dialectic whites and blacks" that repeat this volume's interacting forces, and "the soundtrack's / Treacherous crosscurrent" that seems to slow the action ironically recalls Merrill's own mode. Owing to its age, the film sometimes threatens to be "swept clean / Away by particles that . . . bombard . . . [and] flay an image to the bone-white screen," a "flak fired outward from time's core" that calls up Gabriel's "CAPPD VOLCANO" with its "UPWARD VOLATILE FORCE." Any anxieties that Deren might have shown during her induction, JM surmises, "have been cut, or never filmed," just as he himself prefers, as he has told us earlier, "the happy ending":

> Weren't the endings
> Always happy in books? Barbarity.
> To serve uncooked one's bloody tranche de vie . . .
> Later, if the hero couldn't smile,
> Reader and author could; one called it style.
>
> [*S*, p. 214]

The film ends—interrupting JM's meditation on " 'Paradise' impending"—with "One last shot: dawn, the bare beach," which takes us back to its beginning. "'Happy ending?'" DJ asks with a smile—and he makes the ending happy *by* smiling.

If we ask his question about JM's documentary, the answer must also be yes—and no. Yes, on the emotional level, because MM and the others return to the world so eagerly, as do DJ and JM. (DJ impatiently concludes one philosophical discussion with the shout "Look! This whole world's *a place to live!*" and a rebellious plunge "Into the blue depths of Emmanuel," while JM, for his part, feels a growing urge "to put / These headlong revelations finally / Between the drowsy covers of a book.") Yes, too, on the eschatological level, because Nature and God B leave the gate to Paradise ajar. But also no, on the emotional level, because the relationships with Maria, Wystan, and George have finally ended, and DJ's and JM's world is the poorer without the spirits of those loved ones. And no again, because that "bare beach," the sand over all, prefigures a world blasted clean of all life as easily as it does Paradise. Whether our ending proves happy or not depends on whether it is also a beginning, on whether it turns into the Alpha period. Since the issue cannot be resolved except in time, Merrill's last sentence, when it comes several pages later, remains incomplete, and God B's concluding message begins and ends *in medias res*:

> And should elsewhere
> Broad wings revolve a horselike form into
> One Creature upward-shining brief as dew,
> Swifter than bubbles in wine, through evening air
>
> Up, far up, O whirling point of Light—:
>
> HERS HEAR ME I AND MINE SURVIVE SIGNAL
> ME DO YOU WELL I ALONE IN MY NIGHT
> HOLD IT BACK HEAR ME BROTHERS I AND MINE
>
> [S, p. 235]

3

The final rhyme in *Scripts*—"Light" with "NIGHT"—once more interlocks the positive with the negative and the human voice with the divine. The last three lines themselves might as well be JM's address to his now silent friends—or to the reader, or to posterity. "It's almost as if *we* were dead / And signalling to dear ones in the world," DJ has realized earlier.[12] During Deren's film, watching DJ's face "going white" in the light of the projector, JM thinks *"We* are the ghosts, *hers* the ongoing party." He refers to Deren, but the larger party is hosted by someone else, the third aspect of his Trinity, who appears here, as the result of our tuning in to God B's incessant transmission in the middle of the word "brothers," in the message's startling first word. Even as JM's voice merges with God B's, the term "hers" assigns all existence, from the Pantheon down, to Nature. Beginning and ending with its reciprocal, all-inclusive possessives, revolving around the ambiguous "i" at the middle of its central line, this last message tries one last time to say it all at once, to frame the Word, the single symbol, of which the ornate Arabic phrase, Strauss's ingenious theme, the angels' ideogram, and God's mark are all versions.

In any form, that symbol must be a *"twinned / Emblem,"* simply because, grounded though it is in an intuition of unicity, Merrill's experience of the world demands expression in ambivalent terms. Perhaps no other contemporary American poet would respond as sympathetically to Karl Abel's thesis in "The Antithetical Sense of Primal Words," the pamphlet made famous by Freud's review. Abel argues that since "everything on this planet is relative," and since "every conception is thus the twin of its opposite," it should not surprise us that primal words often said opposite things at once. He cites the parallel thesis of Alexander Bain, the Scottish philosopher, that all mental life must be pervaded by something like that very "duality" that God B instilled in nature. According to Bain,

> The essential relativity of all knowledge, thought, or consciousness cannot but show itself in language. If everything that we can know is viewed as a transition from something else, every experience must have two sides; and either every name must have a double meaning, or else for every meaning there must be two names.[13]

If Merrill were to formulate a language doctrine, it would surely involve propositions like Bain's and Abel's. Merrill's favorite rhetorical and prosodic devices—the pun, the paradox, the oxymoron, the couplet, the ABBA quatrain—either spring from or comport with an intuition of "the essential relativity of all knowledge" and the consequent necessity of two-sided expression. We might even think of his metaphysics as his rhetoric and his prosody writ large, ramified, and reinforced by a physics that seems sometimes to rhyme with them. What the trilogy gives us in the end is not a belief but rather a dialectical process, the process of thought and imagination—a process such that it will not tolerate any single belief, or even species of belief, whether monistic or dualistic, materialistic or idealistic. Unity in duality (or in multiplicity, since dualism propagates) constitutes the poem's fundamental principle, metaphysical and aesthetic alike. The Word is a pun, as Heraclitus and others have suspected.

Merrill delicately reminds us that we must look elsewhere for theological dogma when he echoes, in the lines on the "horselike form" in his conclusion, quoted above, this fable, which Mirabell has told them in "&":

> CIRCA 3000 BC A WIND
> SWEPT DELOS   THE MALE POP RUSHING TO PUT STONES ON THEIR
>   ROOFS
> WERE SWEPT UP UP UP THEN IN A CYCLICAL FREAK MANNER
> RETURND, SET DOWN. ONE CASUALTY: A FAT TEMPLE SCRIBE
> WHO, LEFT ARM BROKEN, DECIDED IT MEANT THEY HAD BECOME
> TOO SOBER TOO WITHOUT LYRIC JOY   SO HE INVENTED
> GREAT PAEANS TO WEIGHTLESS LOFTY & PURELY COMIC LIFE.
> DELOS SET UP A SHRINE & THE SCRIBE'S WORDS 'WE RODE THE AIR,
> WE LAUGHD DOWN AT THE DOMESTIC EARTH' CAUSED A HORSE FIGURE
> TO BE WORSHIPT THERE BY ALL WHO ASPIRED TO THE WORD.
> NOTE THAT THE 'GOD' RESPECTED THE SCRIBE'S RIGHT HAND

[S, pp. 145–146]

The fable illuminates the trilogy: JM and DJ have also been swept up and returned to earth; JM too is a scribe (whose left arm will have felt the effect of long hours with the cup); these volumes are also comic paeans. The "HORSE FIGURE" celebrated by the Greek scribe is a version of Pegasus, the Muses' horse. Trying to ascend to heaven on his back, Bellerophon fell back to Earth, like the scribe, and Pegasus went on alone, like the "horselike form" in this volume's conclusion, to install himself among the stars. If Merrill's own ascent fails, it fails just as it must, because it is finally "only" a fable itself. Asked why he put "'GOD'" in quotes, Mirabell replies

"I BELIEVE U KNOW" and thus hints at the "PURELY COMIC LIFE" of the poem, its fictional nature, its essential agnosticism.

JM also obliquely acknowledges the fiction involved immediately after the last lesson, when he recasts the angels' story of the descent of God B and Nature from the Pantheon in these knowing terms:

> Yet here
> In their New World, this branch at least, these two
> Have fallen on hard times. Their *Mayflower*
> Long run wild, they bend to the poor lamplight,
> Her deft hands full of mending, His roughened ones
> Forming letters which the flame, tipped blue
> As if with cold, breathes fitful life into:
> *I've found work, we get on, Sister keeps house.*
> *Stay well, and please do not abandon us . . .*
>
> [S, p. 212]

To this shrewd translation MM responds, as though with a proud but sad smile, "ALAS ENFANT THERE'S NO DECEIVING U"—which is as much as to say that they have all been treated to an old story tricked out in a new fashion. The angels' cosmogony is no more, if no less, than the New World myth, one more variation on a venerable theme.

He reveals yet another analogue to and possible source for the trilogy a few lines later, when he smoothly turns cosmogony into autobiography (or does so more explicitly, since "these two" in the preceding passage look a good deal like our boarders). His readers will recognize elements of the autobiography from "The Broken Home," "Lost in Translation," and other earlier work. The opening sentence provides the transition, as the primordial broth becomes both the amniotic fluid and a remembered stock; thereafter the personal narrative dominates, though it is always shadowed by the myth:

> Friction made the first thin consommé
> Of all we know. Soon it was time for lunch.
> Between an often absent or abstracted
> (In mid-depression) father and still young
> Mother's wronged air of commonsense the child sat.

> The third and last. If he would never quite
> Outgrow the hobby horse and dragon kite
> Left by the first two, one lukewarm noodle
> Prefigured no less a spiral nebula
> Of further outs. Piano practice, books . . .
>
> [*S*, p. 213]

If Nature and "DISTANT-MINDED" God B, as she has called him earlier, stem from Merrill's own level-headed mother and "absent or abstracted . . . father," humanity's predecessors derive from the poet's older siblings, here given attributes that recall the centaurs and the creatures of the Chinese plain. Even Maria's fate, as we know it from the trilogy, was presaged by JM's early experiences:

> A woman speaking French had joined their sunstruck
> Looking-glass table. Fuels of the cup
> Lowered to her lips were swallowed *up*.
> The child blinked. All now was free to shatter,
> Change or die. Tight wound exposures lay
> Awaiting trial, whose development
> Might set a mirror flowing in reverse
> Forty years, fifty, past the flailing seed
> To incoherence, blackout—the small witness
> Having after all held nothing back?
>
> [*S*, p. 213]

Like the governess in "Lost in Translation," MM speaks French and (having drunk her bitter cup to the dregs) appears at JM's table, "sunstruck" since Michael's entrance—which, the "Coda" reveals, was as Ephraim himself, "Mister E" (mystery) indeed. Both Maria's death and her return to Earth repeat the childhood catastrophe, and these later losses also leave behind them impressions whose poetic "development" entails recollection. Thus JM's different "exposures" to disaster might have given rise to the trilogy, whose very hourglass in which the sand runs up to obliterate the world seems a translation of memory's "mirror flowing in reverse" until it meets the point of its own origin, beyond which lies simple "incoherence, blackout"—the dark force in yet another form.

By candidly exposing these relationships, Merrill has "held nothing back" in the sense that he has once and for all confessed the

possible autobiographical origins of his revelations. Are we per-
haps to read the whole poem, this "spiral nebula," merely as a
wild elaboration of personal experiences? "But by now we know /
Where that will get us," as JM says after he has asked whether
he and DJ were "Literally" *in* the mirror-world during Michael's
fete: "Tutti: Y E S & N O." The suspicion itself that he has "held
nothing back," for instance, turns his self-analysis back into anal-
ogy, since it is identical with the fear that his V work has failed,
that his poem will have altered nothing, that we will give in to the
dark force. The brilliantly equivocal phrase insists on the impor-
tance of the otherworldly communications at the same time that it
challenges their authenticity.

This paradox pays its double tribute to "resistance," one name
for the power at the heart of Merrill's trilogy. On the one hand, he
withstands the temptation to believe that the séances have put him
in touch with the Truth; but on the other, he resists the perhaps
stronger inclination to see the revelations as chimerical projections.
These two forms of resistance coexist in the early comment on the
nature of the schoolroom settings, where *"Real and Ideal study* much
as we / Good luck to them! *compatibility."* But we will not be able to
write Merrill off as a Janusian skeptic who trifles with mystical
notions. That last couplet verges on an understanding of the Real
and the Ideal as *"two floating poles / Of color"* that *"Undulate and
intertwine like snakes."* We can also call his motivating force a vision
of the fabric of existence, in which opposites weave together. Speak-
ing of his father and mother, or of God B and Nature, MM cautions
that "NO MAN'S MIND CAN REACH / BEYOND THAT HIM & HER   THEIR
SEPARATION / REMAINS UNTHINKABLE." But she could be speaking
of the actual and the fictive, the living and the dead, God and
humanity, or A and B. Merrill's vision of things embodies what
Stanley Kunitz has called "The supreme awareness that we can
have": "that all existence is a continuous tissue, a gigantic web of
interconnected filaments so delicately woven that if touched at any
point the whole web trembles."[14]

Perhaps this volume's most dazzling and extended formulation
of that awareness is "Samos," the poem at the beginning of "&."
MM seems to introduce it by way of a bilingual pun at the end of

"Yes," where she endorses DJ's proposal that they at least include a bowl of water in their last rites: "BRAVO ENFANTS   OUR EAU DE V WORK   SMOOTH / SEAS TO SAMOS." "Samos" *is*, at any rate, a sort of ode to V work, written in the form of Auden's "Canzone." As in God B's "Quincunx," the "ghosts of Five and Twelve," two of Mirabell's favorite numbers, rise up here, since "Samos" has five stanzas of twelve pentameter lines each, plus a coda of five lines, and since it uses only five end words (and variants on them): "water," "fire," "land," "light" (the angels' four elements) and "sense" (which points to both the apprehension and the interpretation of these elements). Because of the end words' recurrence, the poem recombines the elements and the sense it makes of them much as the sea it describes reticulates the refracted sunlight. Take this second stanza, which both reflects and extends the web of existence:

> Fire-wisps were weaving a string bag of light
> For sea stones. Their astounding color sense!
> Porphyry, alabaster, chrysolite
> Translucences that go dead in daylight
> Asked only the quick dip in holy water
> For the saint of cell on cell to come alight—
> Illuminated crystals thinking light,
> Refracting it, the gray prismatic fire
> Or yellow-gray of sea's dilute sapphire . . .
> Wavelengths daily deeply score the leit-
> motifs of Loom and Wheel upon this land.
> To those who listen it's the Promised Land.
>
> [S, p. 87]

In its own way, the poem's luminously intricate rhyme scheme also spells out God's name.[15]

Potentially "the Promised Land," and therefore the world in small, Samos inspires in Merrill a feeling akin to Wordsworth's intuition in "Tintern Abbey":

> a sense sublime
> Of something far more deeply interfused,
> Whose dwelling is the light of setting suns,
> And the round ocean and the living air,
> And the blue sky, and in the mind of man . . .

Merrill most nearly approaches Wordsworth's "something"—"a motion and a spirit, that impels / All thinking things, all objects of all thought"—at the canzone's climax:

> Blood's least red monocle, O magnifier
> Of the great Eye that sees by its own light
> More pictures in "the world's enchanted fire"
> Than come and go in any shrewd crossfire
> Upon the page, of syllable and sense,
> We want unwilled excursions and ascents,
> Crave the upward-rippling rungs of fire,
> The outward-rippling rings (enough!) of water . . .
>
> [S, p. 88]

He comes as close here as he did in section X of "Ephraim" to "grasping the naked current" of the immanent "absolute." The "Eye that sees by its own light" and that is itself seen through the "monocle" of the blood cell is clearly not just the sun but the essence of things. Hence the jarring combination of "magnifier" and "great," which renders the concept of size nonsensical. Like Heraclitus the Obscure, that philosopher of pun and paradox, Merrill tries to come to grips here with "the tremendous energy that flows through reality," with the "living fire that supplies the driving force of the universe in endless change."[16]

At such moments, unity takes precedence, and Merrill virtually duplicates the thought of the Sufi mystic, who considers Allah "at once seen, seeing eye, and thing seen." Again, "God becomes the mirror in which spiritual man contemplates his own reality and man in turn becomes the mirror in which God contemplates His Names and Qualities."[17] But division and diversity always get their due in the trilogy. DJ and JM must break the mirror, and its "splinters"—some "aglitter in the boughs" of the cassia, others "facedown, black on soil beneath"—mutely testify to duality, opposition, and destruction in the world. Still—for the poem will not allow us to say the one thing without saying the other—any one of those splinters will be "Able, days hence . . . to rouse / From its deep swoon the undestroyed heartscape." As the echo of the epigraph to Scripts suggests, the very shattering of the looking glass stands for an eternal and sacred union. The epigraph, from Jean

Santeuil, recounts an incident in which Jean confesses to his mother that in a fit of rage he broke a vase of Venetian glass which she had given him. He expects her to be furious, but she responds by wonderfully comparing the vase to the glass ritually broken under heel in the Jewish wedding ceremony: "Ce sera comme au temple le symbole de l'indestructible union."[18] In the trilogy, the broken glass unites DJ and JM and their friends and also humanity, divinity, and Mother Nature, the goddess for whom Merrill has built this later version of Plenorios' temple. For better and for worse, whether we end up saying Yes or No and thus completing the transformation into either God B or God A, we are "HERS."

CHAPTER 10

Merrill and Pynchon:
Our Apocalyptic Scribes

Charles Berger

"WE SPEAK FROM WITHIN THE ATOM," Mirabell and his cohorts de-
clare, thereby placing Merrill's trilogy at the center of our deepest
anxieties since the end of World War II. *Mirabell*'s final sections
eloquently and movingly detail the reasons why JM and DJ were
chosen to receive the vision of things as they are—*de natura rerum.*
But early on in the second poem of the trilogy, Mirabell reveals an
even more urgent fact, the reason why the otherworldly messengers
have chosen this time and place to stage their epic descent: "THE
MUSHROOM CLOUD APPALD YR PRINCIPAL SOUL DENSITY." The drop-
ping of the atomic bomb on Hiroshima threatened the whole struc-
ture of lab work (or V work) by obliterating the gene pool and
thus introducing the specter of annihilation rather than mere death.
"All trace was lost / Of souls that perished in that holocaust," DJ
remembers, referring to a hint left by Ephraim many years earlier.
The message that Mirabell and his superiors are intent on convey-
ing through the medium of the Scribe is a simple one: "THE ATOM
CANNOT BE MAN'S FRIEND." The epigraph to *Mirabell* reinforces the
idea that the trilogy's center of anxious concern, its deep origin,
however clouded by mythic analogue or autobiographical excur-
sus, is the development of the atomic bomb:

> The three men decided they would prepare a letter to President
> Roosevelt, and that Einstein would sign it. . . . Einstein's eyes
> slowly moved along the two full, typewritten pages. . . . "For the

first time in history men will use energy that does not come from the sun," he commented and signed. The scientists operated their pile for the first time on December 2, 1942. They were the first men to see matter yield its inner energy, steadily, at their will. My husband was their leader.

—LAURA FERMI

Merrill's trilogy is an epic of survival. It is also the longest and most self-consciously successful elegy in the language. Some readers are put off by Merrill's apparent lack of eschatological anxiety, his unfaltering graveyard wit. They may be falling into a trap here: by taking the verbal antics of JM, DJ, and WHA as the poet's "authorized" reaction to the news of revelation, they forget that just as we recognize the difference between Dante the Pilgrim and Dante the Poet, so Merrill's role as an actor in the poem needs to be distinguished from the shaping spirit who put the whole structure together. *Mirabell*, in particular, offers sharp contrasts between the anxiety of the spirit world overlooking human history and the players themselves. If we brood upon the whole trilogy, we can see that Merrill's foray into the region of the dead, or their foray into his sphere, is not a parlor game, despite its trappings, but a reaction to the poet's sense of an ending: in other words, an apocalyptic poem.

In the book whose title has now become part of the critical lingua franca, Frank Kermode has a seminal chapter on "The Modern Apocalypse," in which he attempts to discriminate between early and late modernism on the basis of how each responds to apocalyptic pressure.[1] He takes for granted a lasting sense of eschatological anxiety throughout the century, so that what we have is not a moment but an age of crisis. According to Kermode, certain features remain constant in the works of artists acutely conscious of the End, especially when the End is conceived of as a New Beginning. These features include: the certainty that universal bloodshed must accompany the final days, an emphasis upon a phase of transition, periods of decadence and renovation, paradigms of justice or judgment imposed upon historical reality, recognition of an elect who will survive and a demonic host who will perish, and the attempt in the last days to provide a language of renovation. What Kermode finds to be the distinguishing factor between early and late modernism is the emphasis in the former upon our link to the past. Apocalypse, for Yeats, Eliot, or Pound, means restoration of an earlier (superior) order. The newer, or what Kermode calls the schismatic modernism, does not mythologize earlier orders in its quest for a lost stability or hierarchy. The heroes of *The Sense of an Ending*, those who resist the dangerous confusion of ideology and myth, are those supreme artificers Joyce and Stevens. (Thus the temporal distinction gives way to a truer, synchronic struggle between orthodox and schismatic modernism.) They create literary forms that are open to transition and flux; they worship no strange gods, but language; they convey the pathos of endings without any rancor.

Merrill's poetic pantheon might at first incline one to place him with Yeats, and the trilogy is often compared to *A Vision*. But there is nothing hieratic about Merrill's scheme—conversation, even between the upper and lower cases, tends to equalize—though there is much hierarchy. Yeats and even Pound are greater celebrants then Merrill, more attuned to the sacred. Despite everything, Merrill remains a secular epiphanist. He took seriously the injunction to write Poems of Science (which does not mean that he bothered to gather any scientific knowledge). What the Poem or Epic of Science does is to liberate mythology from its grounding in a particular culture. The result is a pure ideology of myth assigned, as we might expect, to a prehistorical era—indeed, to an era preceding the formation of our world. Much of *Paradise Lost*, as well, takes place prior to the creation of Earth, and Milton's emphasis on universal Christian culture was a corrective to the pagan—and Christian Renaissance—focus on the native epic. By mythologizing history, Yeats and Pound open the way to dangerous, even Fascist, notions of past wholeness, lost origins, true cultural centers. V work is Merrill's equivalent of the privileged cultural enterprise, which Yeats assigns to "Byzantium" and Pound to "Provence." The sacred spot becomes an invisible laboratory. (The visual arts matter little to Merrill; in *Mirabell*, Book 3, painters and sculptors are said to be too dependent on the body, as opposed to poets and musicians. Merrill's only icon is the board itself.) And while the ahistorical and impalpable nature of Merrill's central myth reduces its sacramental value, it does grant the prestige of anteriority.

Of course, the nature of V work does require an elect, certain also to be shadowed by what Kermode, following tradition, terms the demonic host. Whether we identify Merrill's corps as the Five, or the Twelve Percent, depending on which account we find more coherent, it is clear that he is at ease with the idea of an elect, despite DJ's democratic protestations. Mirabell's density ratios and his talk of cloning favorable spirits might be excused, if one thinks they need to be, by the urgency of the moment, the need to save the Greenhouse of Earth. Terms such as "Jew-density"—though intended, of course, as the highest compliment—come as a shock in this most civilized of recent literary productions; the shock is healthy, however, if it is taken as a sign or index of the poem's extreme nature, which is ours as well. All sorts of orthodoxies go by the board—no pun?—in crisis, and the apocalyptic text often brims with the energy of the forbidden, especially forbidden knowledge. In the case of Merrill, such knowledge obviously centers on the Ouija board and what it represents as a counter to "legitimate" modes of acquiring information. Merrill's science is a pre-science, but not less legitimate for that. Just as the trilogy labors to ground culture in science, so it authenticates science by stressing its continuity with magic. That "E. German physicist," who is declared an avatar of Montezuma, is not thereby exposed as a fraud. But scientific arrogance does need to be chastened. Laura Fermi's boast in the epigraph—"They were the first men to see matter yield its inner energy, steadily, at their will"—must be corrected, and Mirabell himself does so. Those may have been the first *men*, but they were not the *first*. Mirabell and the fallen spirits can claim priority for that. And since they have gone before, they can legitimately warn us.

The apocalyptic text attempts to counter or ward off total destruction. One of its strategies is to establish a grand heterocosm— a world elsewhere, a rival plenitude designed both to imitate and to preserve the totality of our world, now threatened by extinction. It is no accident that *Ulysses*, for instance, was written during World War I; its encyclopedic scope attempts to protect the world by enclosing it. And yet, although the desired end of such effort might be innocence—the Yes of affirmation—Joyce's heterocosm is hardly innocent. His capacious order is always on the verge of dissolving into disorder, and the strenuous effort to hold things together creates a formal violence of its own. Joyce's rage against the limits of narrative and language is itself a war. Apocalyptic texts, even more than others, must internalize violence. For this reason, as in the case of Blake and Joyce, such texts often veer into savage intellectual satire. This is not Merrill's way. There is nothing Rabelaisian about him. Following Dante, he maintains civility in even the darkest regions, assigning violence to the other, the interlocutor. The message, however, remains clear: save the Greenhouse!

This central anxiety is also shared by the only American work of the last decade that can rival Merrill's trilogy in scope, design, and density: *Gravity's Rainbow*.[2] Neither Pynchon nor Merrill fit into any contemporary movement; it goes without saying that they work worlds apart from each other. Yet each is, or has become, something of an apocalyptic scribe, returning by such different routes to the origin of our impending end.

Mirabell locates that origin in the Fall brought on by the technological *hubris* of Mirabell's own species. They overthrew the Centaurs and seized the secrets of the atom:

> WE SAW THE POWER & WITH IT BUILT A GREAT GREAT GLORY
> A WORLD YOU COULD NOT IMAGINE . . .
>
> [*M*, p. 26]

Then they pushed too far, this race of Master Builders, ruining their own handiwork:

> AND THEN   ONE ATOM TOO MANY   WE WANTED MORE   THE BLACK
> LIGHT ON OUR EYELIDS   OUR BLINDNESS   OUR ARROGANCE   WE CHOSE
> TO MOVE ON INTO SPACE   ABANDONING THE WORLD WE ROSE
> THE CRUST LIKE A VEIL SHREDDED FAR BEHIND US EXPOSING
> THE ALREADY ARID EARTH   WE DESPISD IT & FLUNG BACK
> A LAST BOLT & THE UNIVERSE FELL IN ON US   WE FELL.
>
> [*M*, p. 26]

There is more than a touch of the Mad Scientist in this hyperbole, so that it is crucial to keep "the dark undertone of Hiroshima"

(Helen Vendler's phrase) firmly in mind. Mirabell's attractiveness as epic instructor is also likely to disarm us if we do not remember how wide and imponderable is the gulf between character and deed. The full consequences of an act cannot be gauged by the intentions of the actor; sometimes they can barely be glimpsed. The growing bond between Mirabell and JM cannot blind us to the disasters brought on by the atomic tinkering of Mirabell and his race.

Pynchon shrewdly situates his epic narrative just *before* the beginning of the atomic age proper. The German V-2 rocket, whose presence hovers over *Gravity's Rainbow*, is only a precursor of the greater destructiveness to come. Pynchon's true subject must be the ICBM, but he cannot write directly about it. Instead, he gives us the more "rational" or comprehensible phenomenon of the V-2. The latter becomes a microcosm in which we can study the effects, infinitely reduced, of technological madness. The Zone, the name Pynchon gives to the ruined German sector at war's end, also serves as a laboratory for all the forces that we, as readers located in the 1970s, know will come to dominate the postwar scene. We know that the V-2 rockets will metamorphose into nuclear bombs—indeed, it happens at the very end of the novel—but by taking us back to that moment in history just prior to the transformation, Pynchon makes us experience the Fall all over again. We gather the news of Hiroshima through the eyes of Slothrop, the novel's picaresque protagonist, who glances at a front-page photograph of the phallic cloud and this bit of headline:

MB DRO
ROSHI.

[*GR*, p. 693]

Slothrop is of course baffled by this Ouija-like communiqué. When the puzzle is put together, a new world order will have emerged.

For Pynchon, the villains of this new dispensation are not so much the scientists as the technicians who follow and parody them. To import Blakean terms, the technological end of "sweet science" should be epitomized in the effort to build the New Jerusalem, antithesis to the blind buildings of the tyrannical pharaohs. I think

Merrill, also, tends to center on the demonic distortion of science. Mirabell and his cohorts are the opposites of Blake's Los. Worse yet, they are bureaucrats, for what is the technician but a scientific bureaucrat? One of the more startling aspects of Merrill's other-worldly nexus is the role played there by bureaucratic censorship and control—Dante's hierarchy brought up to date. Pynchon, for whom all forms of bureaucracy partake of sinister beauty, coins a phrase that Merrill might readily subscribe to. Speaking of dreams, Pynchon writes:

> So that the right material may find its way to the right dreamer, everyone, everything involved must be exactly in place in the pattern. It was nice of Jung to give us the idea of an ancestral pool in which everybody shares the same dream material. But how is it we are each visited as individuals, each by exactly and only what he needs? Doesn't that imply a switching-path of some kind? a bureaucracy? Why shouldn't the IG [Farben, that is] go to séances? They ought to be quite at home with *the bureaucracies of the other side.*
>
> [*GR*, pp. 410–411; italics added]

The idea that the unconscious is a vast bureaucracy is not far removed from Merrill's notions of an interlocking system of patrons, representatives, and sorting agents who administer the composition of earthly souls. Nor are we far from Spenser's Garden of Adonis, for that matter. Literary syncretists like Merrill and Pynchon, though they develop highly distinctive styles, tend to efface the role of personality in literary composition; tradition, however disfigured by the avant-gardist, becomes another version of bureaucracy. Some of the more notorious episodes in the trilogy concern revelations of ghostwritten masterpieces. We discover that Dante was dictated to, and that the peculiar physiological combination we refer to as Rimbaud actually wrote "The Waste Land." Pynchon has little use for the literary artist as such, replacing him with the scientist. But the ground rules for scientific creation obviously have much to say about the way writers work. The recipient of the dream material quoted above was Friedrich August Kekulé von Stradonitz, a great German chemist who discovered the structure of the benzene molecule. Kekulé began his studies as an architect and "brought the mind's eye of an architect over into chemistry." He found that the six atoms of carbon and six atoms of hydrogen in benzene are arranged in a closed, ringlike structure resembling a hexagon. Kekulé claimed that the shape of benzene came to him in a dream. Pynchon interprets this episode of inspiration not as a triumph for Kekulé but an example of how the System uses the scientist for its own ends. Kekulé becomes the Scribe of the bureaucracy:

> Kekulé dreams the Great Serpent holding its own tail in its mouth, the dreaming Serpent which surrounds the World. But the meanness, the cynicism with which this dream is to be used. The Serpent that announces, "The World is a closed thing, cyclical, resonant, eternally-returning," is to be delivered into a system whose only aim is to *violate* the Cycle. . . . No return, no salvation, no Cycle—that's not what They, nor Their brilliant employee Kekulé, have taken the Serpent to mean. . . . we had been given certain molecules, certain combinations and not others. . . . we used what we found in Nature, unquestioning, shamefully perhaps—but the Serpent whispered, *"They can be changed,* and new molecules assembled from the debris of the given."
>
> [*GR*, p. 412]

In such a universe, when even a scientist of Kekulé's stature is only an employee, what place is there for the assertion of will, for the individuating choice? Merrill often puzzles over the role of will in the midst of executing his grand arabesques. When we learn what has gone into the programming of even the saving Twelve Percent, we are not likely to regard their achievements as willed. Both Merrill and Pynchon array enormous forces over and against the individual: even the idea of assertion almost begins to seem comical or outmoded, like the dream of narrative continuity. We scan Merrill and Pynchon for those moments in which the will is present, and we take what we can. So we read *Ulysses*, for example, looking for something, anything, that Leopold Bloom might be said to *do*, actually or effectually. His sparing of Molly's suitors, a refusal to "act," becomes Bloom's prime assertion in the course of the novel. Joyce's internalization of the will becomes the norm in the encyclopedic mock-epic. The strength of JM and DJ comes to reside in their being able to provide a space in which things happen: they are loving mediums. They bring about Mirabell's transformation precisely by doing nothing at all. The same negative prescription for the will that we find in Joyce and Merrill—doing nothing—is perhaps the only formula for genuine activity in *Gravity's Rainbow*, a book filled with frenetic semblances of action. Pynchon delights in narrowing the room for action to the point where only refusal fits. And yet this refusal can take on a nobility denied to anything else, as when the Nazi rocket technician Pökler refuses to have intercourse with a young woman whom the SS has provided for him, a young woman who pretends to be his daughter in order to further his delight. "No. What Pökler did was choose to believe she wanted comfort that night, wanted not to be alone. Despite Their game, Their palpable evil, though he had no more reason to trust "Ilse" than he trusted Them, by an act not of faith, not of courage but of conservation, he chose to believe that" (*GR*, p. 421). Nowhere else in *Gravity's Rainbow* is the act of choice so accentuated. Pökler will go on to quit the game and, by doing so, join the Counter-Force.

Stymying the will, yet also committed to the precepts of quest romance, Merrill and Pynchon end up courting the moment of mazy error, to invoke a Miltonism, the moment in which it is recognized that finding the true way means losing oneself to the world, because of either conceptual bewilderment or overcertainty. One can wander in search of the truth through an ever-increasing forest of signals, or one can become blinded by the brightness of a terribly clear message. The first way is typical of Pynchon's characters, the second, of Merrill himself. By saying this I do not mean to imply that the content of Merrill's vision is always clear. Far from it. But the *value* or the *import* of the clues he puts together is never seriously questioned beyond the bound of "The Book of Ephraim." We observe JM in the process of being educated and tested, as a good romance hero should be; much renunciation is demanded of him, politely enough, for the privilege of being chosen. But even though he converses with the avatars of Beelzebub and Co., the sources of JM's revelations remain surprisingly trustworthy. If Mirabell misleads, he does so only because of his lower place in the hierarchy. Merrill's trilogy is, after all, a much more straightforwardly didactic work than *Gravity's Rainbow*. Wandering and error are seen to have their corrections and rewards. Merrill's confessions of his growing isolation avoid the note of terror that would certainly be present were the vision doubted.

> About us, these bright afternoons, we come
> To draw shades of an auditorium
> In darkness. An imagined dark . . .
>   . . . . .
> Lighthouse and clock tower, Village Green and neat
> Roseblush factory which makes, upstreet,
> Exactly what, one once knew but forgets—
> Something of plastic found in luncheonettes;
> The Sound's quick sapphire that each day recurs
> Aflock with pouter-pigeon spinnakers
> —This outside world, our fictive darkness more
> And more belittles to a safety door
> Left open onto light. Too small, too far
> To help. The blind bright spot of where we are.
>
>   [*M*, pp. 53–54]

Merrill's instructors have personalities and they expect their students to possess the same, even if the end of prophecy, as they predict, will be the extinction of self. We hear much throughout the trilogy about this presumed annihilation of self, yet within the poem itself the voices and the selves they embody never really cease:

> JM THE STRIPPING IS THE POINT YR POEM WILL PERHAPS
> TAKE UP FROM ITS WINTRY END & MOVE STEP BY STEP INTO
> SEASONLESS & CHARACTERLESS STAGES TO ITS FINAL
> GREAT COLD RINGING OF THE CHIMES SHAPED AS O O O O O
>
>   [*M*, p. 117]

>   They of course come through
> —It's what, in any Quest, the heroes do—
> But at the cost of being set apart,
> Emptied, diminished. Tolkien knew this. Art—
> The tale that all but shapes itself—survives

By feeding on its personages' lives.
The stripping process, sort of. What to say?
Our lives led *to* this. It's the price we pay.

[*M*, p. 124]

In *Gravity's Rainbow*, on the other hand, we do witness the end
of instruction, quite literally, as the hero of the epic-romance is
finally bombarded into quiescence. In *The Crying of Lot 49*, Oedipa
Maas may or may not fade into the mass of others at novel's end,
but in *GR* there is no question that Slothrop disappears. The puz-
zle is what he disappears into. Maxwell's Demon, the sorting agent
of *Lot 49*, became the guiding spirit of that novel, enabling Oedipa
at least to attempt to sort out her fate, her *sort*. Slothrop, however,
equally assaulted by instruction, comes to a true soldier's end—
he just fades away:

> instructing him, dunce and drifter, in ways deeper than he can
> explain, have been faces of children out the train windows, two
> bars of dance music somewhere, in some other street at night,
> needles and branches of a pine tree shaken clear and luminous
> against night clouds, one circuit diagram out of hundreds in a
> smudged yellowing sheaf, laughter out of a cornfield in the early
> morning as he was walking to school, the idling of a motorcycle at
> one dusk-heavy hour of the summer . . . and now, in the Zone,
> later in the day he became a crossroad, after a heavy rain he doesn't
> recall, Slothrop sees a very thick rainbow here, a stout rainbow
> cock driven down out of pubic clouds into Earth, green wet val-
> leyed Earth, and his chest fills and he stands crying, not a thing in
> his head, just feeling natural. . . .

[*GR*, p. 626]

I think we can read in Slothrop's demise the danger of taking in
all that instruction, all those portents, unaided; and in this danger
might be the motive for Merrill's invention or discovery of the
Instructor. All the classic romance fictions provide a guide for the
hero, and Merrill's trilogy continues this tradition with a vengeance.
He is as guided as any quester since Dante. Even Oedipa Maas had
her precursors along the way to aid her. But much of the darkness
permeating *Gravity's Rainbow* comes from the absence of any such
sponsoring guides. The novel abounds in messages that must be

deciphered in the absence of any guiding ideology, much less any figure of instruction. Slothrop realizes this at long last in a passage just preceding the one quoted above. Wandering through the Zone he gathers a sense of design to it all, a possible legibility to the chaos. "Omens grow clearer, more specific. He watches flights of birds and patterns in the ashes of his fire, he reads the guts of trouts he's caught and cleaned, scraps of lost paper, graffiti on the broken walls where facing has been shot away to reveal the brick underneath—broken in specific shapes that may also be read" (GR, p. 623). Slothrop stumbles into a public latrine abounding in graffiti. Might he now encounter some definitive revelation as to which "Kilroy" had been there, preceding him? But instead of finding the name of his precursor scrawled on the wall, Slothrop finds only the traces of himself: "ROCKETMAN WAS HERE." (Slothrop's nickname is Rocketman.) The uppercase provides no deliverance from the albatross of self.

It is too easy to point out how the reader is tested, constantly, in his ability to decipher the difficult, swirling surfaces of these two epic romances. Merrill and Pynchon have a certain stake in making the very page itself harder to read. The typographic peculiarities of Merrill's trilogy are likely to occupy new readers fully as much as the various realms of being they serve to distinguish. The different type cases and schemes of indentation followed by Merrill may help or hinder his readers, but it should be pointed out that what they literalize—the narrative's frequent and elliptical shifts between kinds of speech—goes on constantly in modern texts, both of poetry and fiction. Merrill's poem is of course difficult to read sequentially, but it is hardly alone in stymying that expectation. Although Merrill has little in common with someone like Pound, one would do well to study the technique each poet adopts to create boundaries of discourse, to mark off intrusive voices. Merrill codifies where Pound often mystifies, but his voices would retain their individuality even if typography did not prepare us to know who was speaking. The trilogy is always a conversational poem. Merrill is able to sustain a modernist revival of that poetic mode by crossing conversation with ellipsis, polite dialogue with sharp interruption. Speakers are always cutting each other off without ever under-cutting what the other says.

Merrill's transitions between speakers never demand that skep-tical distrust of preceding discourse that is the prime function of ellipsis in modernist texts. In other words, Merrill is never struc-turally ironic. His repartee is sprinkled with gentler, passing iron-ies that the reader welcomes as a release from the severity of in-struction, but they do not compel us to suspect what has gone before. This is a crucial point: while it is certainly true that JM and company add piece by piece to their structure of messages, with each new bit revising earlier beliefs, this process of revision is grounded in a growing certainty about the truth. Vergil is su-perseded by Beatrice, but this does not mean that Dante intends Vergil's doctrine to be undercut by the greater instructor. What he knows is amplified by her knowledge; so Mirabell will yield to the angels. Higher authorities supersede lower, while the notion of authority remains intact. The connection between blocks of speech in the trilogy appear more ragged than they really are, primarily for typographical reasons. The cut-and-paste look of the page in-clines one to think of the poem as a disjunctive collage. But its true spirit resides in its formal resolutions, such as the pavane com-posed in praise of V work (*Mirabell*, Book 3), which perfectly blends disparate voices.

Pynchon represents a more savage school of irony. Authority is always put into question in his fiction, error is endless. *Gravity's Rainbow* abounds with false centers of authority, moments that lure the reader into anchoring the quest for certainty, only to slide away like the false bedrock of Leviathan. (Every reader of Pynchon, my-self included, nonetheless believes that there *is* an unassailable passage or two in which the authorial hand betrays itself.)

In its lighter moments, Pynchon's legerdemain resembles Mer-rill's flaunting of poetic conceit. Improvisational wit keeps readers offguard; they know something is up but do not know where it will lead. As a poet, Merrill confines himself more to the local effects of wordplay and, as a mortal, to the lowercase commentary embroidering his blocks of literal truth. (Mirabell's frequent resort to (M), the parenthetical metaphor notwithstanding.) Pynchon's more raucous wit is less susceptible to closure. His improvisations spin off on widening arcs of unpredictability, and his readers are hardly able to tell when or where they have landed. The outrageous pop lyrics that dot the pages of *Gravity's Rainbow* can usually be found at the center of these improvisations. As bits of low culture they might presumably add a touch of stability to the narrative, bringing evidence of a lighthearted world outside the Zone. But Pynchon makes this comfort impossible to derive by skewing the lyrics both to illustrate how malleable they are to any given situation and how unstable or potentially mad they are in their own right.

Take this swatch of narrative from the novel's final section, "The Counter-Force" (*GR*, pp. 634–635). Roger Mexico comes storming into the office of Dr. Pointsman, the sinister Pavlovian, looking for revenge; instead, he finds Pointsman's assistant, Geza Rozsavolgyi. Mexico's anger degenerates into a slapstick session with the latter. But then something strange happens. Rozsavolgyi, retreating from his tormentor, backs into a shadowy corner of the room from whose vantage point "the rest of the room seems to be at more of a distance, as through the view-finder on a camera. And the walls—they don't appear to be . . . well, *solid*, actually. They flow: a coarse, viscous passage, rippling like a piece of silk or nylon, the color watery gray but now and then with a surprise island in the flow." (Compare Merrill's fantasia on the wallpaper in the parlor at Stonington, which opens *Mirabell*.) It is a short step from this "surprise island" to a fantasy about two fighter pilots who crash-land on the island: "We—we're *safe*? We are! Mangoes, I see mangoes on that tree over there! a—and there's a girl—there's a *lotta* girls! Lookit, they're all gorgeous . . . and they're all swingin' those grass skirts, playin' ukuleles and singing (though why are their voices so loud and tough, so nasally like the voices of an American chorus line?): 'White man, welcome to Puke-a-hook-a-look-i I-i-i-island!' Rozsavolgyi's dream vision ends only when one of the pilots raises his goggles and smiles mockingly, familiarly, at the dreamer, thus stepping out of the frame: "I know you, don't you know me? Don't you *really* know me?"

What a Rozsavolgyi sees may only add up to an amusing divertimento, but it is Pynchon's habit throughout *Gravity's Rainbow* to assign even the most seemingly profound visions to peripheral characters. This almost seems a defensive gesture on his part, a reflexive appeal to an irony easily available to the writer of fiction: the untrustworthy narrator, or character, as in this case. But I think a more radical motive is at work. The assignment of these core moments to ephemeral characters seems rather to abolish the perspectives by means of which the reader has been deciding just who is central and who peripheral.

Pynchon's "revelations" often take the form of undoing the mimetic or naturalistic frame of his narratives, calling into question the whole concept of discrete characters or persons. As I have mentioned, the logical denouement of Merrill's schema does the same thing, although his poem cannot bear to eradicate the trace of human personality. Vocal inflections ring true for Merrill even when speech emanates from "WITHIN THE ATOM." Pynchon's character probes of the molecular underworld bring back news of a structuralist's heaven, a realm of law that abolishes the mere subjectivity or intentionality of its subjects. One Blobadjian, a bureaucrat and minor linguist, is abruptly removed from the action (centering on a commission set up to bring the New Turkic Alphabet to an oral tribe in Central Asia) and is brought into touch with the bureaucracy of the other side.

> How alphabetic is the nature of molecules. One grows aware of it down here: one finds Committees on molecular structure which are very similar to those back at the NTA plenary session: "See: how they are taken out from the coarse flow—shaped, cleaned, rectified, just as you once redeemed your letters from the lawless, the mortal streaming of human speech. . . . These are our letters, our words: they too can be modulated, broken, recoupled, redefined, co-polymerized one to the other in worldwide chains that will surface now and then over long molecular silences, like the seen parts of a tapestry."
>
> [GR, p. 355]

"One grows aware of it down here": this conversion of the natural locus of all waste, all loss—the underworld—into a scene of instruction is finally what Pynchon and Merrill have most in com-

mon. "NOTHING IS EVER EVER LOST   THE WATERFALL WILL HOLD / YR
2 BRIGHT DROPS & YOU WILL SPLASH INTO THE GREAT CLEAR POOL"
(*M*, p. 23), are perhaps the most poignant lines in all of Merrill.
This faith justifies the extraordinary feats of conservation, retrieval,
assemblage, that make up the body of *Gravity's Rainbow* or Mer-
rill's trilogy. Pynchon looks upon gravity itself as the preserving
force in nature: "To find that Gravity, taken so for granted, is really
something eerie, Messianic, extrasensory in Earth's mindbody . . .
having hugged to its holy center the wastes of dead species, gath-
ered, packed, transmuted, realigned, and rewoven molecules to be
taken up again by the coal-tar Kabbalists of the other side" (*GR*, p.
590). Something of us will survive, if only as "bright drops" in
gravity's rainbow.

CHAPTER 11

Lending a Hand

David Jackson

JM has covered much of the ground I might venture on. His coverage, however, often tranforms such ground for the uses of the poem. In reading any of the three books and the epilogue I've had the unique experience of coming upon messages I remembered as nearly meaningless, now charged with meaning; what I'd felt was an example of, oh, Mirabell's long-windedness or simply fanciful data emerged from JM's hands as a piece of information useful to the text. A section of transcript (from an April 1976 session) followed by JM's reworking of it may illustrate:

(The oo voice:) BEEZELBOB   WE R CALLED THAT   WE LEFT THE WORK OF CHAOS
WHEN WE SHED OUR FEELINGS   THE FORCES OF BIOL R LIKE WIND & POLLEN
CANNOT LOVE DRIVEN OR NOT BY SEX BE THE GENERATIVE WIND   (JM or
DJ:) So some feelings, not yours perhaps, do work for Biology?   PRE-
HISTORY WE MADE PARABLE & MYTH REAL IN HARD BIOLOGICAL TERMS
ADAM & EVE R IMAGES THAT HAPPENED IN MOLECULAR HISTORY   THERE IS
A WORLD IN THE ATOM NEGATIVE — POSITIVE   Proton and neutron?
YES   NEUTRON ADAM EVE PROTON   SHE HAD TO BE SIMPLIFIED IN PRE
SCIENTIFIC TERMS   LANGUAGE NEEDED TO EXPLAIN MAN TO MAN   EDEN
A STAGE   THE EXPULSION THE DRAMA   THE MISTAKE TO BELIEVE THAT
KNOWLEDGE IS EVIL   THAT MISTAKE PERSISTS

        BEEZELBOB   SYLLABLES THAT TO A CHILD SPELL WICKEDNESS
        BUT WE LEFT THE WORK OF CHAOS WHEN WE SHED OUR FEELINGS
          Have you some chronology for this?
        PREHISTORY   WE MADE PARABLE & MYTH IN HARD
        BIOLOGICAL TERMS   ADAM EVE ARE IMAGES
        FOR DEVELOPMENTS IN THE VERY NATURE OF MATTER
        A WORLD NEGATIVE & POSITIVE DWELLS IN THE ATOM

EDEN A STAGE   THE EXPULSION THE DRAMA   THE MISTAKE
TO BELIEVE THAT KNOWLEDGE IS EVIL   THAT MISTAKE PERSISTS
[M, p. 21]

One understands that JM's concern was not only to make sense of these wordy messages but to fit them into a syllabic line, rewording when necessary and cutting to avoid a poem twice the length of the published one. What he has plucked from here and there to stud the poem is revealed only by a closer look at transcript and text. The phrase "THAT TO A CHILD SPELL WICKEDNESS" has it source in a later transcript (cf. also *Mirabell*, p. 26):

GABRIEL   MICHAEL   THESE NAMES ARE CHILDREN'S NAMES U UNDERSTAND
FOR POSITIVE FORCES   AND THE NEGATIVE   OUR NAMES   BEELZE   WE HAD
NO NAMES   THEY ARE THE INVENTION OF THE SCRIBE

Also the name BEEZELBOB (seen again in the above quotation on the point of becoming BEELZEBUB?). Respelled by JM, it splits easily into two words we have heard before:

> For it seemed that Time—
> The grizzled washer of his hands appearing
> To say so in a spectrum-bezeled space
> Above hot water—Time would not.
>
> [DC, p. 48]

> It's Bob the furnace man. He's on his way.
>
> [DC, p. 135]

The connection is further pointed up by the line JM adds to Wystan's transcript account of the bats: "THESE THE CLERK TYPISTS." This now becomes: "THESE I PRESUME ARE THE CLERK TYPISTS / OR IN YR WORDS THE BOBS   THE FURNACE MEN" (M, p. 37).

As the poem progressed I was always astonished by my own fascination, as if I were listening to an orchestration of what had been a wobbly or unharmonic melody.

In the transcript Wystan explains his death—why, we had asked, was he returning to the mineral world? Maria's radiation treatments, we understood, made *her* soul useless for reincarnation—as follows:

MY DEATH CHEMICAL POISONING   RATHER DRUNKENLY I WENT OFF TO MY
ROOM   I THOUGHT TO WRITE A NOTE TO C   & LIKE MY CHILDHOOD HABIT
SUCKED ON A PENCIL THINKING   & NEXT THING I KNEW I WAS WEIGHTED
DOWN AS IF MY QUILT WERE OF LEAD   WE MAKE OUR DEATHS   I SUSPECT
THAT WILDLY EXPECTED SHY BROTHER WILL TELL US

Months later, having asked for further clarification, we learn:

EACH TIME DEAR BOY I HAD AN XRAY THE DESTRUCTION "RADIATED" BY
MEANS OF AN ACCUMULATED LEAD-BOXED RADIANT WASTE SO TO SPEAK
I BECAME A WALKING "REACTOR"   XRAYS DID NOT DISSIPATE   Due to
the lead in you? YES   A NONCONDUCTOR & THERE4 A "WALL" KEEPING
MINUTE RADIANT ENERGIES IN VARIOUS VITAL ORGANS & BLOODSTREAM.
I SUSPECT THE OLD LEAD PENCIL HAS DESTROYED MANY OF MY GENERA-
TION (& BROKEN UP MANY A HAPPY HOME)   Is graphite just as bad?
SAME ELEMENT   MORE TO THE POINT

Here is how JM telescopes these two passages:

MY DEMISE A FORM OF LEAD
POISONING: I WENT OFF TO MY ROOM
TIDDLY THAT NIGHT BUT HAD IN MIND TO SCRIBBLE
A NOTE TO C, & AS I'D DONE SINCE CHILDHOOD
SUCKED ON A PENCIL THINKING. NEXT I KNEW,
AN ICY SUN SHONE IN UPON THE DEAD
WEIGHT OF MY FEATHER QUILT But how does lead
Destroy the soul? DJ: They don't *use* lead—
Graphite in pencils. LET THE FACT REMAIN
(OR FABLE!) THAT I SIPPED IT GRAIN BY GRAIN.
OVER THE YEARS ANYTHING FROM AN X RAY
TO THE COSMIC RAYS WE'RE ALL EXPOSED TO WD
RESIDE UNDISSIPATED IN MY BLOOD
& VITAL ORGANS: I BECAME A WALKING
NONCONDUCTING LEADEN CASKET THESE
PARTICULAR DESTRUCTIVE ENERGIES
HAD FILLED WITH RADIANT WASTE   Dear God . . . & NO
PANDORA   NO LATTERDAY BASSANIO
TO LIFT THE LID. WE MAKE OUR DEATHS MY DEARS
AS NO DOUBT THAT SHY WILDLY EXPECTED BRO
WILL TELL US

[*S*, pp. 21–22]

So the Scribe took our Senior poet's account and made use of all its
facts, slipped in an allusion to Wystan's Fact versus Fable speech in
Mirabell (9.1) and, by changing the image of the lead box to Bas-

sanio's leaden casket, lightened the heavy news. Perhaps taking her cue from this touch, Maria will ask later (*Scripts*, p. 173) if she may serve as "MAN'S PORTIA."

What of the dictations that JM did *not* use? That last joke about the lead pencil he must have given up most reluctantly. But there were quantities of others, often quite poetic messages that I would be surprised not to find included in the poem as it progressed. Part of this editing was due, as JM has written, to his lower threshold of tolerance for the extraneous passage I couldn't have resisted. Ephraim: U ARE SO DEAR TO ME   I FEEL ALREADY WILLING TO SETTLE IN AN EARTHLY MOOD & LET FOOLISH DESTINY OCCUPY MY PLACE IN HEAVEN. Or, hearing we were off one day to visit an old lady: OLD LADIES R FOOLS   THEY WILL NOT TALK OF SEX WHICH WD BE INSTRUC-TIVE & HARMLESS. Or that whiff of Mary Baker Eddy in his theory of cancer: B4 THE 18TH CENTURY IT WAS RECOGNIZED BY SAINTS & OTHERS AS A WILL TO DIE   CELLS OF BODY RECOGNIZING IF U LIKE LACK OF CONTROL IN THE CAPITAL RUSH IN REBELLION UPON THE BODY OF THE STATE. These and dozens like them made him not only charming to us, a consoling and enlightening friend, but nearly indispensable during many a quiet evening, wherever we happened to find ourselves. In those early years we summoned him only after dinner. Mirabell and the Angels demanded afternoon sessions unblurred by wine.

Our Ouija experience began in Stonington on August 23, 1955, with my wife, Doris Sewell Jackson. Ephraim, we learned right off, was at Stage 6. It never occurred to us (or anyway to me) to con-nect this fact with his later identification as Michael—as Angel of Light, naturally at a stage beyond that of the five senses. Twenty-two years, in fact, passed before we realized that Ephraim had all along been a disguise for our real guide through the winding knowl-edges of the system.

In looking over the earliest transcripts, copied into a small black notebook JM kept, I see that he wrote (on August 30, a week after our first session) that he had "finished, more or less, the ouija board poem" ("Voices from the Other World") and saw it as "the

first in a deepening set, dealing with one's relation to that world."
What was that relation? The question had come up in that very
first session:

> WE CALL THIS SCIENCE A PARTICULAR ONE   WE CALL THOSE WE KNOW WILL
> NOT REFUTE US   Is it Black Magic? What do you do, raise the dead? Can
> we raise you?   YOU HAVE   Where are you?   I AM THE CUP   Can you do
> anything without us?   I CAN IF U WILL PARDON A BAD JOKE SHATTER MYSELF

In "Voices from the Other World" the cup does shatter "in a rage,"
but it never did at our table. Instead, Ephraim went on for several
years, our most amusing houseguest. He brought to the board
patron after patron of those live friends we had for drinks or din-
ner or overnight. Of one, an old and dear friend of mine from
college days: HE RISKS TOO MUCH   PLEASURE IS OFTEN A WALL CRASH-
ING. I think my friend is so witty and penetrating that his life often
makes him desperate. EXACTLY   HE IS MOST PROMISING   STILL PER-
HAPS WE WILL FIND A GENEROUS & QUIETING LOVE. And of another
friend, gruff and intelligent, moving restlessly around in a Lesbian
world: SHE IS A WOMAN IN DISGUISE   LOVE EATS UPON HER   SOCIETY
IS HARDEST ON THE WOMAN WHO CANNOT AS HUNTERS SEEK MEN   A
DIANA TYPE. Rather smoothly Ephraim glazed over inconsistencies.
A third friend: HE HAS HAD 3 LIVES   1ST DEAD AT 10 YEARS 1888   2ND
20 YEARS Are you sure that's not a mistake? If this is our friend's
first life and he is only twenty-seven? U R TESTING NOT ASKING
Forgive us. I ALWAYS HAVE   U SEE IF HE HAD BEEN 20 HE WD HAVE
DOUBLED HIS YEARS   PATRON MUST HAVE AN ORIENTAL COUNTING
SYSTEM (Hmm.)

Most of these readouts weren't used by JM. Indeed their parlor-
game aspect began to weary us, Ephraim always being too gen-
tlemanly to admit his own boredom with it, though complaining
mildly of the increasing swarms of patrons. Yet there is one notable
exception:

> PATRON ENRAGED   RM WAS HIS GREAT HOPE TO ELEVATION BUT FOR RM'S
> CONTACTS WITH CERTAIN LOW TYPES HE SEEMS LASHED TO   RM RARE   IN 3RD
> LIFE   P SAYS 1ST LIFE A RABBI A GREAT MYSTIC OF ENORMOUS POWER   2ND
> LIFE A CHARMING LITTLE PUPIL OF   OH MY DEARS P TOO ANGRY   GOT RM
> INTO SUCH A PLEASANT WOMB & THEN RM JUST THREW IT ALL UP TO FOLLOW

A VIOLINIST TO ITALY   P GAVE RM TWO WARNINGS IN FORM OF HEE HEE
R E M O R S E

Two decades later, Robert Morse would confess to us from the other world that he did not know what his next life would be:

> THEY WON'T TELL:
> MY PUNISHMENT FOR HAVING BLUSHED UNSEEN?
> DJ: *We* saw you, Robert, TRUE   AH WELL
> R(E)MORSE IS USELESS & HAS EVER BEEN
>
> [S, p. 94]

But of course Robert wasn't reborn immediately. They'd had their eye on him since long before that point in *Mirabell* (p. 161) when "Tap on the door and in strolls Robert Morse, / Closest of summer friends in Stonington."

A glimpse here of how an actual message looked when scrawled down by JM, then deciphered: ECCOAROMANMATRONALOVELYSUR PRISE&AREALROMANHEADCH ARMING This friend is an unbeliever. ALLROMANSRRANKCYNICSTHEYRAMUSING4THAT. No, the reader can decipher this one. I found in museums and sites in Greece how easy after the board it was to read the carved inscriptions, those long unseparated lines of immaculate lettering.

Michael's first visit ended with his sun setting. One more time he came to our Stonington tower, the red dining room half-surrounded by windows, with its few randomly spaced oblongs of picture glass. (We'd understood that reflections helped the spirits to "see" and so would often bring a mirror to the table as well.) But the entire dictation of the lessons in *Scripts* took place in Athens. Announcing himself in the West, Michael set up his and his Brothers' workshop in the East closer to sunrise, as it were. The small, tiled entrance hall where we sat was viewless but for a row of high panes giving into a neighboring concrete wall. About us hung a mirror and some largeish glassed-over pictures: two nineteenth-century charcoal studies of sculpture, a Venus and a godlike athlete; a Lear landscape of Corfu; a chromolithograph of Böcklin's *Sport of the Waves*, mermaids and sea gods in an ornate

frame that on first sight had made Maria gasp with recognition—
this very picture had hung for years in her father's study! (No acci-
dent?) A terracotta three-quarter life-size statue—Artemis or Per-
sephone—stood in one corner, holding an apple as if to curry favor
with the teacher in a Schoolroom that was already, so to speak, in
the works. Visible from this hall, in a little room always shuttered
against the noise and fumes of the street, was an upright piano,
then a whole cleverly lit wall that I had frescoed with a trompe-
l'oeil seashore—our only outside view. The hallway thus became a
stage, lit each session by late sun through the front door's frosted
glass, with props and sets adjustable to scenes in the lessons. It
was easy to imagine the volcano erupting (p. 52) from Lear's dis-
tant mountain, or Gabriel's jumble of religious architectures (p. 161)
rising like magic casements from Böcklin's foam.

Only once, for our introduction to Gabriel, did we move to the
upstairs living room, with its fireplace swept bare and its curtains
drawn. Then the farewell to Maria, Wystan, and George took place
on the roof terrace, modest, ringed with big pots of oleander, roses,
and jasmine and the lone warped but golden cassia. There, onto
the underside of an orange awning, a rapid interplay of reflec-
tions—rectangular (the little mirror) and round (the bowl of water)—
was flung up by the sun sinking over St. George's white monastery
on top of Mt. Lykabettos. I'm amplifying JM's stage directions only
because we were a touch dismayed when a young reader of the
poems came to Stonington and confessed he would never have
imagined it as it is. "How did you imagine it?" asked JM. "Oh," he
replied, "as much more Gothic." Despite a tradition of rain-whipped
foggy nights and gloomy castles, we know the better ghost stories
are set in sunny everyday surroundings.

It is of course strange, sitting at the Ouija board—there's no
doubt of that—strange and, whatever results, unbelievable. It's not
unlike an adult at a typewriter waiting for a line to pull the mes-
sage through to its end. Or a fisherman pulling up a fish—in our
case, two.

A certain schism set in during those years, dividing and confus-
ing one's perception of any day's experience: the lived human
hours of meetings and conversations, the hours at the board of

other meetings and conversations, the reading over of the material, the reading of JM's typescript as it approached a finished state. Of course Real (life) remained real. Yet as the final lessons were spelled out, they became realer yet, and these emerging in the final text became the most real of all. A manuscript page with its upper-case and lowercase read rather like some voltage indicator of our newly electrified lives, from DC to AC then back again to DC as our Divine Comedy flowed more and more directly.

In any case, I'm flattered to think I lent a hand, the second hand, to JM's hours of labor.

Would the above do? No, I felt, and suggested to JM that we ask Ephraim for a second opinion. The following three-part message resulted, each speaker somehow never before so clearly a changing aspect of the single light.

MES CHERS, ONE IS QUITE RATTLED GIVING VALEDICTORIALS, NO? SO I CALL ON MY WISER HALF. On Michael? HE COMES:

"NO OBJECT WILL FOR LONG CONCEAL ITS MYSTERY WHEN LIGHT SHINES ON IT. THIS FOR THINGS AND IDEAS. THAT LIGHT CAN BE AS SIMPLE AS MY OWN, REVEALING DAY IN THE WORLD AT DAWN, OR AS COMPLEX AS GOD B'S DARLING'S, THE MIND OF MAN. NO MYSTERY IS ABLE TO PREVAIL, NOR WILL IT. MAN IN TODAY'S FORM OR TOMOR-ROW'S WILL UNMASK IT. THEN THE VOICE OF POETS AND TURTLES WILL BE HEARD AND UNDERSTOOD."

HE MES CHERS TOOK OFF HIS ROBES & DEPARTED SAYING: BASE SELF, CLEAR UP MISUNDERSTANDINGS, ADD IF YOU WILL A NOTE OF YOUR OWN, & SO I DO: "THE MISGUIDED VERB 'TO LOVE' OFTEN MIS-CONSTRUED IN POOR MAN'S EARTHLY SENTENCE, IS AFTER ALL 'TO LIGHT.'"

SIRS? Yes, Uni? MR E TOOK OFF HIS TOGA & DEPARTED SAYING: HORSE, CLEAR UP ANY MISUNDERSTANDINGS & IF YOU LIKE ADD A NAI OF YOUR OWN. (NAI—that ambigious syllable: is it the Greek yes? Is it the English negative?) We're ready—let's have it.

"YES"

Notes

David Lehman / Introduction

1. David Kalstone, *Five Temperaments* (New York: Oxford University Press, 1977), p. 80.
2. John Vernon, *Western Humanities Review*, winter 1973, pp. 107–109.
3. Richard Sáez, "James Merrill's Oedipal Fire," in *Parnassus: Poetry in Review*, fall/winter 1974, pp. 183–184.
4. Helen Vendler, *Part of Nature, Part of Us* (Cambridge: Harvard University Press, 1980), p. 205.

1. David Lehman / Elemental Bravery

1. Helen Vendler, "James Merrill's Myth: An Interview," *New York Review of Books*, May 3, 1979, p. 12.
2. Chaucer, "The Miller's Tale," ll. 349–353; Swift, *Gulliver's Travels*, part 3, chapter 2. In his "Apology for Poetry," Sidney cites as evidence of the limitations of science "that the astronomer looking to the stars might fall into a ditch." From Sidney come the phrases "clayey lodgings," "erected wit," and "infected will."
3. Very much to the point is Helen Vendler's eloquent defense of Merrill from the charge of frivolousness. In her reading, Merrill's moral choice is for the quotidian as opposed to the transcendent: "By taking conversation—from lovers' exchange of vows to friends' sentences in intimacy—as the highest form of human expression (in contrast to the rhapsode's hymns, the orator's harangues, or the initiate's hermetic colloquies with the divine) Merrill becomes susceptible to the charges of frivolity, at least from readers with a taste only for the solemn. But the espousal of the conversational as the ultimate in linguistic achievement is a moral choice, one which locates value in the human and everyday rather than in the transcendent" (*Part of Nature, Part of Us* [Cambridge: Harvard University Press, 1980], p. 217). I would argue that Merrill does not choose the human at the expense of the transcendent experience but that he deliberately situates the latter within everyday contexts. Thus in "From the Cupola," Gertrude comically tells only half the truth when she chides

307

Psyche for spurning "loving kin, in a house crammed with lovely old things," in favor of "the unfamiliar, the 'transcendental'" (*ND*, p. 47).

4. "*Hôte* and *ospite* and *héspide* are as mysteriously equivocal as *hospes*," Max Beerbohm notes in his whimsical "Hosts and Guests." "By the weight of all this authority I find myself being dragged to the conclusion that a host and a guest must be the same thing, after all" (*And Even Now* [London: William Heinemann, 1921], p. 127). On the attractions of *host* as a critical term, see J. Hillis Miller's "The Critic as Host," in *Deconstruction and Criticism* (New York: Seabury Press, 1979).

5. Vendler, "James Merrill's Myth: An Interview," p. 12.

6. David Kalstone, *Five Temperaments* (New York: Oxford University Press, 1977), p. 105.

7. The canzone form is, one might say, like the sestina only more so. It is composed of five twelve-line stanzas and a five-line envoy; each of the end words recurs thirteen times. In "Samos," Merrill sometimes substitutes homophones ("scents" for "sense"), adding prefixes on occasion ("magnifier," "innocence," "alight," "inland"), as if to underscore the "elemental" basis of his words and world.

8. The sentence concludes Pater's essay on Joachim Du Bellay in *The Renaissance* (London: Macmillan, 1919), p. 176.

9. The poems, reprinted in *The Country of a Thousand Years of Peace*, are "The Octopus," "The Greenhouse," "The Wintering Weeds," "Midas among Goldenrod," "The Cruise," "A View of the Burning," "About the Phoenix," and "A Narrow Escape."

10. Thus, in an early assessment of Merrill, Richard Howard introduces "the metaphor of secretion, whether nacre or amber, to represent a part of the self which has become precious by hardening." Having in mind Pound's response to *The Wasteland*, "the artisan's honest resentment of the artist," Howard shrewdly goes on to observe that "the jealous voice of a man capable of no more than objets d'art addressing a man capable of an art transcending objects might easily be the voice of the early James Merrill apostrophizing the writer he was to become: one who managed to make what was merely his poetry into what was necessarily his life" (*Alone with America*, enlarged ed. [New York: Atheneum, 1980], p. 386).

11. Harold Bloom, *Kabbalah and Criticism* (New York: Seabury Press, 1975), pp. 40, 43. It will be remembered that Bloom has diagrammed the relation between defense mechanisms and, in Stevens's phrase, "figures of capable imagination." If the destiny of the strong filial poet calls for him to ward off what he must ultimately aspire to reinvent, then a defensive posture will stand behind his rhetorical gestures—which are, in effect, synecdoches of the subconscious—and the greater the pressure, the more sublime the oblique release will be. So Bloom argues. In this paradigm, divine "emanation" translates into literary "influence," and influence involves a sometimes violent collision of wills. See *Poetry and Repression* (New Haven: Yale University Press, 1976). Bloom has applied his reading of the Kabbalah to critical activity as well: "There is no reading worthy of being communicated to another unless it deviates to break form, twists the lines to form a shelter, and so makes a meaning through that shattering of belated vessels" (in *Deconstruction and Criticism*, p. 22).

12. Appearances are a long-standing concern, judging by the poem entitled

"Mirror" in *The Country of a Thousand Years of Peace*. A pivotal point in the poem is reached when the mirror overhears someone say, "*How super-ficial / Appearances are!*"—and takes it to heart.

13. "Peru: The Landscape Game," in *Prose* 2 (spring 1971), pp. 105–114.

14. Kalstone, p. 79.

15. Complexities of the Proustian influence have been explored by many critics. Consider Kalstone; Vendler, *Part of Nature, Part of Us*, p. 217; Richard Sáez, "James Merrill's Oedipal Fire," in *Parnassus: Poetry in Review*, fall/winter 1974, p. 166; Edmund White, "On James Merrill," in *American Poetry Review*, September/October 1979, p. 9.

16. In *Fields of Light* (New York: Oxford University Press, 1951), p. 116, Reuben Brower writes, apropos of *The Tempest*: "Through a sort of Proustian merging of icon and subject, we experience the blending of states of being, of substantial and unsubstantial, of real and unreal, which is the essence of *The Tempest* metamorphosis." Brower credits Merrill's senior honors thesis at Amherst with bringing "this merging in Proust" to his attention.

17. Susan Sontag, *Against Interpretation* (New York: Dell, 1966), p. 290.

18. Cf. *Mirabell*, p. 163:

> OUR CIRCLE CHARMED BY RM   DID I HEAR
> SOME E F BENSON BABYTALK? Indeed!
> (Alluding to the novels we reread—
> And reenact—each summer.)

19. "[The Midas myth] begins and ends in water—in movement, in process. The first appeal is from ordinary experience to ecstasy, to intoxication, and that is an appeal these poets often acknowledge, though not so frequently as the second appeal from chaos to order, to an ideal pre-sentment of permanence; yet this, too, is no more than an impulse endemic to all poetry—this craving that whatever passes through one's hands shall be immutable, immutably one's own. Rather, what seems to me especially proper to these poets in the myth is the last development, the longing to *lose* the gift of order, despoiling the self of all that had been, merely, *propriety*" (Richard Howard, pp. xii–xiii).

20. Stephen Yenser, "Recent Poetry: Five Poets," *Yale Review*, summer 1979, p. 564

21. *The (Diblos) Notebook* (1965; reprint ed., New York: Atheneum, 1975), p. 55.

22. "The Railway Stationery," one of the most remarkable poems in Kenneth Koch's *Thank You*, is comparable in some ways. Its six sonnets behave like narrative stanzas whose closing couplets amount to comic arias of everyday life: "Now came the truck / Of the postman. 'Hello, Jim.' 'Hello there, Bill.' / 'I've got this—can you take it?' 'Sure, I will.'"

23. Kalstone, p. 105.

24. No doubt the best-known instance is Hedda's incendiary destruction of Eilert Lovborg's major opus in *Hedda Gabler*, but it is a recurrent motif in comic literature also. Confiscation of his book makes possible all of Adam Fenwick-Symes's adventures in Waugh's *Vile Bodies*, and in Huxley's *Crome Yellow* Denis has no choice but to tear up the conventional, life-inhibiting novel he has written.

2. J. D. McClatchy / On *Water Street*

1. Richard Howard, *Alone with America*, enlarged ed. (New York: Atheneum, 1980), p. 401.
2. When the poem was first published in the *Quarterly Review of Literature* (10:4 [1960], pp. 224–225), it was "a frail gold mask." The change may be an improvement, but it is also a presumably unconscious echo of Elinor Wylie's "Sunset on the Spire," which ends "All that I / Could ever ask / Wears that sky / Like a thin gold mask." Merrill has kept the sense of the image, just reversed the time of day.
3. The interview was published in *Contemporary Literature* 9:1 (winter 1968); the quoted statement appears on p. 2.
4. David Kalstone, *Five Temperaments* (New York: Oxford University Press, 1977), p. 88.
5. Ibid., p. 85.
6. *The (Diblos) Notebook* (New York: Atheneum, 1965), p. 9.
7. Wallace Stevens, "The Auroras of Autumn," in *Collected Poems* (New York: Knopf, 1954), p. 411.
8. Ibid., p. 419.

3. Samuel E. Schulman / Lyric Knowledge

1. Helen Vendler, *Part of Nature, Part of Us* (Cambridge: Harvard University Press, 1980), p. 212.
2. Vernon Shetley, "Take But Degree Away," *Poetry* 137 (April 1981), p. 301.
3. Wallace Stevens, "Three Academic Pieces," in *The Necessary Angel* (New York: Knopf, 1951), p. 79.
4. David Kalstone, *Five Temperaments* (New York: Oxford University Press, 1977), pp. 84–85.
5. Alvin Feinman, *Preambles and Other Poems* (New York: Oxford University Press, 1964), p. 3.
6. *The Past Recaptured*, trans. Andreas Mayor (New York: Random House, 1970), p. 176.
7. Kalstone, p. 115.

4. David Kalstone / Persisting Figures

1. See Richard Onorato, *The Character of the Poet: Wordsworth in "The Prelude"* (Princeton: Princeton University Press, 1971).
2. See Harold Bloom, *Poetry and Repression* (New Haven: Yale University Press, 1976).
3. John Ashbery, *Three Poems* (New York: Viking, 1972), pp. 109–110.
4. Ashbery, *Self-Portrait in a Convex Mirror* (New York: Viking, 1976), p. 8.
5. Ibid., p. 81.
6. Ashbery, *Three Poems*, pp. 102–103.
7. Helen Vendler, *Part of Nature, Part of Us* (Cambridge: Harvard University Press, 1980), p. 226.
8. *The Poems of Richard Wilbur* (New York: Harcourt, Brace & World, 1963), p. 72.

9. Adrienne Rich, *On Lies, Secrets, and Silence* (New York: Norton, 1979), pp. 40–41.

10. James Merrill, "These early versions of desire . . . ," *From the First Nine* (New York: Atheneum, 1982).

5. Rachel Jacoff / Merrill and Dante

1. James Merrill, "Divine Poem," *New Republic*, November 29, 1980, pp. 29–34.

2. J. J. Callahan, "The Curvature of Space in a Finite Universe," *Scientific American*, August 1976, pp. 90–100, and Mark A. Petersen, "Dante and the 3-sphere," *American Journal of Physics* 47 (December 1979), pp. 1031–1035.

3. Merrill, p. 32.

4. Auden's "Canzone" is also modeled on Dante's poem, and it too has a five-line congedo. But Auden's shift to the five-line closing stanza is not in any way related to the poem's content. Cf. W. H. Auden, *Collected Poems*, ed. Edward Mendelson (New York: Random House, 1976), pp. 256–257.

5. Cf. John Freccero, "Casella's Song (*Purg.* II, 112)," *Dante Studies* 91 (1973), pp. 73–80; Robert Hollander, "*Purgatorio* II: Cato's Rebuke and Dante's *scoglio*," *Italica* 52:3 (1975), pp. 348–363; and my own "The Post-Palinodic Smile: *Paradiso* VIII and IX," which will appear in *Dante Studies* 98 (1980).

6. Rilke's letter to his Polish translator, Witold von Hulewicz, which is quoted in translation by M. D. Herter Norton in *Sonnets to Orpheus* (New York: Norton, 1942), pp. 132–133.

6. Peter Sacks / The Divine Translation

1. Perhaps it is this sense of greatly augmented rather than merely cleared space that is referred to in the following lines:

> AS, OH, TO MILTON THE DROWNED LYCIDAS,
> SO SOC TO PLATO. . . .
> HIS WHOLE LIFE & DOOM
> FURNISHED THE GOLDEN SCRIBE WITH 'LIVING ROOM'
>
> [S, p. 191]

2. J. D. McClatchy, "*DJ*: A Conversation with David Jackson," *Shenandoah* 30:4 (1979), p. 35.

3. If one examines the elegy as a genre, one notices how such masterpieces as those by Vergil, Spenser, and Milton are empowered by a deeply eclogic device: seemingly "other" voices supersede or break in upon a griever as from a higher or more profound level of experience and authority. Like those of Merrill's dictée, the voices Menalcas, Clorinda, St. Peter, for example, may derive from such subconsciously inspired strata of the mind that their rejoinders and assurances are uttered as though by someone other than the initial griever himself.

4. W. H. Auden and Chester Kallman, *The Rake's Progress* (New York: Boosey and Hawkes, 1951), act III, scene 3, p. 58.

7. Willard Spiegelman / Breaking the Mirror

1. Stephen Yenser, "The Fullness of Time: James Merrill's *Book of Ephraim*," *Conto* 3 (spring 1980), pp. 130–159.
2. Donald Sheehan, "An Interview with James Merrill," *Contemporary Literature* 9 (winter 1968), p. 10.
3. Harold Bloom, *Kabbalah and Criticism* (New York: Seabury Press, 1975), p. 39.
4. Stanley Fish, "*Lycidas*: A Poem Finally Anonymous," *Glyph 8* (Baltimore: The Johns Hopkins University Press, 1981), pp. 1–18. For a more theoretical and fanciful discussion of "interruption," see Louis Marin, "The Autobiographical Interruption: About Stendhal's 'Life of Henry Brulard,'" *MLN* 93 (1978), pp. 597–617.
5. It is perfectly likely, given the self-referentiality of Merrill's oeuvre, that this very sunset and even "Michael" are recalled at the end of *Mirabell* when Michael the angel starkly commands JM at sunset: "LOOK INTO THE RED EYE OF YOUR GOD!" (*M*, p. 182). For the romantic use of biblical paradigms, see M. H. Abrams, *Natural Supernaturalism* (New York: Norton, 1971), especially chapter 3, "The Circuitous Journey: Pilgrims and Prodigals," pp. 141–195.
6. In "Charles on Fire," another poem in *Nights and Days* about the relationship of soul and body, the title character establishes his wholeness by involuntarily looking at himself in a mirror after an eerie experience involving after-dinner drinks set on fire in his hand.
7. Letter to Thomas Poole, January 28, 1810; *Collected Letters of Samuel Taylor Coleridge*, ed. E. L. Griggs, vol. 3 (Oxford: Clarendon Press, 1959), p. 282. A great deal could be said about the importance of parenthetical remarks, not just in Merrill, as "interrupters" that further the development of thought.
8. Cf. Robert Morse's reconstruction of his death (*S*, p. 216) as the reestablishment of wholeness.
9. Many of the major moments in the trilogy are analogous to Thomas Weiskel's definition of "the Wordsworthian sublime" as the "occlusion" of the visible; cf. also his statement that "*resistance* may be identified with what Wordsworth calls imagination" (emphasis mine), in the last chapter, "Wordsworth and the Defile of the Word," of *The Romantic Sublime*: *Studies in the Structure and Psychology of Transcendence* (Baltimore: The Johns Hopkins University Press, 1975), p. 175.
10. The question of whether a rhyme even exists is a puzzling and embarrassing one. The most famous example of "phantom rhyme," I suppose, is Dylan Thomas' "Author's Prologue," where the first line rhymes with the last, the second with the penultimate, the third with the antepenultimate, etc. Not until one reaches a couplet in the middle can one actually "hear" a rhyme, however. Can it be said that the "more" that ends line 1 of *Lycidas* rhymes with anything else in the poem? With the ends of lines 58, 61, 63, 131, 132, 165, 167, 170, 182, or 183?
11. Much could be written on Merrill's specific debts to the romantic poets as well as on his connections with romantic "sublimity." "Hand" and "scribe" surely recall, as does much else in the trilogy, *The Fall of Hyperion* (11.16–18: "Whether the dream now purpos'd to rehearse / Be

poet's or fanatic's will be known / When this warm scribe, my hand, is in the grave.").

8. Richard Sáez / "At the Salon Level": Merrill's Apocalyptic Epic

1. My title comes from the first volume, "The Book of Ephraim," p. 116 (*Divine Comedies*), of Merrill's epic. Throughout my essay, I have tried to use Merrill's own terminology, names, and words.

2. Throughout this essay, I am thinking of some of the distinctions between the private and public aspects of epic and lyric poetry which Northrop Frye makes in the *Anatomy of Criticism* (Princeton: Princeton University Press, 1957). Of particular interest for Merrill's work is Frye's view of "concealment" in the lyric mode.

3. Throughout my essay I refer to the three parts of Merrill's epic with the single names "Ephraim," *Mirabell*, and *Scripts*. For the trilogy or epic as a whole, I have adopted the title *Comedies*. Although the omnibus edition is called *The Changing Light at Sandover*, this lovely title appears to me to be appropriate only for the final volume. *Comedies* is, of course, borrowed from *Divine Comedies*, the title of the volume in which "The Book of Ephraim" appeared. It seems to me a better title for the entire trilogy, and it has the advantage of responding to the epic's all-important camp tonality and tripartite analogy with Dante.

4. The Supplement to the *Oxford English Dictionary* gives the word "camp" a surprisingly long, varied, and "serious" genealogy. But I am thinking most particularly of Susan Sontag's "Notes on 'Camp'" (*Against Interpretation* [New York: Farrar, Straus & Giroux, 1965]). Three aspects of her notes are particularly relevant to Merrill's trilogy: (1) the emphasis on "aestheticism" and "life as theatre," (2) the attempt "to dethrone the serious," and (3) the relationship between "Jewish moral seriousness and homosexual aestheticism and irony."

5. Irvin Ehrenpreis, "Otherwordly Goods," *New York Review of Books*, January 22, 1981, pp. 47–51.

6. Given the way the Ouija board is played *à deux* and the fact that more and more of the pages of Merrill's epic are dictated directly from it as the work progresses, there are interesting questions regarding the authorship of the work and the relationship of JM and DJ. In a later context, I locate the archetype of their relationship in Don Quijote and Sancho Panza, a "quintessential" aspect of which is their exchange of identities. Will the omnibus volume of Merrill's epic be published under the name of David Jackson? And why not?

7. "Chimes at Midnight." The biographical gossip (whether or not true) that this exquisite lyric memorializes a fleeting tryst in a homosexual bathhouse is, of course, not irrelevant to my analysis. Since Auden is gone, one wishes that Merrill would write about the lyric mode and promiscuity. We have much to learn from such an essay, and we have already had intimations of that knowledge in his fine piece on Cavafy ("Marvelous Poet," *New York Review of Books*, July 17, 1975, pp. 12–17).

8. John Huizinga, *Homo Ludens: A Study of the Play Element in Culture* (London: Routledge & Kegan Paul, 1955).

9. The best place to study theodicy is still the complete works of Saint

Augustine. But an excellent introduction, for the less ambitious reader, is to be found in John Hick's *Evil and the God of Love* (London: Macmillan, 1966). Less satisfactory is his essay, "The Problem of Evil," in the *Encyclopaedia of Philosophy* (New York: Macmillan, 1967), vol. 3, pp. 136–140. Especially agile minds will find theodicy dressed in logical-positivist terms in *God, Freedom and Evil* by Alvin Plantinga (London: George Allen & Unwin, 1975).

10. "Chiastic rhyme," the rhyming of words with antithetical meaning, is briefly discussed by W. K. Wimsatt, Jr., in "Rhyme and Reason," *The Verbal Icon* (New York: The Noonday Press, 1958) pp. 162–163. Its most sublime form as thesis, antithesis, and synthesis in Dante's terza rima has never, to my knowledge, been adequately analyzed.

11. The reference to "Mineshafts" appears in *Scripts*, p. 217. "Mineshaft" is the name for what homosexual guides refer to as a "hot" sado-masochistic bar.

12. This is an extremely thorny area of musicology, especially at the moment. One of the problems is the confusion of Bach's straightforward Lutheran point of view with the considerably more fanciful attribution of meaning to musical elements by the adherents of *"affehtlehre"* in the eighteenth-century Mannheim School. Nonetheless, good analyses in English for the way in which the development of Western music is the gradual accommodation of higher degrees of dissonance, that is, the overtone series, and the way in which Bach prepared and anticipated this development can be found in the entries on harmony and Bach in the *New Grove Dictionary of Music and Musicians* (6th edition).

13. The *locus classicus* for this aspect of theodicy is Saint Augustine's *Confessions*, Book X.

14. The most available study of this aspect of Dante is to be found in Erich Auerbach's *Dante: Poet of the Secular World* (Chicago: University of Chicago Press, 1961).

15. I discuss this aspect of Merrill's work, and "18 West 11th Street" in particular, in my essay "Merrill's Oedipal Fire," *Parnassus: Poetry in Review*, fall/winter 1974, pp. 159–184.

16. Ibid., p. 172.

17. Ibid., p. 165.

18. Marcel Proust, À *la recherche du temps perdu* (Paris: Librairie Gallimard, Bibliotheque de la Pléiade, 1954), vol. 3, p. 483. I quote slightly out of context (the release occurs years and pages later), but that is necessitated by the *longueurs* of Proust. My interpretation is subtle but accurate.

19. Merrill describes the "composite" hero in *The (Diblos) Notebook* (New York: Atheneum, 1965; 1975) p. 62.

20. Helen Vendler, "V Works," *The New Yorker*, September 3, 1979, pp. 95–105.

21. Neither is my essay the place for, nor am I qualified to do an analysis of feminine symbols in the films of European homosexual directors. But the interested reader might begin on his own by comparing the script for Franco Zeffirelli's television documentary on Maria Callas (one of the cast of characters in Merrill's *Comedies*) with my discussion of the symbols and language of Merrill's epic. Equally fruitful would be a comparison of Pasolini's counterpoint to the Greek legend in his film *Medea* starring, again, Callas. It is interesting to note that Pasolini, in his own

yes and no dichotomy, also produced the finest cinematic versions of both the gospel (*Il Vangelo secondo Matteo*) and the Marquis de Sade (*Salò*). The latter is particularly orthodox in portraying the slightest Manichaean acknowledgment of evil as leading inexorably to the absolute nadir.

22. Recent scholarship provides a great deal of help in beginning to constitute a phenomenology of male homosexuals and the soprano voice. Of particular interest are the studies by Victor Zuckerkandl, *Sound and Symbol* (Princeton: Princeton University Press, 1956), and Mark Booth, *The Experience of Song* (New Haven: Yale University Press, 1981). These works analyze the tendency of songs to be forms of "self-transcendence," "rituals of solidarity" through which all phenomena and personae concerned are "mystically" joined.

23. The quality of these lyric symbols is, I think, best defined in my own "Oedipal Fire" essay and in David Kalstone's "Transparent Things," *Five Temperaments* (New York: Oxford University Press, 1977), pp. 77–128.

24. There are many references to "plasticity" in Merrill's trilogy, from the loaded presence of the DNA model to fleeting glimpses of the plastic decor of a Stonington luncheonette. In a poet like Merrill, whose lyricism and thematic concerns are so deeply ingrained, the question of conscious choice seems beside the point. But that brings us back to my analysis of the essentially lyric ethos of his oeuvre.

25. The quotation is from A. C. Bradley's justly famous 1904 definition of *Shakespearean Tragedy*. His introduction remains one of the best analyses of theodicy in "secular" literature. Shakespeare's theodicy almost obsessed me in trying to think about theodicy in Merrill's epic. Perhaps the Ouija board–inspired conclusion to my essay explains why.

26. John Bayley, *The Uses of Division: Unity and Disharmony in Literature* (London: Chatto & Windus, 1976).

27. My partner at the Ouija board was E. B., Eric Bernard.

9. Stephen Yenser / The Names of God: *Scripts for the Pageant*

1. In the first lesson in "&" however, MM calls Michael "GOD'S OLDEST CHILD." The following discussion should suggest the reason for this characteristic blurring of identities.

2. Meanwhile we might note that the reference to snakes intertwining, as though on a caduceus, calls up both Mirabell, the earlier "guide" who identified himself and his cohorts with Mercury, and his predecessor, Ephraim, who also merged with the messenger of the gods.

3. The description of Artemis comes from *The Oxford Classical Dictionary*, ed. N. G. L. Hammond and H. H. Scullard, 2d. ed. (Oxford: The Clarendon Press, 1970), pp. 126–127.

4. Thus *Mirabell's* section 0 begins "Oh very well then." Section 1 repeats its number first in French and then for good measure in English: "UNHEEDFUL ONE." And so on.

5. W. H. Auden, *A Certain World* (New York: Viking, 1970), p. 358.

6. The symbolic import of the letter *ba* is discussed in Frithjof Schuon, *Understanding Islam*, trans. D. M. Matheson (London: George Allen & Unwin Ltd., 1963), p. 61, and Annemarie Schimmel, *Mystical Dimensions*

in Islam (Chapel Hill: University of North Carolina Press, 1975), p. 420. The significance of the *a* and *b* in the transliterated *ba* would of course be original with Merrill.

7. For the Sufi interpretations of the diacritical mark, see Laleh Bakhtiar, *Sufi Expressions of the Mystical Quest* (London: Thames and Hudson, 1956), pp. 68, 28, and Schuon, p. 61, n. 4. Merrill's essay is "Divine Poem," *The New Republic*, November 29, 1980, pp. 29–34.

8. Shah Ni'matullah Walli, quoted in Bakhtiar, p. 89.

9. I have discussed the relationship among JM, Ephraim, Rosamund Smith (one of Nature's names in the earlier volume), and Jung's concept of God as he defines it in "Answer to Job" in "The Fullness of Time: James Merrill's *Book of Ephraim*," *Canto* 3 (spring 1980), pp. 130–159. Spinoza's "Deus sive Natura" has its analogue in Whitehead's view that God and the World are different aspects or phases of one another. See Alfred North Whitehead, *Process and Reality: An Essay on Cosmology* (New York: The Free Press, 1929, 1969), esp. pp. 403–413.

10. Evelyn Underhill, *Mysticism: A Study in the Nature and Development of Man's Spiritual Consciousness* (New York: Dutton, 1911, 1963), p. 107.

11. Yūnus Emre, quoted in Schimmel, p. 418.

12. Compare "Ephraim"'s conclusion, which has a similar virtually post-humous ring.

13. Freud quotes Abel's excerpt from Bain's *Logic, Deductive and Inductive* in "'The Antithetical Sense of Primal Words': A Review of a Pamphlet by Karl Abel, *Über den Gegensinn der Urworte*, 1884," *Collected Papers*, trans. Joan Riviere (New York: Basic Books, 1959), vol. 4, p. 189.

14. Stanley Kunitz, "The Life of Poetry," *Antaeus* 37 (spring 1980), p. 153.

15. As in a sestina, the end words in a canzone follow a set order. In the first stanza, they appear in this order: ABAACAADDAEE. The second stanza begins with a linking E and repeats the pattern: EAEEBEECCEDD. And so on, until the coda's lines end ABCDE. That is, as the end words in a sestina's main stanzas recur in the order 615243, so the canzone's end words recur in the order 12, 1, 12, 12, 2, 12, 12, 5, 5, 12, 8, 8.

16. Robert S. Brumbaugh, *The Philosophers of Greece* (New York: Thomas Y. Crowell, 1964), pp. 48–49.

17. Mahmūd Shabistarī, trans. E. H. Whinfield, quoted in Bakhtiar, p. 15; and Ibn 'Arabi, paraphrased by Seyyed H. Nasr, *Three Muslim Sages* (Cambridge, Mass., 1963), p. 116, quoted in Schimmel, pp. 270–271. The eye and the mirror are nearly interchangeable metaphors for the Sufi concept of the unity of Allah and creation. It is interesting that Bakhtiar summarizes the gist of the mirror metaphor by means of a diagram virtually identical to the one that God B traces on the board. Commenting on the diagram, she tells us that mankind "polishes" the mirror that is the macrosmic universe so that there will be a "place for all the particular forms to gather into a unity," a "place for Divine Self to see Self." I do not mean that Merrill must have read Bakhtiar. The closed X or double triangle appears in diverse writers, and many mystics use the mirror and the eye as metaphors. Moreover, Merrill's "Eye" magnified by the blood cell has just as much in common with Boehme ("If thou conceivest a small circle, as small as a grain of mustard seed, yet the Heart of God is wholly and perfectly therein") and Blake ("a World in a

Grain of Sand"). And that is the point: Merrill's symbolism, sometimes superficially esoteric, has venerable precedents.

18. This scene comes at the end of Chapter 7 in Part 3 of *Jean Santeuil* (Paris: Librairie Gallimard, 1952), vol. 1, p. 315. (George D. Painter discusses its biographical origin in his *Marcel Proust: A Biography* [New York: Random House, 1959], vol. 1, pp. 214–215.) Proust's note to this passage tells us that after his confession, Jean went to his room to revise his will, in order to leave most of his furnishings to his father and mother. While he was doing so, his mother came to his room and asked him to go out. Proust concludes, "Il cessa de songer à la mort pour jouir de la vie." Just as the bequest might serve indirectly to dedicate the trilogy to God B and Nature, so that last sentence might serve as an oblique farewell to the other world. At the same time, however, since the hero goes off with his mother, that sentence could vicariously imply, once more, the bond between humanity and Nature and thus between the trilogy's two worlds. "Pour jouir de la vie": the trilogy's V work is "vie" work, a work in the service of life, a life's work.

10. Charles Berger / Merrill and Pynchon

1. Frank Kermode, *The Sense of an Ending* (New York: Oxford University Press, 1976).
2. Thomas Pynchon, *Gravity's Rainbow* (New York: Viking, 1973). All page numbers in text refer to this paperback edition.

Bibliography

Literary Works by James Merrill

First Poems. New York: Alfred A. Knopf, 1951.
Short Stories. Pawlet, Vt.: Banyan Press, 1954.
"The Immortal Husband" (play). In *Playbook: Plays for a New Theater*. New York: New Directions, 1956. The play was produced in New York in 1955.
The Seraglio (novel). New York: Alfred A. Knopf, 1957.
The Country of a Thousand Years of Peace. New York: Alfred A. Knopf, 1959; rev. ed., New York: Atheneum, 1970.
"The Bait" (play). In *Artists' Theatre*, ed. Herbert Machiz. New York: Grove Press, 1960. The play was produced in New York in 1953.
Water Street. New York: Atheneum, 1962.
"Driver" (short story). In *Partisan Review*, fall 1962; reprinted in *The Poet's Story*, ed. Howard Moss. New York: Macmillan, 1973.
The (Diblos) Notebook (novel). New York: Atheneum, 1965.
Nights and Days. New York: Atheneum, 1966.
The Fire Screen. New York: Atheneum, 1969.
"The Landscape Game" (short story). In *Prose* 2 (spring 1971).
Braving the Elements. New York: Atheneum, 1972.
The Yellow Pages. Cambridge, Mass.: Temple Bar Bookshop, 1974.
Divine Comedies. New York: Atheneum, 1976.
Mirabell: Books of Number. New York: Atheneum, 1978.
Scripts for the Pageant. New York: Atheneum, 1980.
"Palme" (poem by Paul Valéry, translated by James Merrill). In *New York Review of Books*, March 18, 1982, p. 10.
From the First Nine: Poems 1946–1976. New York: Atheneum, 1982.
The Changing Light at Sandover. New York: Atheneum, 1982.

Unless otherwise indicated, titles refer to volumes of poetry. The list is not comprehensive; it omits, among other things, Merrill's essays and reviews.

Interviews with James Merrill

"An Interview with James Merrill," conducted by Donald Sheehan. *Contemporary Literature* 9 (winter 1968).

"An Interview with James Merrill," conducted by Ashley Brown. *Shenandoah* 19 (summer 1968).

"The Poet: Private," with David Kalstone. *Saturday Review/The Arts,* December 2, 1972.

"James Merrill's Myth: An Interview," conducted by Helen Vendler. *New York Review of Books,* May 3, 1979.

"James Merrill at Home: An Interview," conducted by Ross Labrie, *Arizona Quarterly* 38 (spring 1982).

"The Art of Poetry XXXI: James Merrill," with J. D. McClatchy. *Paris Review* 84 (summer 1982), pp. 184–219.

Selected Criticism of James Merrill's Poetry

BISHOP, JONATHAN. *Who Is Who,* pp. 90–101. Ithaca, N.Y.: Glad Day Press, 1975.

DICKEY, JAMES. "James Merrill." In *Babel to Byzantium,* pp. 97–100. New York: Farrar, Straus & Giroux, 1968.

DONOGHUE, DENIS. "Waiting for the End." *New York Review of Books,* May 6, 1971, pp. 27–31.

EHRENPREIS, IRVIN. "Otherworldly Goods." *New York Review of Books,* January 22, 1981, pp. 47-51.

ETTIN, ANDREW V. "On James Merrill's 'Nights and Days.'" *Perspective,* spring 1967, pp. 33–51.

HARMON, WILLIAM. "The Metaphors and Metamorphoses of M." *Parnassus: Poetry in Review,* spring 1980, pp. 29–41.

HOLLANDER, JOHN. "A Poetry of Restitution." *Yale Review* 70 (winter 1981), pp. 161–186.

HOWARD, RICHARD. "James Merrill." In *Alone with America,* enlarged edition, pp. 386–411. New York: Atheneum, 1980.

KALSTONE, DAVID. "Transparent Things." In *Five Temperaments,* pp. 77–128. New York: Oxford University Press, 1977.

KENNEDY, X. J. "Translations from the American." *Atlantic Monthly,* March 1973, pp. 101–103.

McCLATCHY, J. D. "Lost Paradises: The Poetry of James Merrill." *Parnassues: Poetry in Review* fall/winter 1976, pp. 305–320.

———. "DJ: A Conversation with David Jackson." *Shenandoah,* 30:4 (1979), pp. 23–44.

MOFFETT, JUDITH. "What Is Truth?" *American Poetry Review,* September/October 1979, pp. 12–16.

———. "Sound without Sense: Willful Obscurity in Poetry: With Illustrations from James Merrill's Canon." *New England Review* 3 (1980), pp. 294–312.

Nemerov, Howard. "The Careful Poets and the Reckless Ones," *Sewanee Review* 60 (spring 1952); reprinted in *Poetry and Fiction: Essays*, by Howard Nemerov, pp. 188–199. New Brunswick, N.J.: Rutgers University Press, 1963.

Parisi, Joseph. "Ghostwriting." *Poetry* (December 1979), pp. 161–173.

Pettingell, Phoebe. "Voices from the Atom." *New Leader*, December 4, 1978, pp. 14–15.

Sáez, Richard. "James Merrill's Oedipal Fire." *Parnassus: Poetry in Review*, fall/winter 1974, pp. 159–184.

Sloss, Henry. "James Merrill's 'Book of Ephraim.'" *Shenandoah*, summer 1976, pp. 63–91, and fall 1976, pp. 83–110.

Spender, Stephen. "Can Poetry Be Reviewed?" *New York Review of Books*, September 20, 1973, pp. 8–14.

Steiner, Robert. [Review of Merrill's trilogy.] *The American Book Review*, July–August 1981, pp. 2–3.

Vendler, Helen. "James Merrill." In *Part of Nature, Part of Us*, pp. 205–232. Cambridge: Harvard University Press, 1980.

White, Edmund. "On James Merrill." *American Poetry Review*, September/October 1979, pp. 9–11.

Yenser, Stephen. "Feux d'Artifice." *Poetry* (June 1973), pp. 163–168.

———. "The Fullness of Time: James Merrill's *Book of Ephraim*." *Canto* 3 (spring 1980), pp. 130–159.

Contributors

CHARLES BERGER, coeditor of this volume, teaches at Yale University. He has written on modern and contemporary poetry and is the author of a critical study of Wallace Stevens.

DAVID JACKSON, novelist, has been James Merrill's close companion for more than three decades. He figures significantly as a character in Merrill's trilogy; the three volumes were, Merrill tells us, generated out of "a Thousand and One Evenings Spent / With David Jackson at the Ouija Board."

RACHEL JACOFF, a Dante scholar, teaches at Wellesley College, where she is chairman of the Italian department. She has recently received fellowships from the National Endowment for the Humanities and from the Bunting Institute of Radcliffe College.

DAVID KALSTONE, professor of English at Rutgers University, is the author of *Five Temperaments* (New York: Oxford University Press, 1977), a study of the autobiographical impulse in the poetry of Elizabeth Bishop, Robert Lowell, James Merrill, Adrienne Rich, and John Ashbery.

DAVID LEHMAN, coeditor of this volume, has published poems and critical essays in *Poetry, Paris Review, Shenandoah,* and *Parnassus.* In 1980 Cornell University Press published *Beyond Amazement: New Essays on John Ashbery,* which Lehman edited.

J. D. McCLATCHY is the author of *Scenes from Another Life*, a book of poems, and editor of *Anne Sexton: The Artist and Her Critics*. He has taught at Yale and Princeton Universities.

PETER SACKS teaches at The Johns Hopkins University. His poems have appeared in the *New Yorker* and the *New Republic*.

RICHARD SAEZ, associate professor of comparative literature at the City University of New York, has written on seventeenth-century European literature as well as on modern and contemporary poetry. "Merrill's Oedipal Fire," his essay on *Braving the Elements*, appeared in *Parnassus* in 1974.

SAMUEL E. SCHULMAN teaches English at Boston University, where he is associate editor of *Studies in Romanticism*.

WILLARD SPIEGELMAN, associate professor of English at Southern Methodist University, has published critical essays on Auden, Elizabeth Bishop, and Charles Tomlinson.

STEPHEN YENSER, professor of English at the University of California, Los Angeles, has written on Merrill for *Poetry, Canto,* and the *Yale Review*. He is the author of *Circle to Circle: The Poetry of Robert Lowell* (Berkeley: University of California Press, 1975).

Index of Merrill's Works

Index of Names

JAMES MERRILL

Designed by G. T. Whipple, Jr.
Composed by Eastern Graphics
in 10 point Palatino (Linotron 202), 3 points leaded,
with display lines in Palatino.
Printed offset by Thomson-Shore, Inc.
on Warren's Number 66 Text 50 pound basis.
Bound by John H. Dekker & Sons
in Holliston book cloth
and stamped in Kurz-Hastings foil.

Library of Congress Cataloging in Publication Data

Main entry under title:

James Merrill, essays in criticism.

    Bibliography: p.
    Includes index.
    1. Merrill, James Ingram—Criticism and inter-
pretation—Addresses, essays, lectures.   I. Lehman,
David, 1948–   .   II. Berger, Charles, 1950–   .
PS3525.E6645Z73   1983   811'.54   82-71603
ISBN 0-8014-1404-0